Noel Whelan is the author or co-author of a number of previous books on politics, elections and electoral law in Ireland. These have included the series of *Tallyman's Guides* to Irish elections and most recently he was author of *Showtime or Substance: A Voter's Guide to Election 2007*. He writes a weekly political column for *The Irish Times* and is a regular commentator on politics and current affairs for the broadcast media. He previously worked as a political organiser at Fianna Fáil headquarters and then as a special advisor to the Minister for European Affairs at the Departments of An Taoiseach and Foreign Affairs. He currently works as a barrister practising on the Dublin and South Eastern circuits.

GU00543964

The Tallyman's Campaign Handbook: Election 2007

Noel Whelan

NEW ISLAND

The Tallyman's Campaign Handbook: Election 2007
First published 2007
by New Island
2 Brookside
Dundrum Road
Dublin 14

www.newisland.ie

ISBN 1 905494 13 0

British Library Cataloguing in Publication Data. A CIP catalogue record for this book is available from the British Library.

Printed in the UK by Athenaeum Press Ltd., Gateshead, Tyne & Wear
Cover design by Inka Hagen @ New Island

10 9 8 7 6 5 4 3 2 1

CONTENTS

PREFACE

This is only the second guide ever published in advance of an Irish election, the first having been the similar guide I worked on in advance of the 2002 contest. I have been fortunate both times that the government has run full term and that my instinct – at least to the extent of predicting when the election is likely to be called – has proven correct. I was taken aback at the response to and demand for the first version of this pre-election book. What had begun as a personal pastime of collating the details for the various candidates and of the results of the previous election for each constituency developed into a small-scale book at the suggestion of a number of journalists who found the information useful when I showed it to them. What I had underestimated was the demand for a book of this type from political activists and politics watchers generally who were anxious to have all the minutiae of the electoral contest between one set of covers.

I am therefore obliged to New Island for giving it a more professional structure and taking on a project which, because of the vagaries of the electoral cycle, has its particular challenges. Jonathan Williams had the foresight to recognise the wider potential of this book. Edwin Higel at New Island also saw the potential and he, and the editor Deirdre Nolan, have ensured that it is a much improved product in its final published form than we could have envisioned. A great deal of thanks must also go to Kathryn Marsh and Bríd Ingoldsby, who worked tirelessly and skilfully on the original text to give it greater coherence and who checked and cross-checked so much of the data. Thanks also to Mairéad Whelan, who diligently gathered and reworked much of the material on the constituencies. Again, no word here or elsewhere could thank Sinéad McSweeney adequately for her considerable assistance with this book and for putting up with the various projects I lumber myself (and her) with. Thanks also to the extended Whelan family for so much.

There were many opinions from readers about what additional features should be in this pre-election guide. This book contains more information about the constituencies and more details about more of the candidates. This has been helped by the fact that the parties have selected their candidates even earlier this time round, although of course any book like this operates within the constraints that the full line-up of candidates will not be finalised until the close of nominations. The other feature which people asked for most was somewhere for readers themselves to write in the details of the 2007 counts as they come in. We have added this feature, along with space for readers to make their own predictions, in the hope that, as well as being a reference point during the election campaign itself, this book can be a useful companion during the long hours of election count coverage which, thankfully, we will again be able to enjoy in the days and nights after polling day 2007. An opinion piece at the front of the 2002 Tallyman's pre-election guide warned of the damage which the introduction of electronic voting might do to confidence about, participation in and enjoyment of our election process. That was a minority opinion in political circles then – thankfully those concerns are now more widely appreciated. For another election, at least, the Tallyman lives!

Noel Whelan, April 2007

FEW CHANGES IN THE 29th DÁIL

For the last 15 years, Ireland has settled into a stable pattern in which our parliament has run its full term. The last time we had a surprise Dáil election in this country was in November 1992, when acrimony between Albert Reynolds and Dessie O'Malley over evidence at the Beef Tribunal led to the collapse of the Fianna Fáil–Progressive Democrats government. By law the Dáil can run for a maximum of five years from the date it first meets after the election. The 27th Dáil ran from December 1992 to May 1997, some seven months shorter than the permitted 60 months. However, during the lifetime of that Dáil there was, in January 1995, a change of government without an election. The 28th Dáil sat from 26 June 1997 to 25 April 2002, just two months short of a full term. The current Dáil, which is the 29th, has been sitting since 6 June 2002 and, depending on the precise date on which Bertie Ahern chooses to dissolve it, will again last for at least 58 months.

Although it has had a long life, the current Dáil has seen relatively little change in the make-up of the parliamentary parties or of the Cabinet during its term. There has been one Taoiseach throughout and the configuration of the government has also been consistent. The government majority has been composed of Fianna Fáil and the Progressive Democrats, although it has also enjoyed the consistent support of three independent deputies. There has been only one cabinet reshuffle. The line-up of ministers after the 2002 election was relatively unchanged in terms of both personnel and portfolios from that which had been in place before the election. The most significant change was the allocation of an additional seat at the cabinet to the Progressive Democrats, which reflected the increase in the number of their seats from four to eight. Mary Harney returned to the Department of Enterprise, Trade and Employment, while Michael McDowell was assigned to the Justice, Equality and Law Reform portfolio. The only significant re-ordering of ministers and portfolios was the reshuffle in September 2006 when, following the appointment of Charlie McCreevy to the European Commission, there were relatively dramatic changes. These included the allocation of most of the important government departments to new ministers and the promotion of three newcomers to the Cabinet.

The other significant change in the allocation of responsibilities has been the change in the leadership of the Progressive Democrats and the consequent movement of the title Tánaiste around the cabinet table from Mary Harney to Michael McDowell. This change was also achieved relatively calmly, without a leadership contest or any change in the Progressive Democrats' ministerial personnel. There was also a minor innovation at the Cabinet table when it was provided, from January 2006 onwards, that the Minister of State for Children could attend all cabinet meetings as of right.

The more dramatic personnel changes have taken place on the opposition side of the house. Much of this was a consequence of the results of the 2002 election itself. Michael Noonan, the then leader of Fine Gael, resigned on the evening that the results of the 2002 election were announced and the Labour leader, Ruairi Quinn, resigned some weeks later. Both Fine Gael and Labour will therefore contest this election with new leaders – Enda Kenny and Pat Rabbitte, respectively. The 2002 electoral contest also saw the election of six Green Party deputies, five Sinn Féin deputies and a record number of independents. The 'Balkanisation' of the opposition benches is reflected when the Taoiseach, Bertie Ahern, faces three more opposition leaders in the chamber at the twice weekly Leaders' Question Time. He must now take questions on a rotating basis from either the leader of the Green Party, Trevor Sargent, the leader of Sinn Féin in the Dáil, Caoimhghín Ó Caoláin, or Joe Higgins, as the nominee of the 'Technical Group', the ad hoc grouping of the independents which came together to utilise their collective Dáil strength to secure speaking and other rights, as well as facing those of the Fine Gael leader, Enda Kenny, and the Labour leader, Pat Rabbitte.

Other minor changes have also occurred in the make-up of the various parliamentary parties since the 2002 election. Among these was the decision of the Wexford TD Liam Twomey, elected as an independent in 2002, to join Fine Gael in autumn 2004 and to immediately assume a position on the Fine Gael frontbench in the high-profile role of spokesperson on Health. In July 2006 the independent Donegal North East deputy Niall Blaney joined the Fianna Fáil parliamentary party, thereby ending a split which had lasted more than 30 years. The subsequent amalgamation of the Blaneyite Independent Fianna Fáil organisation and Fianna Fáil itself is likely to have a significant impact on the 2007 election in Donegal. This will be felt not only in Blaney's own constituency of Donegal North East, where he will join the two sitting deputies, Jim McDaid and Cecilia Keaveney, on the Fianna Fáil ticket, but also in the neighbouring Donegal South West constituency, where Independent Fianna Fáil also had a significant electoral presence.

Although it gained one independent TD, Fianna Fáil also lost three of its sitting TDs during the lifetime of this Dáil. The party's Mayo deputy, Beverley Flynn, was expelled from the parliamentary party and ultimately from the party itself following a libel action she took against RTÉ about a report they broadcast on controversial activities in the National Irish Bank, where she worked before coming into politics. Flynn is contesting the 2007 election in Mayo as an independent candidate. Fianna Fáil's Limerick West deputy, Michael Collins, resigned the party whip in 2003 because of controversies about his tax affairs. He is not contesting the 2007 election, although his nephew, Niall Collins, is standing as a Fianna Fáil candidate in Limerick West.

The party also lost a seat following the appointment of Charlie McCreevy to the European Commission in 2004. In the subsequent by-election in Kildare North in March 2005, Fianna Fáil failed to retain the seat, which went instead to new independent deputy Catherine Murphy.

The lifetime of the 29th Dáil was unusual in that there were no deaths among its membership. The only other vacancy arose because of the appointment of the Fine Gael deputy and former Taoiseach John Bruton to the position of European Union ambassador to the United States. The resulting by-election was held in Meath East in March 2005 on the same day as that in Kildare North but, in this instance, Fine Gael comfortably retained the seat; their new deputy was Sean McEntee.

THE BALANCE OF POWER IN THE OUTGOING DÁIL

THE DIVISION OF SEATS	
Fianna Fáil	78 Deputies[*]
Fine Gael	32 Deputies
Labour Party	21 Deputies
Progressive Democrats	8 Deputies
Green Party	6 Deputies
Sinn Féin	5 Deputies
Socialist Party	1 Deputy
Independents	15 Deputies[**]

[*] includes Rory O'Hanlon, Ceann Comhairle

[**] includes Beverly Flynn and Michael Collins, ex-FF

VOTE FOR BERTIE AHERN FOR TAOISEACH – 6 JUNE 2002			
Fianna Fáil	80	Fine Gael	31
Progressive Democrats	8	Labour Party	21
Jackie Healy Rae (Ind)	1	Sinn Féin	5
Mildred Fox (Ind)	1	Green Party	6
Niall Blaney (Ind)	1	Tony Gregory (Ind)	1
Paddy McHugh (Ind)	1	Joe Higgins (SP)	1
Paudge Connolly (Ind)	1	Michael Lowry (Ind)	1
		Finian McGrath (Ind)	1
		Séamus Healy (Ind)	1
TÁ	**93**	**NÍL**	**68**

Rory O'Hanlon, as Ceann Comhairle, abstained on the vote for Taoiseach.

Independent deputies James Breen, Marian Harkin, Liam Twomey and Jerry Cowley also abstained.

LOCAL AND EUROPEAN ELECTIONS 2004

There have been relatively few elections during the lifetime of the current Dáil. Apart from two by-elections in March 2005, the only nationwide elections have been the local and European elections held on 11 June 2006.

The need for a presidential election, which had been due for October 2004, was avoided. The incumbent, Mary McAleese, nominated herself for a second term. Fine Gael leader, Enda Kenny, had wisely said earlier in the year that if she did so, his party, which was unlikely to find a candidate capable of beating her, would not oppose her re-election. There were tentative proposals from the Labour Party to run Michael D. Higgins and from the Green Party that Eamon Ryan should run, but the ruling bodies of both parties decided against entering the fray. An attempt by the independent Dana Rosemary Scallon to again contest the presidential election also fizzled due to lack of necessary support for her nomination from the county councils or Oireachtas members. Consequently, when nominations closed, President McAleese was the only candidate nominated and was deemed re-elected for another seven-year term without the need for a poll.

The local and European elections, or at least their results, were, however, dramatic. The delegation of MEPs from the Republic of Ireland which made its way to the new European Parliament elected in June 2004 was markedly different from that which had represented the country in the previous parliament. First, it was a smaller delegation since, as a result of the enlargement of the European Union to 25 states, the Republic of Ireland's representation in the European Parliament was reduced from 15 to 13. The resultant redrawing and renaming of the Euro-constituencies gave rise to a reduction in the Leinster constituency, now called East, from four seats to three and the same reduction in the Munster constituency, now called South.

Of the 15 MEPs from the Republic of Ireland elected to the European Parliament in 1999, two were from the Green Party, one was from the Labour Party, four were from Fine Gael and six were from Fianna Fáil. There were also two independents – Dana Rosemary Scallon from the Connacht Ulster constituency and Pat Cox from the Munster constituency, who went on to become the President of the European Parliament for the second half of its term from 2001 to 2004. After the June 2004 elections, however, the Republic of Ireland had 13 MEPs. Fine Gael is now the largest component of the delegation, with five of the 13 seats. Only four MEPs are from Fianna Fáil. The Labour Party still has one MEP but, for the first time, Sinn Féin has one also. There are still two independents: Marian Harkin, who replaced Dana Rosemary Scallon in the North and West constituency, and Kathy Sinnott, who replaced Pat Cox in the newly named South constituency. Ireland now has no Green MEP.

Eight of the 15 MEPs who served from 1999 to 2004 did not contest the 2004 elections and three more were unsuccessful in their efforts to be elected. Brian Crowley, Prionsias De Rossa and Avril Doyle were therefore the only MEPs who had won in June 1999 and were re-elected in June 2004. As a result, nine of the 13 going to Brussels were newcomers to the European Parliament.

EUROPEAN ELECTION 2004 – SEATS WON

	DUBLIN	EAST	SOUTH	NORTH and WEST	NATIONAL 2004	NATIONAL CHANGE
Fianna Fáil	1	1	1	1	4	-2
Fine Gael	1	2	1	1	5	+1
Labour	1	-	-	-	1	-
Green	-	-	-	-	-	-2
Sinn Féin	1	-	-	-	1	-1
Others	-	-	1	1	2	-

EUROPEAN ELECTION 2004 – % VOTE SHARE

	DUBLIN	EAST	SOUTH	NORTH and WEST	NATIONAL 2004	NATIONAL CHANGE
Fianna Fáil	23.22	25.08	41.02	27.10	29.3	- 9.1
Fine Gael	21.51	40.55	24.56	23.96	27.6	+3.2
Labour	22.53	13.05	4.12	3.31	10.8	+1.9
Green	9.59	5.64	2.25	-	4.4	-2.4
Sinn Féin	14.32	8.68	6.74	15.50	11.3	+4.8
Others	8.84	6.99	21.30	30.13	16.8	+1.8

The local elections were also dramatic. As well as giving rise to a change in the balance of power in Irish local government, the 2004 local elections also saw a dramatic influx of new faces. This was the first election held since the introduction of a statutory prohibition on simultaneous membership of either House of the Oireachtas and a city or county council (the 'dual mandate ban'). This factor, together with a dramatic shift in voter patterns and, in particular, the loss of almost a fifth of its seats by Fianna Fáil, means that there are literally hundreds of new faces sitting in city and county council chambers across the country. As will be seen in the following pages, many of these are contesting this Dáil election.

For the purposes of this book, the 2004 local elections are significant not only for what they reveal about whether the vote share of the different parties is holding up, but also because the local elections allowed for some road testing of new candidates for the Dáil contest, particularly for the non-government parties. Some indications of the likely strength of those candidates can be garnered from how well they did in their local electoral areas in the local elections, which were only three years ago. Those details are given, where relevant, in the constituency pages. Of course, this comes with the rider that such results are only indicative of their support in their immediate political base, and that because of the dual mandate ban they are not a test of their electoral strength in a fight with the local TDs.

Nationally, the local election results showed a large drop in seat numbers and vote share for Fianna Fáil on the county and City Councils, while Fine Gael not only managed, against expectations, to hold the seats it had on these councils, but actually increased its seat numbers slightly. Fianna Fáil's vote share declined from 38.9% in the 1999 local elections to 31.9% in the 2004 local elections. In the four city and council elections the party suffered dramatically reduced representation. Overall, its number of seats fell by 80 and, significantly, the gap between Fine Gael and Fianna Fáil in terms of seats was reduced to eight. After the 1999 local and European elections the party had a majority on eight of the county and City Councils, but after the 2004 local elections the party has no outright majority on any city or county council.

In the 1999 local elections Fine Gael got a seat bonus in that it secured more seats than it was strictly entitled to on its first preference share. In 1999 it won 277 of the 883 seats on these councils with just 28% of the first preference vote. However, in the 2002 election, it not only managed to hold these seats, but also increased its seat total to 293. The Labour Party had a good local election in that it increased its seat numbers on these councils from 83 to 101. The Green Party did well and managed to double its seat tally on the councils, albeit from a low base of eight to 17. Sinn Féin did very well, increasing its seats from 21 in 1999 to 54 in 2004 and doing spectacularly well in Dublin city.

LOCAL ELECTIONS 2004

SEATS WON

	1999	2004	CHANGE
Fianna Fáil	382	302	−80
Fine Gael	277	293	+16
Labour	83	101	+18
PDs	25	19	−6
Green Party	8	18	+9
Sinn Féin	21	54	+33
Others	94		

% VOTE

	1999	2004	CHANGE
Fianna Fáil	39	32	−7
Fine Gael	28	27	−1
Labour	11	11	−
PDs	3	4	+1
Green Party	2	4	+2
Sinn Féin	4	8	+4
Others	13	17	+4

% FIRST PREFERENCE VOTES SHARE 2004 LOCAL ELECTIONS

COUNCIL	FF	FG	LAB	PD	GP	SF	OTHS
Carlow	36.32	32.91	17.19	3.38	6.86	1.54	1.79
Cavan	41.16	43.97	0.76	-	-	11.62	2.49
Clare	41.51	28.83	3.32	3.84	4.51	1.85	16.08
Cork Co.	32.93	37.19	10.19	1.32	4.26	6.14	7.96
Cork City	29.1	22.1	13.2	4.7	6.8	10.4	13.8
Donegal	40.02	22.95	1.14	0.58	2.19	13.51	19.59
Dublin City	23.20	16.94	20.45	3.63	6.42	18.51	10.8
Dun Laoghaire Rathdown	24.86	24.05	20.30	8.40	10.34	3.67	7.38
Fingal	21.47	22.53	18.71	5.98	8.20	5.20	12.71
Galway County	34.54	28.06	3.37	9.03	0.73	4.04	20.23
Galway City	19.2	17.1	16.5	22.6	7.3	8.4	9.0
Kerry	37.47	24.82	11.50	0.63	1.01	7.86	8.85
Kildare	32.01	20.81	18.89	3.77	6.07	0.73	17.72
Kilkenny	33.93	38.23	14.76	1.77	4.61	2.68	3.99
Laois	37.78	33.92	4.09	10.06	0.72	3.75	9.67
Leitrim	40.13	38.14	2.17	-	0.61	11.17	7.79
Limerick County	38.60	38.07	3.80	8.24	2.01	1.49	7.80
Limerick City	15.9	26.6	14.0	8.4	0.3	3.8	31.0
Longford	35.28	38.92	1.77	6.91	0.51	3.69	12.93
Louth	29.67	23.35	4.67	3.91	4.71	16.88	16.81
Mayo	37.02	43.18	2.26	1.38	0.46	4.24	11.47
Meath	38.36	26.62	6.51	1.12	4.3	9.45	13.64
Monaghan	29.37	29.89	-	-	-	31.05	9.69
North Tipperary	41.28	21.50	10.32	-	-	2.88	24.01
Offaly	33.78	29.31	3.88	7.23	0.78	1.27	23.76
Roscommon	36.19	35.88	1.87	2.47	0.66	2.85	20.09
Sligo	37.41	36.77	10.42	-	-	7.73	7.68
South Dublin	25.70	13.70	18.49	6.70	8.38	13.45	9.68
South Tipperary	34.86	27.87	9.58	1.41	1.24	4.09	20.95
Waterford County	35.88	36.21	14.63	0.98	1.82	2.95	7.53
Waterford City	13.9	18.5	15.2	3.0	4.2	13.5	31.6
Westmeath	35.30	31.12	25.14	-	1.10	5.06	2.28
Wexford	30.43	33.07	8.76	1.12	1.95	8.92	15.43
Wicklow	25.02	22.50	21.78	3.45	4.65	6.66	15.94

CONSTITUENCY CHANGES

The significant demographic change which Ireland has experienced in the last decade will have only a modest impact on the electoral landscape. The return of Irish emigrants to live in Ireland has been a feature of that landscape, although not as marked a feature in the period since 2002 as it was in the decade from 1992 to 2002. The most significant population shift in the last five years will actually have no bearing on the make-up of the electorate, as the large number of non-nationals who have come to live and work in Ireland over the last four years have no vote in Dáil elections. Estimates put the portion of the population who are born abroad at about 10% of the general population and perhaps as much as 12% of the population over 18 years of age. Although immigration may be one of the issues to feature in the election campaign, this portion of the population will exert no direct influence on the election itself since they are, by law, prohibited from voting in Dáil elections.

The more significant demographic shift has been a continuation in the rapid rise in population on the outskirts of Dublin and particularly those parts of Dublin which border Meath and Kildare. It is this shift which has exerted most influence on the redrawing of constituencies undertaken since the 2002 election. A population census was conducted in April 2002 and, after the publication of the detailed figures for that census, a constituency commission was established to review the Dáil constituency boundaries in 2004. A constituency commission is an independent statutory boundary commission which comes into being after the final results of each census are published. It is chaired by a High Court judge – in this instance, Mr Justice Lavin – and its other members are the Clerks of the Dáil and Seanad, the Comptroller and Auditor General and the Secretary General of the Department of the Environment. The commission then deliberates on the potential shape of the map of constituencies, and the number of deputies to be elected for each. In this work it is assisted by the franchise section of the Department of the Environment, which has a particular expertise in electoral matters, by the Central Statistics Office, which provides it with the localised population data, and by the Ordnance Survey Office, which develops the necessary cartography for the redrawing of the electoral map.

When the report of the Constituency Commission was published in 2005 it presented a relatively extensive reconfiguration of the constituencies. Additional seats were given to Dublin Mid West and Kildare North. An additional seat was also given to the county of Meath, where the existing five-seat constituency was divided in two and an eastern portion of County Westmeath included to create two new three-seat constituencies, Meath East and Meath West. Since the commission decided not to increase the number of TDs – it could by law have recommended an increase from 166 to 168 – the allocation of additional seats to those areas of most rapid population growth in the south west of Dublin and the bordering counties necessitated the taking of three seats from some other parts of the country.

One seat was taken from north of the Liffey, where the relative growth in population has been slowest. This was achieved by reducing Dublin North Central from a four-seat constituency to a three-seat constituency, with some consequent redrawing of boundaries to give parts of its existing territory to Dublin North Central and Dublin North West.

Another seat was found by taking one from the county of Cork. As a result, Cork North

Central was reduced from five to four seats and part of its existing territory was given to Cork South Central by restoring the Lee as the border between these two constituencies.

The most significant aspect of the redrawing of constituencies, however, was to take another seat from those counties in the area of north west Leinster and Connacht. The redrawing in this part of the country was most controversial since it involved splitting the county of Leitrim into two constituencies. The existing five-seat constituency of Sligo–Leitrim was reduced from five to four seats and a large portion of Leitrim in the south amalgamated with Roscommon into the new Roscommon–South Leitrim three-seat constituency. The domino effect of this was the abolition of the Longford–Roscommon constituency, which was anomalous in that it was the only constituency to cross a provincial and Euro constituency boundary. There was a re-emergence of the old Longford–Westmeath constituency. A portion of Westmeath was put with the western party of County Meath to create a new Meath West constituency, with the balance of the county becoming the new Meath East constituency, each with three seats.

Of course, it is impossible to discern precisely which of the parties will gain or lose most from the effect of the redrawing of constituencies. The parties have shown themselves particularly adept at recalibrating their constituency machines and reconfiguring their candidate line-ups to take account of constituency redrawings. Fianna Fáil is certainly down a seat in Cork North Central as a result of the reduction of that constituency from five seats to four seats and has accepted that reality by running two candidates on this occasion, although of course it would have struggled to hold three out of five in any case. There is also a risk for Fianna Fáil that it will lose out because of the reduction of seats in north Dublin, since one of its deputies may be the casualty of the reduction of Dublin North Central from four seats to three. The newly configured constituencies covering the counties of Sligo, Leitrim and Roscommon will be watched with particular interest. Again, on balance it is probably Fianna Fáil which has suffered here.

Whether the impact of the loss of seats as a consequence of the reduction of seats in Cork, North Dublin and the Leinster–Connacht region can be offset by gaining one of the three new seats in Meath, Kildare South and west Dublin remains to be seen. The increase in seats in Kildare North from three to four means that Fianna Fáil will win back the seat in North Kildare which it lost in the by-election in 2005. There is some bullish talk of winning two seats there. In Dublin Mid West either Labour or Fine Gael are likely to be the beneficiary of the new seat, while in Meath East either Labour or an independent are likely to win the additional seat.

Even where redrawing leaves party positions unaffected, it can have a pronounced impact on the individual representatives of those parties. Some have suffered the splitting or breaking away of their political base. The person most significantly affected in this manner is Fianna Fáil's outgoing Cork South Central TD Batt O'Keeffe, who saw much of his original political base in the Ballinacollig part of the Carrigaline local electoral area redrawn into the Cork North West constituency, where Fianna Fáil already has two out of the three sitting TDs. O'Keeffe is the person who has had to make the most significant adjustment since the redrawing and he has actually decided to transfer constituencies and contest in Cork North West for this election. Others affected are John Ellis, the sitting Fianna Fáil TD for Sligo–Leitrim, who gets almost his entire vote in the county of Leitrim. This time he must contest the newly created Roscommon–South Leitrim. However, as the only sitting Leitrim deputy contesting, he is likely to be the beneficiary of a determination by voters from Leitrim that their county will have at least one representative in the next Dáil.

Another Fianna Fáil TD affected by the redrawing of constituencies is Donnie Cassidy in Westmeath, who has seen a portion of the hinterland of his Castlepollard base drawn into the new Meath West constituency. He has opted to stay with Westmeath in the new four-seat Longford–Westmeath constituency, where he may feel the absence of this territory in what would always have been a difficult battle for him against a strong challenge from his running mate, Mary O'Rourke. Independent Finian McGrath is also affected by the redrawing. Not only is he competing to hold his first-term seat as one of four sitting deputies contesting a constituency which is now a three-seater, he is doing so without some of the area where his support is strongest. In Dublin North Central, Labour's Derek McDowell, and indeed Fianna Fáil councillor Deirdre Heney, who got a very large first preference vote in 2002, also have reason to feel aggrieved at this particular redrawing.

The census of population due in 2001 was postponed to 2002 because of the outbreak of foot and mouth disease. In order to keep the census within a relatively consistent five-year gap for comparative purposes, another census of population was conducted in April 2006. This, together with the fact that the current Dáil has run a full term, means that, unusually, two sets of census figures will have been produced during the lifetime of the current Dáil. The preliminary figures for the 2006 census published in September 2006 again revealed significant population movements. The most important electoral implications are in west and south west Dublin and adjoining counties. However, since the final results of the 2006 census are not due to be published until April 2007, they will have no bearing on the shape of the constituencies for this election. This does, however, mean that there will be very large quotas in those under-represented constituencies for the 2007 contest.

CANDIDATES 2007

The full line-up of candidates in each of the 42 constituencies will only be finalised when nominations close, which will not be until 10 days before the final polling date chosen by Bertie Ahern. However, the lead-in to this election has been characterised by the fact that all of the parties have selected more of their candidates earlier. Inevitably, knowledge of the intentions of independent candidates is more limited at this early stage and so the focus of the following pages of constituency detail is in the main confined to party candidates or incumbent independents who are known to be contesting the 2007 election. One hundred and thirteen independent candidates contested the 1997 election and 95 contested the 2002 election. The number of independents contesting on this occasion is likely to be in or about the same number.

ESTIMATED NUMBER AND GENDER OF CANDIDATES, 2007

		Total 2007		Male 2007		Female 2007
Fianna Fáil		107		94		13
Fine Gael		93		78		15
Labour		51		43		9
Greens		35		29		6
Sinn Féin		37		31		6
PDs		21		16		5

The most vulnerable time for any party's seat is when the sitting deputy is retiring. While the main political parties have got better at retaining seats when a sitting deputy is stepping down, it still presents particular challenges. Parties are addressing the difficulty by putting new candidates in the field earlier. This is something which can be done when one has an idea of when the election will be held. One of the difficulties which the retirement of a sitting deputy presents is illustrated by the fact that four deputies who had announced they were not contesting the election changed, or were prevailed upon to change, their minds.

In the case of Fine Gael, deputies Padraig McCormack in Galway West and Dinny McGinley in Donegal South West are returning to the fray for the 2007 election, having been persuaded by concerns that in their absence the party would not hold its seats in those constituencies. In the case of Breeda Moynihan Cronin, Labour also feared, with some justification, that it would lose its seat in Kerry South if she were not a candidate. She had previously announced her retirement on health grounds in mid-2006, but is now well enough to contest. The circumstances surrounding the reversal of the decision of Jim McDaid to retire in Donegal North East are more complex and are dealt with in some detail in the relevant constituency pages.

Fianna Fáil, as the party with most sitting deputies, is also the one most affected by retirements. Fianna Fáil deputies are stepping down in 10 constituencies and in one, Dublin North, both of the party's sitting deputies are stepping down. Fine Gael is also affected, particularly in the highly competitive, newly recreated constituency of Longford–Westmeath, where their sitting deputy, Paul McGrath, has decided to step down. Labour has also been affected by the retirement of Seán Ryan in Dublin North and Joe Sherlock in Cork East, although the party is hoping that the fact that they are running Sean Ryan's brother, Brendan, in Dublin North, and Joe Sherlock's son, Seán, in Cork East will enable them to hold on to their seats.

A number of deputies who were elected to the European Parliament in June 2004 have decided not to contest the 2007 Dáil elections. Recent legislative changes have introduced a prohibition on members of the European Parliament from the Republic of Ireland simultaneously being members of the Oireachtas. As a result, any member of the European Parliament who is elected to Dáil Éireann in this election will automatically cease to be a member of the European Parliament. Fianna Fáil backbenchers Liam Aylward from Carlow–Kilkenny and Eoin Ryan from Dublin South East are not contesting this election. To the surprise of many, the Fine Gael deputy for Dublin South Central, Gay Mitchell, has also decided to stay in the European Parliament and to step down from the Dáil at this election. Also giving up her Dáil career, in her case after one term, is the independent deputy for Sligo–Leitrim, Marian Harkin, who was elected to the European Parliament for the North and West constituency in 2004.

On the other hand, three sitting members of the European Parliament – all of them elected for the first time in the 2004 European election – are contesting the 2007 Dáil election. All three of them are in real contention to win Dáil seats and, if they do so, will forfeit their seats in the European Parliament to less well-known substitutes who were designated at the time of the European election. Mairead McGuinness, who topped the poll for Fine Gael in the East constituency in the 2004 European election, will automatically vacate that seat if she is elected to the Dáil for Louth. Another Fine Gael poll topper, Simon Coveney, who took the first seat in the South constituency, will automatically vacate his seat if he is re-elected to Dáil Éireann in Cork South Central. Mary Lou McDonald will vacate her seat in the Dublin constituency if she is elected to Dáil Éireann in Dublin Central.

OUTGOING DEPUTIES NOT CONTESTING

Deputy	Party	Constituency	Years in Dáil
Joe Jacob	FF	Wicklow	20
Dan Wallace	FF	Cork North Central	25
Tony Dempsey	FF	Wexford	5
Joe Walsh	FF	Cork South West	30
Liam Aylward	FF	Carlow–Kilkenny	30
Eoin Ryan	FF	Dublin South East	15
Síle De Valera	FF	Clare	24
Noel Davern	FF	Tipperary South	28
Jim Glennon	FF	Dublin North	5
GV Wright	FF	Dublin North	12
Dermot Fitzpatrick	FF	Dublin Central	10
Paul McGrath	FG	Westmeath	18
Gay Mitchell	FG	Dublin South Central	26
Joe Sherlock	Lab	Cork East	11
Sean Ryan	Lab	Dublin North	18
Seamus Pattison	Lab	Carlow–Kilkenny	46
Michael Collins	Ind (ex FF)	Limerick West	10
Mildred Fox	Ind	Wicklow	15
Marian Harkin	Ind	Sligo–Leitrim	5

The notion of the Seanad as a resting home for previous TDs pending their next Dáil challenge or as a launch pad for new Dáil careers is also confirmed by the candidate line-up for this election. At least 25 of the current members of the Seanad are contesting this election, nine of whom are former members of the Dáil. Interestingly, six of the 11 people who are members of the Seanad as Taoiseach's Nominees are contesting this Dáil election.

This election will also have a significant impact on the composition of local government. Even if one confines oneself to a consideration of the members of county and City Councils who are contesting, then one can see that even if only some of them end up getting elected, there will be a noticeable impact in council chambers. The 'dual mandate' ban not only exerted a dramatic influence on the 2002 general election, it will now affect the outcomes of the 2004 local elections.

POLITICAL STATUS OF CANDIDATES 2007

	Sitting TD	Sitting Senator	Former TD	First Dáil Election	City or County Council Members
Fianna Fáil	67	8	73	23	22
Fine Gael	28	9	40	35	35
Labour	18	4	20	16	16
Greens	6	–	7	17	9
Sinn Féin	5	–	5	21	11
PDs	8	3	8	8	1

As always there are a lot of newcomers contesting for the parties. In addition to turnover of membership being affected by retirements, many sitting deputies will lose their seats.

TURNOUT

Estimating the likely turnout in this election is nearly impossible. Turnout in elections is generally measured in Ireland as the percentage of persons registered to vote who actually come out to do so. On the basis of that measure, then, the turnout in recent Irish Dáil elections has been taken to be falling, and falling dramatically.

However, the use of this measure rests on a number of assumptions. These assumptions are that all eligible voters were registered, that only eligible voters were registered, and there were no multiple registrations. All these assumptions are wrong and significant errors have been revealed on the electoral register.

It has now been accepted by the Minister for the Environment that, previous to efforts to improve the accuracy of the register in advance of the 2007 election, there could perhaps have been as many as 400,000 more names than there were voters entitled to be registered. Since it appears there were perhaps hundreds of thousands of people who were registered at least twice, the percentage of people said not to have voted at recent Irish elections has been overstated and the turnout figure understated. Turnout in Irish elections therefore has been significantly underestimated. The true extent of this is difficult to determine but it could be as high as 20% and is more likely to be in the region of a 10% underestimate.

In light of the controversy about the state of the electoral register arising from some detailed media exploration of the defects in the registering system – most usefully by Shane Colman and Odrain Flynn in the *Sunday Tribune* – the government promised to improve the system. The compilation of the 2007 register, which will be in effect for this election, was accompanied by an extensive public relations campaign and because improved guidelines on how data for the registered was to be gathered were issued to local authorities. When the changes to the compilation method gave rise to some voters being deleted from the register who were probably entitled to be on it, the government announced an extension of time for the finalisation of the 2007 register. However, there are many indications that there are still considerable defects with the register and an element of double registration, and there may be many eligible voters who are still not registered.

TURNOUT IN IRISH DÁIL ELECTIONS, 1967–2004

YEAR	ELECTION	% TURNOUT
2004	Local Euro Elections (and Ref)	59.9
2002	**Dáil Election**	**62.7**
1999	Local and European (and Ref)	50.3
1997	**Dáil Election**	**65.2**
1992	**Dáil Election**	**67.4**
1991	Local Elections	55.7
1989	**Dáil Election**	**67.6**
1987	**Dáil Election**	**72.7**
1985	Local Election	63.0
1981/82*	**Dáil Election**	**72.0 –73.0**
1979	Local and European Election	66.0
1977	**Dáil Election**	**75.6**
1974	Local Election	67.0
1973	**Dáil Election**	**75.5**
1969	**Dáil Eireann**	**76.0**
1967	Local Elections	69.0

* Three elections held in 18 months

ELECTION DAY, MAY 2007

The latest possible polling day

The Constitution provides that the same Dáil shall not continue for a period longer than seven years. It also provides that a shorter period can be fixed by law. Section 33 of the Electoral Act 1992 currently provides a maximum period of five years.

The Dáil term runs from the date that the House first meets after an election. The 29th Dáil first met on 6 June 2002. Consequently, the current Dáil does not legally have to be dissolved until 6 June 2007 and, technically, the election could be held any day up to the 4th of July.

The dissolution of the Dáil

The President, on the advice of the Taoiseach, may dissolve the Dáil any time, and where a Taoiseach retains the majority support of the Dáil the President must assent to the Taoiseach's request. This is traditionally done by the Taoiseach making a statement in the Dáil that he proposes to go to Áras an Uachtaráin to seek dissolution. However, it should be noted that there is no legal restriction on where or when this announcement is made. Indeed, there is no legal requirement that the Taoiseach even announce in advance that he intends to travel to the Áras to seek a dissolution. There is also no requirement that his announcement and the request for dissolution should occur on the same day.

The election date

Article 16.4.2 of the Constitution provides that the election of members to the new Dáil must take place not later than 30 days after dissolution. However, the Electoral Acts limit this further by requiring that the election take place not less than 17 days and not more than 25 days (excluding Sundays and bank holidays) after the dissolution. There are no legal restrictions on the day of the week on which polling can be held. The polling date will be designated by an order made by the Minister for the Environment and Local Government.

The first meeting of the new Dáil

The Constitution provides that the proclamation issued by the President bringing about the dissolution must set out the date on which the new Dáil will meet. The new Dáil elects a Ceann Comhairle at its first meeting. However, there is no obligation on the new Dáil to select a new government at its first meeting. Indeed, three of the last five Dáil have failed to select a government on their first meeting.

TRANSFER PATTERNS

Internal transfer patterns

The following table shows the internal transfer patterns within the three main parties. The internal transfer rate effectively shows the rate of transfers to a fellow party candidate (when one is available). Interestingly, apart from a minimal decline in the case of Fianna Fáil, in 2002, it was effectively unchanged on the 1997 election.

	Fianna Fáil	Fine Gael	Labour Party
Internal Transfer Rate 2002	62.4%	64.2%	49.4%
Internal Transfer Rate 1997	67.3%	64.5%	48.1%

Obviously, the smaller parties have limited internal transfers since in most constituencies where they contest they will have only one candidate.

Terminal transfer rates

The following table sets out the destination of each party's vote when another candidate of the same party is no longer in contention.

To \ From	Fianna Fáil	Fine Gael	Labour Party	PDs	Green Party	Sinn Féin	Others
Fianna Fáil	——	20.2%	22.7%	34.6%	19.7%	24.8%	29.4%
Fine Gael	30.7%	——	37.5%	28.2%	16.6%	12.9%	28.7%
Labour Party	26.1%	32.1%	——	22.8%	29.4%	13.5%	7.1%
PDs		1.9%	2.5%	——	2.4%	1.6%	0.9%
Green Party	10.3%	13.4%	8.0%	1.9%	——	10.1%	3.3%
Sinn Féin	1.6%	1.1%	5.2%	1.5%	5.3%	——	10.4%
Others	3.1%	16.5%	14.0%	3.5%	12.6%	17.2%	——
Non-Transferable	28.1%	14.8%	10.1%	7.5%	13.9%	20.0%	20.0%

CARLOW–KILKENNY

Outgoing Deputies: Séamus Pattison (Lab), Liam Aylward (FF), Phil Hogan (FG), John McGuinness (FF), MJ Nolan (FF).

Séamus Pattison (Lab) as outgoing Ceann Comhairle of the 28th Dáil was automatically re-elected to the 29th Dáil in the 2002 election. He is not contesting the 2007 election.

Liam Aylward was elected to the European Parliament in 2004 and is not contesting the 2007 Dáil election.

The Constituency: This **five-seater** includes the county of Kilkenny and all of the county of Carlow except an area in east Carlow which is in the Wicklow constituency. The boundaries of this constituency are unchanged since 2002.

Party	Votes 2002	Quota 2002	% Vote 2002	% Vote 1997	Swing
Fianna Fáil	30,543	2.5	50.20%	42.19%	8.01%
Fine Gael	13,309	1.1	21.87%	29.19%	−7.31%
Labour	8,004	0.7	13.15%	15.19%	−2.03%
PDs	–	–	–	5.64%	−5.64%
Green Party	4,961	0.4	8.15%	5.52%	2.63%
Sinn Féin	2,078	0.2	3.42%	–	3.42%
Others	1,949	0.16	3.20%	2.27	0.93%

2007 Candidates will include: Bobby Aylward (FF), John McGuinness (FF), MJ Nolan (FF), Fergal Browne (FG), Phil Hogan (FG), John Paul Phelan (FG), Michael O'Brien (Lab), Jim Townsend (Lab), Mary White (GP), Walter Lacey (PD), Kathleen Function (SF)

In Brief: With two of the sitting deputies not contesting, this is a key target for a Fine Gael or Green Party gain at the expense of Fianna Fáil. The fact that the long-time Labour incumbent, Séamus Pattison, is stepping down makes the Rainbow's overall challenge more difficult, although all the indications are that Labour's Carlow-based candidate, Jim Townsend, will hold the seat for the party. MJ Nolan is likely to be the weaker of the Fianna Fáil candidates and a switch of counties for the Labour seat and another strong challenge from the Green Party's Mary White will make him even more vulnerable. Kilkenny-based John McGuinness is safe, while Bobby Aylward is likely to hold the seat being vacated by his brother, Liam Aylward, who is now an MEP. Fine Gael is hoping their big name, Phil Hogan, can manage the vote to bring Carlow-based Senator Feargal Browne or Kilkenny-based Senator John Paul Phelan into Dáil Éireann with him.

Fianna Fáil: Fianna Fáil made a key gain here in 2002 when they regained their Carlow seat, an achievement which was all the more remarkable since the presence of the Ceann Comhairle meant that the constituency was in reality a four-seater for that election. Indeed, Carlow–Kilkenny was Fianna Fáil's best performance in the country in 2002, and the party attained its best vote share ever in this constituency. The Fianna Fáil vote increased by 8% from 42.19% in 1997 to 50.19% in 2002. During the campaign the *Carlow Nationalist* published reports of a controversial poll suggesting that Carlow would be without a TD after the election and this may also have exerted influence in Nolan's favour on the final outcome. While the retirement of their long-term deputy Liam Aylward will hinder Fianna Fáil's chances of holding their three sitting TDs, the retirement of Labour's sitting deputy, Séamus Pattison, helps them.

The party's Kilkenny City-based incumbent is deputy John McGuinness. McGuinness, who was first elected to Dáil Éireann in 1997, is a prominent businessman in the city. He was a member of Kilkenny Corporation from 1979 to 2004 and of Kilkenny County Council from 1991 to 2004. He is a former mayor of Kilkenny and increased his vote by over 3,000 first preferences in 2002. He is Deputy Chairman of the Committee of Public Accounts in the outgoing Dáil and revels in occasionally being a controversial backbencher.

The party's other sitting Dáil deputy in Kilkenny is Liam Aylward, who was elected to the European Parliament in 2004 and is not contesting the 2007 Dáil election. Liam was first elected to Dáil Éireann in 1977 and topped the poll in 2002 with one of the largest first preference votes in the country at 12,489 votes. He was a Minister of State in the Department of Agriculture from 2002 to 2004. His brother Bobby, who is replacing him in the 2007 Dáil contest, has been a member of Kilkenny County Council since 1992, representing the Piltown local electoral area, like Liam before him. In the 2004 local elections Bobby Aylward topped the poll in this area with 1,478 first preferences.

The party's sitting deputy in Carlow is MJ Nolan. He was first elected to Dáil Éireann in 1982 but lost his seat in 1997 and regained it in 2002. He is a son of the former TD and Minister, Tom Nolan. MJ was a member of Seanad Éireann from 1981 to 1982 and from 2001 to 2002. He received 8,711 first preferences in 2002 and was in third position on the first count. His brother, Enda Nolan, is a member of Carlow County Council for the Muinebeag local electoral area, where he polled 636 when the quota was 880.

Fine Gael: The retirement of their outgoing deputy, John Browne, was the occasion of the loss of a seat by Fine Gael here in 2002. Their vote fell from 29% in 1997 to 21.9% in 2002 and the party was left with only one seat.

Fine Gael's big player in this constituency is their national director of organisation, Phil Hogan, who is also currently their spokesperson on Enterprise, Trade and Employment. Hogan, who is an auctioneer, is based in Kilkenny City. He was first elected to Dáil Éireann in 1989 and has been re-elected on each occasion since. His first preference performance in 2002, at 7,841 votes, was well down on his 1997 achievement of 9,642, but that may be due in part to a vote management strategy in the constituency. Hogan was Minister of State at the Department of Finance from December 1994 to February 1995 when he resigned, accepting responsibility for a premature publication of budget details by his office. He was chairman of the Fine Gael parliamentary party from 1995 to 2001 and he was an unsuccessful candidate for the party leadership in June 2002.

The party's other Kilkenny-based candidate is Senator John Paul Phelan. Phelan is on the Agriculture panel and at 28 years of age is the youngest member of Seanad Éireann, where he is the party spokesperson on Finance. He is based near Tullogher and was a member of Kilkenny County Council for the Piltown electoral areas from 1999 to 2002.

Fine Gael's Carlow-based candidate is Senator Fergal Browne. A former primary school teacher, he contested the 2002 Dáil election when his father, John Browne, who was a member of Dáil Éireann from 1989 to 2002, retired. Fergal polled 5,468 first preferences and was eliminated on the sixth count. He was subsequently elected to Seanad Éireann on the Labour panel. He was a member of Carlow urban district council from 1999 to 2004.

Labour Party: Labour's long-serving deputy, Séamus Pattison, was Ceann Comhairle when the 2002 election was called and, as such, was returned automatically in that election. Pattison is currently 'Father of the House', the longest-serving member of the outgoing Dáil, having first been elected in 1961. His retirement therefore makes Labour's seat in this constituency vulnerable. Séamus Pattison's nephew, Eoin Pattison, was unsuccessful in his attempt to be selected as one of the party's candidates for the 2007 election.

In the 2002 election, because of Pattison's automatic re-election in that year, Labour ran two candidates, Jim Townsend in Carlow and Michael O'Brien in Kilkenny. Jim Townsend had also contested the 1997 election as Pattison's running mate. Impressively, in Pattison's absence Labour's vote only declined by 500 votes.

Jim Townsend was a member of Seanad Éireann from 1993 to 1997. He is Leas Cathaoirleach of Carlow County Council and Chairman of Carlow Town Council. In the 2004 local elections he was again elected to Carlow County Council, polling 965 first preferences and taking the first seat in the Muinebeag electoral area. Townsend was the stronger of the party's two candidates in the 2002 Dáil election, when he polled 4,272 first preferences – 540 votes more than Michael O'Brien.

Michael O'Brien has been a member of Kilkenny County Council since 2004 representing the Thomastown local electoral area. In the 2004 local elections he polled 964 first preferences, taking the third of the five seats there. In the 2002 Dáil election he polled 3,732 first preferences. O'Brien works as a distribution manager and is a former chairman of the South Eastern Health Board.

Green Party: The party's deputy leader, Mary White, is the candidate in this constituency. She was the candidate in the 2002 election, when she polled 4,961 first preferences, and in the 1997 election, when she polled 3,116 first preferences. White has been a member of Carlow County Council since 1999, representing the Borris electoral area. In June 2004 she was the party's candidate in the East constituency in the European Elections, where she polled 25,576 first preferences. On the same day she was re-elected to Carlow County Council, polling 610 (quota 757) first preferences and taking the third seat in the Borris electoral area. She has been a deputy leader of the Green Party since 1991.

Progressive Democrats: The party's candidate is Walter Lacey, who is a councillor for the Carlow No. 2 local electoral area. He polled 730 votes there in the 2004 local elections and took the third of the five seats. The last candidate to contest a Dáil election for the party here was Jim Gibbons, then a senator who stood in 2002. He polled 3,184 first preferences.

Sinn Féin: Kathleen Function is a 24-year-old who is the party's Equality Officer for the Leinster area. She is originally from Callan and now lives in Kilkenny City. This is her first electoral contest.

CARLOW KILKENNY 2007 FIGURES

Candidate	Party	1st Count	2nd Count	3rd Count	4th Count	5th Count	Later counts

YOUR PREDICTION 2007

	Candidate Elected	Party
1		
2		
3		
4		
5		

RESULT 2007

	Candidate Elected	Party
1		
2		
3		
4		
5		

NOTES/UPDATES

CARLOW–KILKENNY 2002 FIGURES

5 seats (4 for election) Quota: 12,169

Candidate	Party	1st	2nd	3rd	4th	5th	6th	7th	8th
Transfer of			Nolan	Collins-Hughes	Kiernan	O'Brien	Browne	Akward surplus	White
Liam Aylward*	FF		**12,489**						
John McGuinness*	FF	**9,343**	*+28* **9,371**	*+286* **9,657**	*+428* **10,085**	*+442* **10,527**	*+127* **10,654**	*+224* **10,878**	*+1,233* **12,111**
MJ Nolan	FF	**8,711**	*+61* **8,772**	*+115* **8,887**	*+253* **9,140**	*+64* **9,204**	*628* **9,832**	*+63* **9,895**	*+1,114* **11,009**
Philip Hogan*	FG	**7,841**	*+11* **7,852**	*+222* **8,074**	*+165* **8,239**	*+664* **8,903**	*3,335* **12,238**		
Feargal Browne	FG	**5,468**	*+62* **5,530**	*+140* **5,670**	*+92* **5,762**	*+132* **5,894**	*Elim'd*		
Mary White	GP	**4,961**	*+42* **5,003**	*+398* **5,401**	*+654* **6,055**	*+641* **6,696**	*+633* **7,329**	*+26* **7,355**	
Jim Townsend	Lab.	**4,272**	*+58* **4,330**	*+85* **4,415**	*+153* **4,568**	*+2,057* **6,625**	*+1021* **7,646**	*+7* **7,653**	*+2,962* **10,615**
Michael O'Brien	Lab.	**3,732**	*+7* **3,739**	*+207* **3,946**	*+274* **4,220**	*Elim'd*			
Tom Kiernan	SF	**2,078**	*+20* **2,098**	*+118* **2,216**	*Elim'd*				
Eddie Collins-Hughes	IND	**1,614**	*+30* **1,644**	*Elim'd*					
Billy Nolan	IND	**353**	*Elim'd*						
Non-Transferable			16	73	197	22	150	0	2,046

* Outgoing Deputy

CAVAN–MONAGHAN

Outgoing Deputies: Caoimhghín Ó Caoláin (SF), Brendan Smith (FF), Paudge Connolly (Ind), Rory O'Hanlon (FF), Seymour Crawford (FG).

As the outgoing Ceann Comhairle of the 29th Dáil, Rory O'Hanlon (FF) will, if he chooses, be automatically returned to the 30th Dáil in the 2007 election.

The Constituency: This **five-seater** comprises the counties of Cavan and Monaghan. The boundaries of this constituency are unchanged since 2002.

Party	Votes 2002	Quota 2002	% Vote 2002	% Vote 1997	Swing
Fianna Fáil	21,614	2.1	34.95%	38.44%	−3.49%
Fine Gael	15,571	1.5	25.18%	34.67%	−9.49%
Labour	550	0.1	0.89%	3.96	−3.07%
PDs	1,131	0.1	1.83%	–	1.83%
Green Party	1,100	0.1	1.78%	–	1.78%
Sinn Féin	10,832	1.1	17.51%	19.37%	−1.85%
Others	11,049	1.07	17.51%	3.21	14.30%

2007 Candidates will include: Brendan Smith (FF), Margaret Conlon (FF), Seymour Crawford (FG), Joe O'Reilly (FG), Caoimhghín Ó Caoláin (SF), Paudge Connolly (Ind), Des Cullen (Lab).

In Brief: This will in effect be a four-seater, since Fianna Fáil's Monaghan-based deputy, Rory O'Hanlon, as the outgoing Ceann Comhairle, will automatically be re-elected. In this four-seat scenario both Fianna Fáil and Fine Gael are hopeful of gaining an extra seat. Both parties face an uphill task, however. Sinn Féin's leader in Dáil Éireann, Caoimhghín Ó Caoláin, will comfortably hold his seat. Much interest will focus on the prospects of Monaghan-based independent, Paudge Connolly, who won a seat in 2002 on the back of the local controversy about Monaghan Hospital. Fine Gael's Seymour Crawford is also likely to hold his seat in Monaghan, although his Cavan running mate, Joe O'Reilly, cannot be ruled out of contention, not least because only one of the five seats would go to Cavan if he doesn't win a seat. If O'Reilly does win a seat, however, it is more likely to be at the ultimate cost of the Monaghan Hospital candidate.

Fianna Fáil: Fianna Fáil had three out of the five seats here until 1997. It lost a seat in 2002, when its veteran Monaghan-based deputy Jimmy Leonard retired. This time the automatic return of Rory O'Hanlon as outgoing Ceann Comhairle guarantees Fianna Fáil one seat in Monaghan. Their other sitting deputy is Cavan-based Minister of State Brendan Smith, who is also likely to be safe. In order to win three seats Fianna Fáil will have to win a second seat in Monaghan.

The party's Monaghan-based candidate in 2002 was young urban councillor Robbie Gallegher, who polled just 3,731 first preference votes. The extent to which the Fianna Fáil vote in Monaghan holds up in the absence of O'Hanlon, who has been comfortably returned in each election since 1997, will be interesting. On 16 March 2007 Fianna Fáil headquarters announced that the party's other candidate in this constituency would be Margaret Conlon. Originally from the Lough Egish area, Ms Conlon is currently assistant principal at the St Louis convent in Monaghan town. She is chairwoman of the Fianna Fáil organisation in Monaghan.

Brendan Smith is Minister of State at the Department of Agriculture with special responsibility for food and horticulture. He was a long-time constituency manager and political adviser to the former Tánaiste, John Wilson, and he was first elected to Dáil Éireann on Wilson's retirement in 1992. Smith was comfortably re-elected in 2002, topping the poll with 10,679 first preferences, almost 2,000 more than in 1997.

Fine Gael: This was one of Fine Gael's disaster constituencies in 2002. Their vote fell by 5,000 first preferences and they lost one of their two seats. In 2002 they ran three candidates, Cavan-based outgoing deputy Andrew Boylan, outgoing Monaghan deputy Seymour Crawford and Cavan-based Paddy O'Reilly, who was from the Ballyjamesduff area. When Paddy O'Reilly was eliminated it took a three-day recount to determine whether Crawford or Boylan would win the single Fine Gael seat. In the end Crawford beat Boylan for the seat by just 121 votes.

Fine Gael's only outgoing deputy is therefore Seymour Crawford, who is based near Aghabog in County Monaghan. Crawford was first elected to Dáil Éireann in 1992. He is a former member of Monaghan County Council for the Clones electoral area and is also a former county chair of Monaghan IFA. He was appointed Deputy Spokesperson on Agriculture and Vice-Chairperson of the British-Irish Parliamentary Body in October 2004.

Fine Gael's second candidate in 2007 is Joe O'Reilly. Based in Ballieboro in County Cavan, O'Reilly was a member of Seanad Éireann from 1989 to 1992 on the Cultural and Educational Panel. He is a member of Cavan County Council, representing the Ballieboro local electoral area, where in the 2004 local elections he topped the poll with 1,291 first preferences. He is a national school teacher.

Labour Party: This is not a strong constituency for Labour. In 1997 former senator Ann Gallagher polled 2,359 first preference votes. Their candidate on this occasion is again Des Cullen. In 2002 he polled 550 first preferences, which is just 0.9% of the vote. Cullen was a member of Cavan Town Council from 1994 to 1999 and was once again elected to that council in 2004.

Progressive Democrats: In 2002 the party decided to contest this constituency the month before the election and nominated Gerry McCaughey, chief executive of Century Homes. He polled just 1,943 first preferences. They will have no candidate in this constituency in this election.

Sinn Féin: Sinn Féin's single candidate on this occasion is again their outgoing deputy, Caoimhghín Ó Caoláin. Ó Caoláin is based in Monaghan town. He was first elected to Dáil

Éireann in 1997. In that election he topped the poll with 11,531 first preferences and became the first Sinn Féin TD to be elected since the party abandoned its policy of abstentionism. He again topped the poll in the 2002 Dáil election, this time with 10,832 first preferences. Ó Caoláin was a member of Monaghan County Council from 1985 to 2004 for the Monaghan local electoral area. The party had a particularly good performance in Monaghan in the 2004 local elections, winning six seats on Monaghan County Council. In the lead-in to the 2007 election there was some speculation that the party might run a second candidate and there had been similar speculation in advance of the 2002 election, but Sinn Féin has stuck with its one-candidate strategy.

Others: Independent Paudge Connolly was first elected to Dáil Éireann in 2002. He was then a SIPTU representative and a psychiatric nurse working in Monaghan General Hospital. He is a former member of the North Eastern Health Board. In 2002 he polled 7,227 first preference votes. He voted for Bertie Ahern in the vote for Taoiseach when the Dáil first convened after the 2002 election.

CAVAN–MONAGHAN 2007 FIGURES

Candidate	Party	1st Count	2nd Count	3rd Count	4th Count	5th Count	Later counts

YOUR PREDICTION 2007

	Candidate Elected	Party
1		
2		
3		
4		
5		

RESULT 2007

	Candidate Elected	Party
1		
2		
3		
4		
5		

NOTES/UPDATES

CAVAN–MONAGHAN 2002 FIGURES

5 Seats   Quota: 10,308

Candidate	Party	1st	2nd	3rd	4th	5th	6th	7th	8th	9th	10th	11th	12th
Transfer of			Ó Caoláin surplus	B.Smith surplus	Cullen T.Smth	Brennan	McCaughey	McCabe	Martin	Gallagher	O'Hanlon surplus	Connolly surplus	O'Reilly
Caoimhghín Ó Caoláin*	SF	10,832											
Brendan Smith*	FF	10,679											
Paudge Connolly	IND	7,722	+145 7,867	+4 7,871	+75 7,946	+429 8,375	+239 8,614	+359 8,973	+705 9,678	+1,192 10,870			
Rory O Hanlon*	FF	7,204	+91 7,295	+184 7,479	+62 7,541	+107 7,648	−159 7,807	136 7,943	719 8,662	2,370 11,032			
Seymour Crawford*	FG	6,113	+23 6,136	+3 6,139	+39 6,178	+108 6,286	+111 6,397	+112 6,509	+294 6,803	+275 7,078	+314 7,392	+310 7,702	+1,463 9,165
Andrew Boylan*	FG	4,819	+36 4,855	+34 4,889	+172 5,061	+23 5,084	+127 5,211	+163 5,374	+142 5,516	+117 5,633	+211 5,844	+61 5,905	+3,139 9,044
Paddy O'Reilly	FG	4,639	+28 4,667	+31 4,698	+119 4,817	19 4,836	119 4,955	153 5,108	212 5,320	109 5,429	199 5,628	82 5,710	Elim.
Robbie Gallagher	FF	3,731	+58 3,789	+85 3,874	+47 3,921	+83 4,004	+193 4,197	+122 4,319	+216 4,535	Elim.			
Vincent P. Martin	IND	1,943	+49 1,992	+5 1,997	+90 2,087	+178 2,265	+106 2,371	+275 2,646	Elim.				
Marcus McCabe	GP	1,100	+38 1,138	+5 1,143	+158 1,301	+84 1,385	+128 +1513	Elim.					
Gerard McCaughey	PD	1,131	+13 1,144	+10 1,154	+65 1,219	+42 1,261	Elim.						
Joe Brennan	IND	1,026	+20 1,046	+1 1.047	+67 1,114	Elim.							
Des Cullen	LAB	550	+16 566	+6 572	Elim.								
Tony Smith	CSP	358	+7 365	+3 368	Elim.								
Non-Transferable			0	0	46	41	79	193	358	472	0	109	1,108

*Outgoing Deputy

CLARE

Outgoing Deputies: James Breen (Ind), Pat Breen (FG), Tony Killeen (FF), Síle de Valera (FF).

Síle de Valera is retiring and therefore will not be contesting the 2007 election.

The Constituency: This is a **four-seater** encompassing the county of Clare except for a part of the county in the Parteen area, which is in the Limerick East constituency. In the revision of constituencies since 2002 a small area in the electoral division of Ballyglass has been moved from Limerick East back into the Clare constituency, giving Clare an additional population (on 2002 figures) of 1,025.

Party	Votes 2002	Quota 2002	% Vote 2002	% Vote 1997	Swing
Fianna Fáil	22,602	2.3	45.38%	50.36%	–4.98%
Fine Gael	12,680	1.3	25.46%	30.08	–4.62%
Labour	1,720	0.2	3.45%	3.59%	–0.14%
PDs	–	–		6.93%	–6.93%
Green Party	2,903	0.3	5.83%	3.59%	2.24
Others	9,897	0.99	19.87%	5.44	14.43%

2007 Candidates will include: Brendan Daly (FF), Timmy Dooley (FF), Tony Killeen (FF), Pat Breen (FG), Joe Carey (FG), Tony Mulcahy (FG) Madeleine Taylor-Quinn (FG), Pascal Fitzgerald (Lab), Brian Meaney (GP), Anna Prior (SF), James Breen (Ind).

In Brief: Fianna Fáil will probably hold its two seats, Fine Gael are likely to win one, and the independent (but former Fianna Fáil councillor) James Breen is likely to hold his seat. If James Breen proves weaker than published constituency polls suggest, then Fine Gael could win a second seat or Fianna Fáil a third, with the former more likely than the latter. Outgoing Minister of State Tony Killeen is likely to be joined by former minister Brendan Daly, who will return to Dáil Éireann taking the seat left vacant by the retirement of Síle De Valera, although their running mate, Timmy Dooley, cannot be ruled out of contention. This is also a constituency where there is an outside chance that the Green Party could cause an upset.

Fianna Fáil: Fianna Fáil had three seats going into the 2002 election but lost one of them to the independent candidate James Breen, a former Fianna Fáil councillor who resigned from the party after he failed to get a nomination for that election. As a result Fianna Fáil's vote dropped nearly 5%. This time the party's outgoing Fianna Fáil deputy, Síle de Valera, is retiring. A former Minister and Minister of State and granddaughter of the party founder, Eamon de Valera, she has represented Clare since 1987. In her absence the party's ticket is Minister of State Tony Killeen, former deputy Senator Brendan Daly and Senator Timmy Dooley, for whom this will be his first Dáil contest.

Tony Killeen was first elected to Dáil Éireann in 1992 and has held the seat in each subsequent election. He was appointed Minister of State at the Department of Enterprise and Employment with special responsibility for Labour Affairs in September 2004. He lives in the Corofin end of the constituency, and also operates a constituency office in Ennis. From 1985–1997 he was a member of Clare County Council, representing the Ennistymon local electoral area. Killeen was chair of the Shannon Airport status committee from 1989 to 1991. He is a former primary school teacher.

Brendan Daly was first elected to Dáil Éireann in 1973. He held his seat in each election until 1992 when he lost it to the Labour Party's Moosajee Bhamjee. Daly narrowly regained this seat in 1997. However, in 2002 he lost the seat again, this time to the independent James Breen. Daly has been a member of Seanad Éireann since 2002 and was also a senator from 1993 to 1997. He has been a Minister in the Departments of Marine, Defence, Social Welfare, and Fisheries and Forestry. Now 67 years of age, he enjoys a strong political base in the Kilrush end of the constituency.

Timmy Dooley is 38 years of age and this is his first Dáil contest. He has been a member of the Seanad on the Administrative Panel since 2002. He is the party's spokesperson on Transport in the upper house. He had previously been a prominent member of Fianna Fáil's National Executive's Committee of Fifteen and before that of the party's National Youth Committee. He worked previously in sales and marketing and business development.

Fine Gael: Fine Gael, somewhat curiously, is running four candidates in this five-seat constituency where it currently has only one seat.

Pat Breen is the party's sitting deputy. He was elected to Dáil Éireann for the first time in 2002 on his first attempt, taking the seat previously held by outgoing deputy Donal Carey. He is currently the party's deputy spokesperson on Enterprise, Trade and Employment with Special Responsibility for EU Internal Market Development and Small and Medium Enterprises. He was a member of Clare County Council from 1999 to 2004 for the Kilrush electoral area.

Joe Carey is a member of Clare County Council and topped the poll in the Ennis electoral area in the 2004 local elections, where he polled 1,939 first preferences, which was 420 votes over the quota. He has been a member of the council since 1999. His father, Donal Carey, was a member of Dáil Éireann from 1981 to 2002. Joe's sister, Leonora Carey, is Vice-Chairperson of the Party's National Executive, while his younger brother, Donal Jnr, is Chairperson of Ennis District Fine Gael and his cousin, Sinead Carey, is Vice-President of Young Fine Gael.

Tony Mulcahy has been a member of Clare County Council for the Shannon electoral area and of Shannon Town Council since 1999. He polled 1,195 votes in the 2004 local elections. He is vice-chairperson of the Clare Federation of People with Special Needs.

Madeleine Taylor-Quinn was a member of Dáil Éireann from June 1981 to February 1982 and from November 1982 to 1989. She was a member of Seanad Éireann from 1993 to 2002 and from April to November 1982. A former secondary school teacher, she is a daughter of former deputy Frank Taylor, who was a member of Dáil Éireann from 1969 to 1981. She was a candidate for Fine Gael in the North West constituency in the 2004 European elections, in which she polled 41,570 preferences. She is a member of Clare County Council for the Kilrush electoral area, where she polled 1,079 first preferences in the 2004 local elections.

Labour: Labour's heyday in this constituency was 1992 when, on the back of the Spring tide, the psychiatrist Moosajee Bhamjee won a surprise seat. Bhamjee decided to retire from politics in advance of the 1997 election and, as a result, the party lost its seat here. The party's candidate in 2002 was councillor Michael Corley, an urban district councillor in Ennis and a former president of the ASTI. He polled just 1,720 first preference votes. The party's new candidate for this election is councillor Pascal Fitzgerald. Fitzgerald represents the Killaloe electoral area on Clare County Council, where he polled 940 first preferences in the 2004 local elections.

Green Party: Brian Meaney is again the party's candidate. An engineer, he just failed to get elected to Clare County Council in the local elections of 1999 but was elected in the Ennis electoral area in the 2004 local elections, where he polled 1,011 first preferences. In the 1997 Dáil election he polled 1,682 votes and in 2002 he increased that to 2,903 first preferences.

Sinn Féin: The party's candidate is Anna Prior and this is her first electoral contest.

Others: James Breen was a long-time Fianna Fáil activist and councillor. He was first elected to Clare County Council in 1985. He topped the poll for the party in the Miltown Malbay area in the 1991 local elections and transferred to the Ennis electoral area in the 1999 local election, where he polled 1,300 first preferences. After failing to persuade the party to place him on the ticket for the 2002 general election, Breen resigned and contested as an independent.

During the 2002 election the key planks of Breen's campaign became retaining services at Ennis Hospital and protecting the status of Shannon Airport. In that election he polled 9,721 first preference votes, just 333 votes short of the quota, and he took the first seat comfortably on the second count. He is a farmer by profession and is most remembered in the current Dáil for speeches in which he highlighted the issue of MRSA, the hospital infection from which he himself suffered.

CLARE 2007 FIGURES

Candidate	Party	1st Count	2nd Count	3rd Count	4th Count	5th Count	Later counts

YOUR PREDICTION 2007

	Candidate Elected	Party
1		
2		
3		
4		
5		

RESULT 2007

	Candidate Elected	Party
1		
2		
3		
4		
5		

NOTES/UPDATES

CLARE 2002 FIGURES

4 seats   Quota: 9,961

Candidate	Party	1st	2nd	3rd	4th	5th
Transfer of			Whelan Corley	Meaney	Carey	Taylor- Quinn
James Breen	IND	**9,721**	*+333* **10,054**			
Tony Killeen*	FF	**8,130**	*+122* **8,252**	*+388* **8,640**	*+424* **9,064**	*+418* **9,482**
Síle De Valera*	FF	**7,755**	*+111* **7,866**	*+598* **8,464**	*+355* **8,819**	*+551* **9,370**
Brendan Daly*	FF	**6,717**	*+69* **6,786**	*+128* **6,914**	*+172* **7,086**	*+597* **7,683**
Patrick Breen	FG	**4,541**	*+160* **4,701**	*+564* **5,265**	*+1,669* **6,934**	*+4,462* **11,396**
Madeleine Taylor-Quinn	FG	**4,124**	*+225* **4,349**	*+685* **5,034**	*1,692* **6,726**	*Elim'd*
Donal Carey*	FG	**4,015**	*+212* **4,227**	*+364* **4,591**	*Elim'd*	
Brian Meaney	GP	**2,903**	*+605* **3,508**	*Elim'd*		
Michael Corley	LAB	**1,720**	*Elim'd*			
Derek J Whelan	CSP	**176**	*Elim'd*			
Non-Transferable			59	781	279	698

*Outgoing Deputy

CORK EAST

Outgoing Deputies: Ned O'Keeffe (FF), Michael Ahern (FF), David Stanton (FG), Joe Sherlock (Lab).

The Constituency: This **four-seat** constituency is entirely within the county of Cork and stretches from Mallow in the north east to Cobh in the south west. The boundaries of this constituency are unchanged since 2002.

Party	Votes 2002	Quota 2002	% Vote 2002	% Vote 1997	Swing
Fianna Fáil	18,914	2.1	41.31%	36.44%	4.87%
Fine Gael	13,322	1.5	29.09%	30.12%	−1.03%
Labour	9,605	1.0	20.98%[1]	18.83%	2.12%*
PDs	–	–	–	4.25%	−4.25%
Green Party	1,136	0.1	2.48%	–	2.48%
Sinn Féin	2,624	0.3	5.73%	3.56%	2.17%
Others	187	0.02.	0.41%	0.78%	−6.37%

2007 Candidates will include: Michael Ahern (FF), Ned O'Keeffe (FF), Paul Bradford (FG), David Stanton (FG), John Mulvhill (Lab), Seán Sherlock (Lab), Sarah Iremonger (GP), Sandra McLellan (SF).

In Brief: For almost two decades the outcome in this constituency has been two Fianna Fáil seats and two seats for the Fine Gael–Labour combination, although there has been some change of personnel on the 'Rainbow' side and, on occasion, Fine Gael has won both seats. Currently, Fianna Fáil holds two seats and Fine Gael and Labour have one each. This time Fianna Fáil is again running its two sitting deputies, Ned O'Keeffe and Michael Ahern, who, bar an upset, should hold their seats. For Fine Gael the outgoing deputy David Stanton and former deputy Senator Paul Bradford are the candidates. Labour's candidates are Seán Sherlock, a son of the sitting deputy Joe Sherlock, and the party's former deputy, John Mulvihill. Realistically, Labour can only hope to win one seat and locally some are suggesting that Labour may not even take one seat, meaning that Fine Gael may win two.

Fianna Fáil: In 2002 Fianna Fáil again easily retained its two seats. Each of the two sitting TDs has a solid constituency profile and distinct geographic base.

Ned O'Keeffe is a successful farmer and businessman from Mitchelstown. He was first elected to Dáil Éireann in 1982 and has been re-elected in each election since. O'Keeffe was appointed Minister of State at the Department of Agriculture following the 1997 general election. However, he resigned in 2001, following allegations that he had failed to comply with the requirement to make certain declarations under the Ethics in Public Office Act. Subsequently, a Public Office Commission inquiry held that O'Keeffe had breached the Ethics Act but that he had not intended to do so. This controversy ensured that Ned O'Keeffe had a political point to prove in 2002 and he topped the poll, with his vote increasing from 8,737 in 1997 to 10,574 in 2002. He was a member of Cork County Council from 1985 to 1997. His son Kevin O'Keeffe has been a member of Cork County Council for the Fermoy electoral area since 1999. Kevin topped the poll there in the 2004 local election with 3,671 first preferences.

Michael Ahern was first elected to Dáil Éireann in February 1982 and has held his seat on every occasion since. He is currently Minister of State at the Department of Enterprise, Trade and Employment with special responsibly for Trade and Commerce. He was Minister of State at the Department of Industry and Commerce with special responsibility for Science and Technology from 1992 to 1993. Living in Carrigtwohill and operating off a Midleton base, he significantly increased his vote in the 2002 election, going from 6,959 first preferences in 1997 to 8,340 in 2002. Ahern is an accountant by profession.

Fine Gael: Fine Gael won two seats here in 1997 but was left with only one when the high-profile deputy and outgoing chief whip, Paul Bradford, lost his seat in 2002. Even though the other outgoing deputy, David Stanton, received less first preferences than Paul Bradford on the first count, Stanton picked up enough transfers to take the last seat. The decisive count involved transfers following the elimination of the Labour Party candidate, John Mulvihill, whose geographic base was close to Stanton's.

David Stanton was first elected to Dáil Éireann in 1997 on his first attempt. Based in Midleton, he is a former teacher and career guidance counsellor. He is currently the party's front bench Spokesperson on Social and Family Affairs and Equality. He was the party's deputy spokesperson on Education and Science with special responsibility for the Information Society from 2002 to 2004. He has been chairman of the Fine Gael Oireachtas Committee on disability issues since December 2002. He is a director of Midleton and District Day Care Center Ltd.

Paul Bradford is currently a member of Seanad Éireann having been elected on the Agricultural panel in 2002. He was a Dáil deputy from 1989 to 2002 and was Fine Gael chief whip during Michael Noonan's leadership. He was previously a senator from 1987 to 1989. A farmer, he was a member of Cork County Council for the Mallow electoral area from 1985 to 2004. He was first elected to Cork County Council at the age of 21, to Seanad Éireann at the age of 23 and to Dáil Éireann at the age of 25. He is a former Co-Chair of the British–Irish Inter Parliamentary Body.

Labour Party: In 2002 this constituency was a crucial test for the amalgamated Labour Party and it was hoped that the synergy from the Labour and Democratic Left merger would enable the party to take a seat from Fine Gael. In 1997 the Democratic Left and Labour Party candidates combined had a total of 8,122 first preferences, just about 500 votes short of a quota, but neither of them won a seat. In 2002, with both Joe Sherlock and John Mulvihil running under the Labour Party banner, their combined vote was up to 9,605. The two candidates were 21 votes apart on the first count, with Mulvihill slightly ahead. However, Sherlock was much stronger in attracting transfers than Mulvihill and by the third count had not only overtaken him but had opened a 633 vote gap. Mulvihill was eliminated and Sherlock took the third of the four seats. This time Joe Sherlock is retiring and his son, Seán Sherlock, joins Mulvihill on the party's ticket.

John Mulvihill, based in Cobh, was a member of Dáil Éireann from 1992 to 1997. He has been a member of Cork County Council for the Midleton electoral area since 1991. He polled 2,821 first preferences in the Midleton area in the 2004 local elections. He polled 5,703 first preferences in the 1992 Dáil election, 3,500 in the 1997 election and 4,813 first preferences in the 2002 election.

Seán Sherlock has been a member of Cork County Council since 2004. He topped the poll in the Mallow local electoral area in the 2004 local elections with 3,184 first preference votes. His father, Joe Sherlock, has been a candidate in this constituency in every election since 1973, first for Sinn Féin The Workers Party, then the Workers Party, Democratic Left and, after the merger, the Labour Party. He was a member of Dáil Éireann from November 1981 to November 1982 and from 1987 to 1992 and since 2002.

Green Party: In 2002 the Green Party ran a candidate here for the first time; Martin O'Keeffe polled 1,136 first preferences. The party candidate in 2007 is Sara Iremonger. She was an unsuccessful candidate for Cork County Council in the 2004 local elections. She stood in the Midleton electoral area, where she polled 737 votes when the quota was 3,176.

Sinn Féin: Their candidate is Sandra McLellan, who is a Youghal Town Councillor. In 2002 they ran Mitchelstown-based June Murphy, who polled 2,624 first preferences.

CORK EAST 2007 FIGURES

Candidate	Party	1st Count	2nd Count	3rd Count	4th Count	5th Count	Later counts

YOUR PREDICTION 2007

	Candidate Elected	Party
1		
2		
3		
4		
5		

RESULT 2007

	Candidate Elected	Party
1		
2		
3		
4		
5		

NOTES/UPDATES

CORK EAST 2002 FIGURES

4 Seats   Quota 9,158

Candidate	Party	1st	2nd	3rd	4th
Transfer of			N.O'Keeffe's surplus	Murphy M.O Keefe Manning	Mulvihill
Ned O Keeffe*	FF	10,574			
Michael Ahern*	FF	8,340	+864 9,204		
Paul Bradford*	FG	7,053	+171 7,224	+494 7,718	+513 8,231
David Stanton*	FG	6,269	+55 6,324	+654 6,978	+1,460 8,438
John Mulvihill	LAB	4,813	+25 4,838	+721 5,559	Elim'd
Joe Sherlock	LAB	4,792	+223 4,838	+721 5,559	+2,468 8,660
June Murphy	SF	2,624	+61 4,838	+721 5,559	Elim'd
Martin O'Keeffe	GP	1,136	+15 1,151	Elim'd	
Patrick Manning	CSP	189	+2 189	Elim'd	
Non-Transferable			0	979	1,118

*Outgoing Deputy

CORK NORTH CENTRAL

Outgoing Deputies: Noel O'Flynn (FF), Bernard Allen (FG), Billy Kelleher (FF), Dan Wallace (FF), Kathleen Lynch (Lab).

Dan Wallace (FF) is retiring and is therefore not contesting the 2007 election.

The Constituency: This is now a **four-seat** constituency, having lost one seat in the redrawing of constituencies since 2002. The redrawing transferred an area south of the Lee, with a population of 25,918 (on 2002 census figures), back into Cork South Central, restoring the Lee as the border between the two city constituencies. The redrawing also involved the transfer of the electoral divisions of Carrigcrohane Beg, Dripsey, Firmount and Matehy from the former Cork rural district and Gowland from the Macroom rural district with a total population of 7,001 in the area to the east and north of Cork North West into this constituency.

Party	Votes 2002	Quota 2002	% Vote 2002	% Vote 1997	Swing
Fianna Fáil	18,725	2.5	41.48%	35.53%	5.95%
Fine Gael	9,202	1.2	20.38%	30.16%	–9.78%
Labour	5,313	0.7	11.77%	5.27%	–0.65%**
PDs	3,126	0.4	6.92%	14.65%	–0.58%
Green Party	1,155		2.56%	3.04%	–0.49%
Sinn Féin	2,860	0.4	6.34%	3.76%	2.58%
Others	4,763		10.55%		2.97%

2007 Candidates will include: Billy Kelleher (FF), Noel O'Flynn (FF), Bernard Allen (FG), Gerry Kelly (FG), Kathleen Lynch (Lab), Chris O'Leary (GP), Jonathan O'Brien (SF), Mick Barry (SP), Ted Tynan (WP).

In Brief: This constituency has been reduced from a five-seater in 2002 to a four-seater in 2007. One of the sitting Fianna Fáil deputies, Danny Wallace, is retiring, so Fianna Fáil is running just two candidates this time – the other two incumbents, Noel O'Flynn and Billy Kelleher – thereby accepting the reality that the redrawing has reduced their seat share here from three to two. With Fine Gael's Bernard Allen and the Labour Party's Kathleen Lynch likely to hold their seats, the result will most probably see the four sitting deputies who are contesting returned. Fine Gael talks of winning a second seat here. In the unlikely event of this happening, it is more probable that it will be achieved by taking the Labour seat than by reducing Fianna Fáil's representation further to just one seat.

Fianna Fáil: Fianna Fáil won three seats when this was a five-seater in 1997. Although the party polled just 36% of the first preference vote, a tight vote management strategy and the decisive Progressive Democrat transfers enabled the party to win three seats here. In 2002 the party retained the three seats with the help of a six percentage point increase in its first preference vote. Dan Wallace was the veteran of Fianna Fáil's three outgoing deputies, having been first elected to the Dáil in 1982, but he is retiring at this election. The reduction of seats in the constituency from five to four means that the party is running just two candidates on this occasion.

Noel O'Flynn was first elected to Dáil Éireann in 1997. In 2002 he increased his first preference vote dramatically, from 4,943 in 1997 to 7,387, which put him at the top of the poll, just 138 votes below the quota. He is currently chairman of the Dáil Committee on Communications, Marine and Natural Resources. He came to national prominence in the months before the 2002 election with remarks about non-nationals and asylum seekers, which earned him an unusual public rebuke from Taoiseach Bertie Ahern. He was a member of Cork City Council from 1991 until 2003 for the Cork North Central ward. He is also a businessman.

Billy Kelleher was first elected to Dáil Éireann in 1997. He came extremely close to winning a seat on his first attempt in 1992, when he lost out by just 25 votes. He was also an unsuccessful candidate in the 1994 by-election in this constituency caused by the death of Labour's Gerry O'Sullivan. In 2002, Kelleher polled 5,801 first preferences, which was up marginally on his vote in 1997, and he took the fourth seat on the last count. He is a former member of Cork City Council for the North East ward. He has been Fianna Fáil assistant chief whip since 2002.

Fine Gael: In the 2002 election Fine Gael's Bernard Allen comfortably retained his seat but the party lost its second seat, which had been held by Liam Burke, who retired at that election. The party's vote was down considerably. In 1997 the party had polled 30.16% but in 2002 that dropped by a third to 20.38%.

Bernard Allen was first elected to Dáil Éireann in 1981 and has been returned on each occasion since. He was a member of Cork City Council from 1979 to 1995 and was Mayor of Cork for the year 1988–89. Allen was Minister of State at the Department of Education from 1994 to 1997. He was the party's spokesperson on the Environment and Local Government from June 2002 to October 2004 and is currently their spokesperson on Foreign Affairs. Bernard Allen's own personal vote was down from 7,746 first preferences in 1997 to 5,458 in 2002.

Gerry Kelly is again running in this election. In the 2002 election he polled 3,744 first preferences. He has been a member of Cork County Council for the Blarney local electoral area since 1999. He topped the poll in the 2004 local elections with 3,402 first preferences.

Labour Party: This constituency was another important testing ground for the merger between the Labour Party and Democratic Left in 2002. Both of the parties had a seat here in 1989. Kathleen Lynch, then a Democratic Left deputy, lost her seat in the election that year but won it back in the 1994 by-election which followed the death of the Labour Party's Gerry O'Sullivan. However, she lost the seat again in 1997. In 2002, after the merger, she was the sole Labour candidate and this, combined with the weakness of Fine Gael, enabled her to regain her seat. She polled 5,313 first preferences and attracted a significant number of Green Party, Sinn Féin and indeed Progressive Democrat transfers to take the second of the five seats.

Lynch's achievement in 2002 was particularly impressive because the former Labour Party councillor Joe O'Callaghan, who was expelled from the party after controversial remarks about non-nationals and asylum seekers, ran as an independent and polled 3,154 first preferences. Lynch is based in Farranree and was a member of Cork City Council from 1985 to 2004, most recently for the Cork North Central ward. She is currently the party spokesperson on Consumer Affairs.

Progressive Democrats: When Máirín Quill decided not to contest the 2002 election, party chairman John Minihan switched from Cork South Central to contest this constituency. Of the 3,286 votes which Minihan had when he was eliminated on the fifth count in 2002, just under 40% went to the two remaining Fianna Fáil candidates. For the 2007 election Minihan has returned to Cork South Central and the party is not running a candidate in this constituency.

Green Party: The party candidate here in 2002 was Nicholas McMurray, who polled just 1,155 first preferences. In 2007 the candidate is Chris O'Leary, who is based in Mahon. He has been a member of Cork City Council since 2002. He was was co-opted to the council in 2002 to replace Dan Boyle, who had been elected to Dáil Éireann. O'Leary retained the seat in the 2004 local elections, polling 1,086 first preferences in the Cork South East ward .

Sinn Féin: The party candidate in 2002 was Jonathan O'Brien, who polled a credible first preference vote of 2,860. He has since been elected to Cork City Council, having topped the poll in the North West ward in the 2004 local elections with 1,150 first preferences. Now 35 years of age, he is likely to improve the party vote share in this election but is unlikely to be in contention for a seat.

Others: Mick Barry is again the Socialist Party candidate in this constituency. In the 2002 election he polled 936 first preferences. He has been a member of Cork City Council since 2004, when he topped the poll in the Cork North Central local electoral area with 1,390 first preferences and took a seat. He is a member of the Cork Householders against Service Charges campaign and secretary of Cork Independent Workers Union home helps branch. He was jailed for failing to pay refuse charges in 2001.

Ted Tynan (WP) is a former city councillor. Based in the Mayfield area, he contested the 1992 general election, when he polled just 446, and the 2002 general election, when he polled 458 first preferences. He was jailed twice in the 1990s for failing to pay service charges and is also a member of the Householders against Service Charges group.

CORK NORTH CENTRAL 2007 FIGURES

Candidate	Party	1st Count	2nd Count	3rd Count	4th Count	5th Count	Later counts

YOUR PREDICTION 2007

	Candidate Elected	Party
1		
2		
3		
4		
5		

RESULT 2007

	Candidate Elected	Party
1		
2		
3		
4		
5		

NOTES/UPDATES

CORK NORTH CENTRAL 2002 FIGURES

5 seats   Quota: 7,525

Candidate	Party	1st	2nd	3rd	4th	5th	6th	7th
Transfer of			Tynan Duffy	Barry	McMurray	Minihan	O'Brien	O'Callaghan
Noel O'Flynn*	FF	7,387	+54 7,441	+54 7,495	+30 7,525	7,525	7,525	7,525
Billy Kelleher*	FF	5,801	+48 5,849	+36 5,885	+55 5,940	+690 6,630	+339 6,969	+487 7,456
Dan Wallace*	FF	5,537	+71 5,608	+24 5,632	+43 5,675	+560 6,235	+342 6,577	+610 7,187
Bernard Allen*	FG	5,458	+45 5,503	+94 5,597	+75 5,672	+512 6,184	+417 6,601	+1,049 7,650
Kathleen Lynch	LAB	5,313	+89 5,402	+226 5,628	+514 6,142	+541 6,683	+813 7,496	+922 8,418
Gerry Kelly	FG	3,744	+23 3,767	+51 3,818	+93 3,911	+493 4,404	+164 4,568	+369 4,937
Joe O'Callaghan	IND	3,154	+68 3,222	+97 3,319	+138 3,457	+248 3,705	+760 4,465	Elim'd
John Minihan	PD	3,126	+26 3,152	+21 3,173	+113 3,286	Elim'd		
Jonathan O Brien	SF	2,860	+105 2,965	+258 3,223	+182 3,405	+78 3,483	Elim'd	
John Minihan	PD	3,126	+26 3,152	+21 3,173	+113 3,286	Elim'd		
Nicholas McMurray	GP	1,155	+41 1,196	+133 1,329	Elim'd			
Mick Barry	SP	936	+90 1,026	Elim'd				
Ted Tynan	WP	458	Elim'd					
Gerry Duffy	CSP	215	Elim'd					
Non-Transferable			13	32	86	164	648	1,028

CORK NORTH WEST

Outgoing Deputies: Michael Moynihan (FF), Donal Moynihan (FF), Gerard Murphy (FG).

The Constituency: This is a **three-seat** constituency. In the redrawing of constituencies since the 2002 election, it has gained an area in Ballincollig (which had a 2002 population of 15,119) from the Cork South Central constituency. However, it lost Carrigcrohane Beg, Dripsey, Firmount, Matehy and Gowland in the east and north of the constituency to Cork North Central.

Party	Votes 2002	Quota 2002	% Vote 2002	% Vote 1997	Swing
Fianna Fáil	19,433	2.0	50.06%	46.50%	3.56%
Fine Gael	16,335	1.7	42.08%	41.12%	0.96%
Labour	2,668	0.3	6.87%	7.4%	–0.53%
Others	383	0.0	0.99%	0.99	–

2007 Candidates will include: Donal Moynihan (FF), Michael Moynihan (FF), Batt O'Keeffe (FF), Michael Creed (FG), Gerard Murphy (FG), Martin Coughlan (Lab).

In Brief: This is a key Fine Gael target for a gain from Fianna Fáil. The sitting deputy, Gerard Murphy, and the former deputy, Michael Creed, are the two candidates for Fine Gael. However, the intensity of the competition within the Fianna Fáil ticket, which includes the two sitting Moynihan deputies and the sitting Cork South Central deputy, Batt O'Keeffe, whose Ballincollig base has been redrawn into this constituency, will increase that party's chances of holding its two seats. Whatever happens, one of the four Dáil deputies contesting will lose his seat.

Fianna Fáil: Fianna Fáil won two of the three seats here for the first time in 1997. In 2002 they held them comfortably and in fact took the first two seats.

Donal Moynihan was first elected to Dáil Éireann in 1982. He held on to his seat in 1987. However, in 1989 he lost his seat to his party colleague Laurence Kelly. Moynihan regained the seat from Kelly in 1992 and has held it since. He enjoys an established base in the southern end of the constituency and in particular in Macroom. He increased his support from 7,867 first preferences in 1997 to 8,893 in 2002.

Michael Moynihan was elected to Dáil Éireann in 1997 on his first attempt and he topped the poll in that election. He has a particular base in the northern end of the constituency and in the urban centres of Kanturk and Millstreet. He is a former national chair of the party's youth wing, Ógra Fianna Fáil. In 2002 he again topped the poll, dramatically increasing his first preference vote from 8,299 in 1997 to 10,540, which was comfortably over the quota. He is a farmer and lives just outside Kanturk.

Batt O'Keeffe is the outgoing Dáil deputy for the neighbouring constituency of Cork South Central. He won a seat in that constituency in 1987, lost it in 1989 but regained it in 1992 and has held it since. He was appointed Minister of State at the Department of the Environment, Heritage and Local Government with special responsibility in the area of Environmental Protection in September 2004. He is a former chairperson of the Southern Health Board and was chairman of the Oireachtas Committee on Health and Children from 1997 to 2002. In the redrawing of constituencies since 2002 his Ballincollig base has been transferred into this Cork North West constituency and that is why he is contesting here on this occasion. A former lecturer at what is now the Cork Institute of Technology, he was a member of the Seanad from 1989 to 1992. He is also a former member of Cork County Council, on which he represented the Carrigaline electoral area from 1985 to 2002. His son, Mark O'Keeffe, was co-opted to his Cork County Council seat and held it in the 2004 local elections, polling 3,094 first preferences.

Fine Gael: Veteran Fine Gael deputy Frank Crowley lost his seat here in 1997, which was the first time Fine Gael had failed to win two seats since the constituency was created. The Fine Gael vote was actually up marginally in 2002, but this was due in no small part to the absence in 2002 of one of the independents who had run in 1997. However, the party still only won one seat, with the outgoing frontbencher Michael Creed losing his seat to his party colleague Gerard Murphy, albeit by just 47 votes.

Gerard Murphy was elected to Dáil Éireann on his first attempt in 2002. Based in Newmarket, he was a member of Cork County Council from 1991 to 2004 for the Kanturk electoral area. He is currently the party's deputy spokesperson on Justice, Equality, Defence and Women's Rights. He was previously deputy spokesperson on Enterprise, Trade and Employment from 2002 to October 2004.

Michael Creed was a member of Dáil Éireann from 1989 to 2002. During Michael Noonan's leadership, Creed was frontbench spokesperson on Education. He is currently a member of Cork County Council for the Macroom electoral area, where he topped the poll with 3,710 first preferences in the 2004 local elections. He is also a farmer. His father, Donal Creed, was a Dáil deputy for Mid Cork from 1965 to1981 and for Cork North West from 1981 to 1989.

Labour Party: The party candidate again is Macroom urban district councillor Martin Coughlan. Coughlan is a member of Cork County Council for the Macroom electoral area, where he polled 1,393 and took the third of three seats in 2004. In the 2002 Dáil election the party's vote was down just over half a percentage point on their 1997 vote share. In that election Coughlan polled 2,668 first preferences.

CORK NORTH WEST 2007 FIGURES

Candidate	Party	1st Count	2nd Count	3rd Count	4th Count	5th Count	Later counts

YOUR PREDICTION 2007

	Candidate Elected	Party
1		
2		
3		
4		
5		

RESULT 2007

	Candidate Elected	Party
1		
2		
3		
4		
5		

NOTES/UPDATES

CORK NORTH WEST 2002 FIGURES

3 Seats   Quota 9,705

Candidate	Party	1st	2nd	3rd	4th
Transfer of			M.Moynihan's surplus	Duffy Coughlan	D.Moyniha's surplus
Michael Moynihan*	FF	**10,540**			
Donal Moynihan*	FF	**8,893**	+592 **9,485**	+669 **10,154**	
Gerard Murphy	FG	**8,548**	+181 **8,729**	+688 **9,417**	+90 **9,507**
Michael Creed*	FG	**7,787**	+30 **7,817**	+1,340 **9,157**	+303 **9,460**
Martin Coughlan	LAB	**2,668**	+26 **2,694**		
Gerry Duffy	CSP	**383**	+6 **389**		
Non-Transferable			0	386	56

CORK SOUTH CENTRAL

Outgoing Deputies: Micheál Martin (FF), Simon Coveney (FG), Batt O'Keeffe (FF), Dan Boyle (GP), John Dennehy (FF).

Batt O'Keeffe (FF) is contesting this election in the Cork North West constituency.

The Constituency: This large **five-seat** constituency includes all of the Cork City Council administrative area south of the River Lee and most of the county council area of Carrigaline. In the redrawing of constituencies since 2002, Cork South Central gained an area near the Lee, with a population (on 2002 census figures) of 25,918, from Cork North Central, thereby restoring the river as the boundary between the two city constituencies. However, it lost an area at the Ballincollig end, with a population of 15,119, to Cork North West, and an area east of Kinsale and in the area of Warners Crossroads, with a population of 3,757, to Cork South West.

Party	Votes 2002	Quota 2002	% Vote 2002	% Vote 1997	Swing
Fianna Fáil	26,879	2.9	48.57%	42.62%	5.96%
Fine Gael	10,735	1.2	19.49%	30.57	−11.17%
Labour	3,286	0.4	5.94%	8.92%	−2.98%
PDs	–	–	–	4.19	−4.19%
Green Party	4,956	0.5	8.96%	6.58%	2.38%
Sinn Féin	2,073	0.2	3.75%	0	3.75%
Others	7,409	0.8	13.39%	7.13	6.26%

2007 Candidates will include: John Dennehy (FF), Micheál Martin (FF), Michael McGrath (FF), Jerry Buttimer (FG), Deirdre Clune (FG), Simon Coveney (FG), Ciaran Lynch (Lab), John Minihan (PD), Dan Boyle (GP), Henry Cremin (SF).

In Brief: This large five-seat constituency was the last in which the result was declared in 2002. John Dennehy beat the independent Kathy Sinnott by just a handful of votes to win the last seat after a lengthy recount. This time the constituency is a key Fine Gael target for a gain from Fianna Fáil. Fine Gael's chances are helped by the fact that one of the sitting Fianna Fáil deputies, Batt O'Keeffe, is contesting Cork North West in this election. Fine Gael's prospects are also helped by the fact that their sitting deputy, Simon Coveney, who was also elected an MEP in 2004, has opted to recontest for the Dáil. The former Fine Gael deputy Deirdre Clune is likely to be the second strongest of the three Fine Gael candidates running. The Green Party's

Dan Boyle, likely to be high profile as the party's finance spokesperson during the campaign, should safely hold his seat.

Fianna Fáil: In 2002 Fianna Fáil retained the three seats they won in 1997, but only by the skin of their teeth. The party's vote rose from 42.62% in 1997 to 48.6% in 2002, but the division of votes between their three candidates made it difficult to win three seats in a five-seater on this vote share. Minister Micheál Martin's first preference vote rocketed from 9,652 in 1997 to 14,764 in 2002. This left him 5,540 votes over the quota on the first count. Although 3,394 votes of Martin's surplus transferred on the next count to his two Fianna Fáil colleagues, this was an internal transfer rate of 61%, which was just slightly short of the national average. The party's third candidate, John Dennehy, was left with a margin of only six votes over the independent candidate Kathy Sinnott for the last seat.

Micheál Martin was first elected to Dáil Éireann in 1989 on his second attempt and has been returned in each election since. He has been Minister for Enterprise, Trade and Employment since September 2004, was Minister for Health from 2000 to 2004 and was Minister for Education from 1997 to January 2000. He was a member of Cork City Council from 1985 to 1997 and Mayor of Cork for the year 1992–93. His brother Seán has been a member of Cork City Council in the Cork South Central ward since 1997 and polled 1,191 first preferences there in the 2004 local elections.

John Dennehy was first elected to Dáil Éireann in 1987 but lost his seat in 1992. He won it back in 1997 and then came very close to losing it in 2002. He also unsuccessfully contested the 1977 Dáil election in the Mid Cork constituency and unsuccessfully contested by-elections in the Cork City constituency in 1979 and in Cork South Central in 1994. Dennehy is a former co-chair of the British-Irish Interparliamentary Body and was assistant government chief whip from 1989 to 1991. He was a member of Cork City Council from 1979 to 2003. His son Fergal was co-opted in his stead to Cork City Council and retained the seat in the 2004 local elections, when he polled 1,408 first preferences in the Cork South West ward.

The party's new candidate is 30-year-old Michael McGrath. He first became an elected representative in 1999 at the age of 22, when he was elected to Passage West Town Council. McGrath has been a member of Cork County Council since 2004, when he topped the poll in the Carrigaline electoral area with 3,951 first preferences on his first attempt. He qualified as a chartered accountant with KPMG and was previously Head of Management Information and Systems in University College Cork.

Fine Gael: Although the party had two of the biggest political names in Cork on their ticket in this constituency, its share of the first preference vote collapsed from 30.57% in 1997 to 19.4% in 2002. It was a close call as to which of the party's then outgoing Dáil deputies, Deirdre Clune or Simon Coveney, would win the one seat available on that vote share. Clune actually increased her vote marginally, from 4,602 first preferences 1997 to 5,538 in 2002, and she was ahead of Coveney, who polled 5,197 first preferences, on the first count. However, Coveney attracted more transfers and by the sixth count was a crucial 54 votes ahead of Clune. As a result she was eliminated and Coveney went comfortably over the quota. This time the party is again running Coveney and Clune and they are joined by a new candidate, Jerry Buttimer.

Simon Coveney was first elected in October 1998 in a by-election following the death of his father, Hugh Coveney, who was a Dáil deputy for this constituency from 1981 to 1987 and again from 1992 to 1998, holding ministerial office from 1993 to 1997. Simon Coveney held his Dáil seat, although after a close shave as mentioned above, in 2002 and in 2004 was elected to the European Parliament for the South constituency, which covers all of Munster except Clare. He was a member of Cork County Council for the Carrigaline electoral area from 1999 to 2003 and the party's frontbench spokesperson on Communications, Marine and Natural Resources from 2002 until 2004. If re-elected to Dáil Éireann in this election he will automatically cease to be a member of the European Parliament.

Deirdre Clune was elected to Dáil Éireann on her first attempt in 1997 but lost the seat in 2002 even though she was ahead of Coveney on the first count. She is a member of Cork City Council and in the 2004 local elections topped the poll in the Cork South East ward. Her chances of regaining her seat will have been helped by the fact that she was the Lord Mayor of Cork for the year 2005–2006. Her father is the former Minister for Foreign Affairs and deputy leader of Fine Gael, Peter Barry, who was a member of Dáil Éireann from 1969 to 1997.

Jerry Buttimer has been a member of Cork City Council since 2004. He represents the Cork South West ward, where he topped the poll with 1,968 first preferences in the 2004 local elections and is based in Bishopstown. He is a secondary school teacher and Director of Adult Education at Ballincollig Community School and is a former Youth and Development Officer of Cork County GAA Board. He writes a weekly education column in the *Cork Independent*.

Labour Party: The party's candidate here in 2002 was the formerly independent National University of Ireland senator, Brendan Ryan. He polled 3,282 first preference votes and was never in contention for a seat. He did, however, later retain his Seanad seat on the NUI Panel and is currently the Labour Party's leader in Seanad Éireann.

In the 2007 election, the party's candidate in this constituency is the Cork City councillor Ciaran Lynch. He has been a member of Cork City Council since 2004, when he took the second seat in the Cork South Central ward, polling 1,226 first preferences. He is an adult literacy officer with Cork Vocational Education Committe

Green Party: The party's outgoing deputy, Dan Boyle, is expected to hold on to the Dáil seat he finally won in 2002. He was an unsuccessful candidate in 1992, when he polled 2.1%, and again in 1997, when he polled 6.5%. In 2002 he polled 4,952, which represented 9% of the vote. He was a member of Cork City Council for the South East ward from 1991 to 2002. He is currently the party's spokesperson on Finance, Social and Family Affairs, Rural Development, the Gaeltacht and the Islands.

Progressive Democrats: The party's Cork senator, John Minihan, is again engaging in some constituency hopping across the Lee for this election. Minihan was a candidate in Cork North Central in the 2002 general election, where he polled 3,126 first preferences. He was, however, a member of Cork City Council for the South East ward (which is within this constituency) from 1999 to 2004. He has been a Taoiseach's nominee to Seanad Éireann since 1997. A relatively high-profile senator, he has been prominent in his anti-Sinn Féin stance and is party spokesperson on Justice and Finance issues in the Seanad. He was chairman of the Progressive Democrats from 1999 to 2002. He is a former army officer and is also involved in a pharmacy business.

Sinn Féin: Tom Hanlon, a Passage West town councillor, was the party's candidate in 2002 when he polled just 2,063 first preferences. The party's candidate in 2007 is Henry Cremin, who first stood at the by-election following the death of Hugh Coveney and gained 1,020 first preference votes in the Cork South West ward in the 2004 local elections.

Others: Kathy Sinnott was an independent candidate in this constituency in 2002, when she polled 4,984 first preferences. She has since been elected a member of the European Parliament for the South constituency, where she took the third seat in the 2004 European elections.

CORK SOUTH CENTRAL 2007 FIGURES

Candidate	Party	1st Count	2nd Count	3rd Count	4th Count	5th Count	Later counts
Boyle		4945					
Buttimer		5180					

YOUR PREDICTION 2007

	Candidate Elected	Party
1		
2		
3		
4		
5		

RESULT 2007

	Candidate Elected	Party
1		
2		
3		
4		
5		

NOTES/UPDATES

CORK SOUTH CENTRAL 2002 FIGURES

5 seats   **Quota: 9,207**

Candidate Transfer of	Party	1st	2nd Martin's surplus	3rd Neville O'Sullivan	4th O'Connell	5th Hanlon	6th Ryan	7th Clune	8th Coveney's surplus	9th O'Keeffe's surplus	10th Boyle
Micheál Martin*	FF	14,742									
Batt O Keeffe*	FF	6,556	+1,668 8,224	+55 8,279	+114 8,393	+301 8,694	+203 8,897	+215 9,112	+219 9,331		
Deirdre Clune*	FG	5,535	313 5,848	+38 5,886	+96 5,982	+93 6,075	+518 6,593	Elim'd			
John Dennehy*	FF	5,533	+1,723 7,256	+39 7,295	+402 7,697	+364 8,061	+220 8,281	+199 8,480	+204 8,684	+82 8,766	+23 8,789
Simon Coveney*	FG	5,183	+574 5,757	+36 5,793	+113 5,906	+132 6,038	+596 6,634	+4.939 11,573			
Kathy Sinnot	IND	4,984	+409 5,393	+98 5,491	+418 5,909	+541 6,450	+765 7,215	+509 7,724	+930 8,654	+42 8696	+87 8783
Dan Boyle	GP	4,952	+442 5,394	+112 5,506	+260 5,766	+568 6,334	+1,427 7,761	+543 8,304	+1.013 9,317		
Brendan Ryan	LAB	3,282	+179 3,461	+48 3,509	+234 3,743	+223 3,966	Elim'd				
Tom Hanlon	SF	2,063	+113 2,176	+78 2,254	+226 2,480	Elim'd					
Con O Connell	IND	1,821	+93 1,914	+90 2,004	Elim'd						
Ted Neville	IND	372	+11 383	Elim'd							
Michael O'Sullivan	SWP	217	+10 227	Elim'd							
Non-Transferable		0	16	141	258	237	188				

*Outgoing Deputy

CORK SOUTH WEST

Outgoing Deputies: Denis O'Donovan (FF), Joe Walsh (FF), Jim O'Keeffe (FG).

Joe Walsh is retiring and is therefore not contesting the 2007 election.

The Constituency: This **three-seat** constituency is entirely within the county of Cork and includes the towns of Clonakilty, Bandon and Skibbereen. In the redrawing of constituencies since 2002 it has gained an area east of Kinsale (2002 census population 3,757) and a smaller area around Warner's Crossroads from Cork South Central.

Party	Votes 2002	Quota 2002	% Vote 2002	% Vote 1997	Swing
Fianna Fáil	14,882	1.6	39.48%	39.05%	0.42%
Fine Gael	12,189	1.3	32.33%	44.18%	−11.85%
Labour	3,442	0.4	9.13%	6.75%	2.38%
Sinn Féin	2,207	0.2	5.85%	–	5.85%
Others	4,978	0.5	13.20%	6.52%	6.68%

2007 Candidates will include: Denis O'Donovan (FF), Christy O'Sullivan (FF), Jim O'Keeffe (FG), PJ Sheehan (FG), Michael McCarthy (Lab), Cionnaith Ó Suilleabhain (SF), Quentin Gargan (GP).

In Brief: This constituency is another key Fine Gael target for a gain from Fianna Fáil. It had traditionally been a predictable two Fine Gael, one Fianna Fáil constituency but threw up a surprise in 2002, when Fine Gael lost one of their two seats to Fianna Fáil. Fine Gael's former deputy, the veteran PJ Sheehan, is again their candidate, along with their incumbent deputy, Jim O'Keeffe. Fianna Fáil's former minister, Joe Walsh, is retiring and this will considerably weaken the party's prospects of holding its two seats, although it has a strong ticket with the former independent Christy O'Sullivan as well as the high-profile backbencher, Denis O'Donovan.

Fianna Fáil: After many attempts Fianna Fáil made their long hoped for breakthrough to win two seats here in 2002. Their candidates in both 2002 and 1997 were the outgoing deputy Joe Walsh and the then senator Denis O'Donovan and, although the party's vote was up only marginally, the vote management between them was better and the party actually took the first two seats.

O'Donovan was first elected to Dáil Éireann in 2002 on his third attempt. He polled 4,268 first preferences in 1992, increased that to 6,081 in 1997 and increased it further to 7,695 votes in 2002. He was a member of Seanad Éireann from 1989 to 1992 and from 1997 to 2002. He is currently chairman of the All-Party Oireachtas Committee on the Constitution. He was also chair of the committee set up to report to the Houses of the Oireachtas on whether to impeach Judge Brian Curtin. A Bantry-based solicitor, O'Donovan was a member of Cork County Council for the Bantry electoral area from 1985 to 2004.

Fianna Fáil did not select its second candidate here until January 2007, reflecting the difficulty it had finding a candidate who could hope to retain the seat held by Joe Walsh since 1977. They solved their problem by persuading the independent councillor Christy O'Sullivan to join the party and to contest for them in this election. Previously a Fianna Fáil councillor, O'Sullivan ran as an independent in the 2002 Dáil elections and polled 3,609 first preferences. He has been a member of Cork County Council for the Skibbereen local electoral since 1999. He polled 2,510 first preferences there in the 1999 local elections and 2,859 first preferences in the 2004 local elections.

Fine Gael: In 1997 Fine Gael deputies PJ Sheehan and Jim O'Keeffe won the first two seats in Cork South West with 8,008 and 7,454 first preferences, respectively. In 2002, however, the party's vote share dropped by almost 12 percentage points and consequently it lost a seat, with O'Keeffe's vote falling less dramatically than Sheehan's – O'Keeffe was 527 votes ahead of Sheehan on the first count. Sheehan managed to narrow this gap over subsequent counts, not least by attracting twice as many transfers as O'Keeffe did on the fifth count, when Labour's Michael McCarthy was eliminated. However, O'Keeffe was still 35 votes ahead of Sheehan on the last count and won the seat.

Jim O'Keeffe was first elected to Dáil Éireann in 1977 and has held the seat on each occasion since. He was a Minister of State at the Department of Finance from 1986 to 1987 and at the Department of Foreign Affairs from November 1981 to March 1982 and then from 1982 to 1986. He has also held a number of portfolios on the Fine Gael frontbench when in opposition. In 2001 he was appointed by Michael Noonan to be the party's spokesperson on Foreign Affairs, but he was not initially included in Enda Kenny's first frontbench line-up in 2002. However, he was given the high-profile Justice portfolio in April 2004, when the Waterford deputy John Deasy was sacked from the position. O'Keeffe is based in Bandon and was formerly a solicitor.

PJ Sheehan was a member of Dáil Éireann from 1981 to 2002. He lives in Goleen and has a local political base that extends to Bantry. He was always a colourful contributor to Dáil proceedings. Notwithstanding the fact that his vote sharply declined from 8,008 first preferences in 1997 to just 5,831 in 2002 and that he is 74 years of age going into the 2007 election, Sheehan has a strong chance of regaining his seat. He has been a member of Cork County Council for almost 40 years, representing the Bantry electoral area. He again topped the poll in the Bantry electoral area in the 2004 local elections with 2,101 first preferences.

Labour Party: In 2002 the party was very excited about the prospects of its new young candidate, Skibbereen-based councillor Michael McCarthy. Then aged 25, he was one of the youngest candidates in the country and was seen as being in serious contention for a seat. He polled 3,442 first preferences, which was credible but far from being enough to make a Dáil breakthrough. He was subsequently elected to Seanad Éireann on the Labour panel and is the party spokesperson on Agriculture and Food, Social and Family Affairs and Environment and Local Government. He is a former process operator with the Schering Plough pharmaceutical company in Bandon. He was a member of Cork County Council from 1999 to 2004 for the Skibereen electoral area. His sister Phyllis ran in his stead in the 2004 local election, when she polled 829 votes but did not win a seat. Their cousin is the former senator Michael Calnan, who was based in Dunmanway and was Labour's Dáil candidate in the 1997 election.

Green Party: The high-profile environmental activist Quentin Gargan is the party's new candidate. Gargan co-founded Genetic Concern, which opposed the introduction of genetically engineered food. He was the unsuccessful plaintiff in a High Court case against Monsanto and the Environmental Protection Agency, attempting to prevent sugar beet trials. Based in Bantry, he is a farmer and is involved in Eco Logistics, a solar water heaters distributor. He may be the only candidate running his campaign from an electrically powered car.

Sinn Féin: Unusually, the party ran two candidates in this constituency in 2002, Ann O'Leary and Cionnaith Ó Suilleabháin, who polled 899 and 1,308, respectively. Ó Suilleabháin is the party's only candidate on this occasion. He has been a member of Clonakilty Town Council since 1994 and was an unsuccessful candidate for Cork County Council in the 1999 and 2004 local elections. In 2004, he polled 1,244 first seats and was eighth in a seven-seat electoral area.

CORK SOUTH WEST 2007 FIGURES

Candidate	Party	1st Count	2nd Count	3rd Count	4th Count	5th Count	Later counts

YOUR PREDICTION 2007

	Candidate Elected	Party
1		
2		
3		
4		
5		

RESULT 2007

	Candidate Elected	Party
1		
2		
3		
4		
5		

NOTES/UPDATES

CORK SOUTH WEST 2002 FIGURES

3 seats   Quota: 9,425

Candidate	Party	1st	2nd	3rd	4th	5th	6th	7th
Transfer of				Ó Súilleabháin		O'Donovan's		
			Butler	Heaney	O'Leary	McCarthy	O'Sullivan	surplus
Denis O'Donovan	FF	7,695	+79 7,774	+88 7,862	+415 8,277	+586 8,863	+1,316 10,179	
Joe Walsh*	FF	7,187	+84 7,271	+124 7,395	+311 7,706	+413 8,119	+878 8,997	+390 9,387
Jim O Keeffe*	FG	6,358	+118 6,476	+146 6,622	+213 6,835	+889 7,724	+772 8,496	+95 8,591
PJ Sheehan*	FG	5,831	+33 5,864	+68 5,932	+224 6,156	+831 6,987	+1,300 8,287	+269 8,556
Christy O Sullivan	IND	3,609	+75 3,684	+165 3,849	+454 4,303	+841 5,144	Elim'd	
Michael McCarthy	LAB	3,442	+63 3,505	+131 3,636	+394 4,030	Elim'd		
Cionnaith Ó Súilleabháin	SF	1,308	+21 1,329	+43 1,372	Elim'd			
Anne O'Leary	SF	899	+9 908	+72 945	Elim'd			
Theresa Heaney	IND	748	+166 864	Elim'd				
Edmund Butler	IND	621	Elim'd					
Non-Transferable			23	62	306	470	878	

*Outgoing Deputy

DONEGAL NORTH EAST

Outgoing Deputies: Jim McDaid (FF), Cecilia Keaveney (FF), Niall Blaney (FF).

Niall Blaney (FF) was elected as an Independent Fianna Fáil deputy in the 2002 election and joined Fianna Fáil in July 2006.

The Constituency: This is a **three-seat** constituency. It is entirely within the county of Donegal. The boundary with Donegal South West is in the main a line from the Errigal Mountains to the Finn Valley. In the redrawing of constituencies since 2002 this constituency lost an area in the Lifford-Raphoe area (2002 population 5,386), which was transferred to Donegal South West.

Party	Votes 2002	Quota 2002	% Vote 2002	% Vote 1997	Swing
Fianna Fáil	17,954	2.0	49.40%	41.81%	7.59%
Fine Gael	7,637	0.8	21.01%	18.87%	2.14%
Labour	1,021	0.1	2.81%	5.48%	–2.67%
Sinn Féin	3,611	0.4	9.93%	8.11%	1.83%
Others	6,124	0.7	16.85%	25.7 %	–8.88%

2007 Candidates will include: Niall Blaney (FF), Cecilia Keaveney (FF), Jim McDaid (FF), Joe McHugh (FG), Siobhan McLaughlin (Lab), Frank Gallagher (GP), Pádraig Mac Lochlainn (SF), Jimmy Harte (Ind), Ian McGarvey (Ind).

In Brief: It is almost certain that the 'pro-Ahern' voting bloc in this constituency will be down at least one seat. There will be a seat gain for either Sinn Féin or Fine Gael and maybe even for both. In 2002 Fianna Fáil won two seats here and the Independent Fianna Fáil organisation's Niall Blaney won the other. Blaney joined Fianna Fáil in 2006 and Fianna Fáil now holds all three outgoing seats, a scenario which is not electorally sustainable. After an internal row over candidate selection and the reversal of Jim McDaid's decision to retire, Fianna Fáil has ended up running the three incumbent deputies in the 2007 election. The Fine Gael challenger for a seat is Senator Jim McHugh. His prospects will be hampered by the decision of Jim Harte, son of the party's former deputy, Paddy Harte, to run as an independent. Pádraig MacLochlainn is again Sinn Féin's candidate and will also be in contention for a seat.

Fianna Fáil: In the 2002 election the overall Fianna Fáil vote went up from 41.8% in 1997 to 49.4%. Both of the party's outgoing deputies, Jim McDaid and Cecilia Keaveney, were comfortably returned. In the same election the legendary Independent Fianna Fáil machine safely managed the succession from outgoing deputy Harry Blaney to his son, Niall Blaney.

In April 2006 Jim McDaid, one of the sitting Fianna Fáil deputies, announced that he would not be contesting the 2007 election. In July 2006 Niall Blaney joined the Fianna Fáil parliamentary party and his Independent Fianna Fáil organisation merged with the Fianna Fáil organisation in Donegal. In the months following the merger, however, there was considerable controversy within Fianna Fáil, mainly arising from the insistence of the party organisation in Letterkenny that a candidate from that area should contest the election. This culminated in McDaid announcing that he was reversing his decision to retire and that he would contest the selection convention. The possibility was even raised that McDaid would run in the election as an independent. In November 2006 party headquarters announced that there would be no selection convention and instead three candidates – Cecilia Keveney, Niall Blaney and Jim McDaid – were selected by the party's national executive.

Jim McDaid was elected to Dáil Éireann on his first attempt in 1989 and has held the seat since, although he struggled in 1997, when he was just 515 votes ahead of Fine Gael's Paddy Harte for the last seat. McDaid was the subject of national media attention during the 2002 campaign because of reported remarks he made to students about suicide. Perhaps because of the associated controversy, local support rallied to him and he topped the poll in that election with 9,614 votes, taking a seat on the first count. He was Minister for Tourism, Sport and Recreation from 1997 to 2002 but was demoted to Minister for State at the Department of Transport in 2002 and further demoted from that position to the back benches in 2004. He pleaded guilty to a drink driving incident on the Naas dual carriageway in April 2005. He is also a medical doctor.

Cecilia Keaveney is based in Moville in the Inishowen Peninsula. A former music teacher, she was first elected to Dáil Éireann in April 1996 in a by-election caused by the death of the Independent Fianna Fáil deputy Neil T. Blaney. Keaveney retained the seat comfortably in the 1997 election and again in 2002. She was a member of Donegal County Council from 1995 to 2004 for the Inishowen electoral area. Her father, Paddy Keaveney, was an Independent Fianna Fáil TD from 1976 to 1977.

Niall Blaney was elected to Dáil Éireann on his first attempt in 2002. He was a member of Donegal County Council from 1999 to 2004 for the Milford electoral area. Based in Rossakill, Blaney formerly worked as a civil engineering technician with Donegal County Council. He is the son of Harry Blaney, who was a Dáil deputy from 1997 to 2002, and a nephew of Neil T. Blaney, who was a Dáil deputy from 1948 to 1997, a member of the European Parliament from 1948 to 1996 and a former Fianna Fáil minister. In 2002 as an Independent Fianna Fáil candidate, Niall Blaney polled 6,124, which was two-thirds of a quota. In that election the combined vote of the two Fianna Fáil candidates was 17,954, which was almost two quotas.

Fine Gael: The party's veteran deputy, Paddy Harte, lost his seat in 1997, and the party has been left with no TD in this constituency since then. In 2002 Fine Gael put together a diverse candidate slate in its effort to regain a seat when it selected Bernard McGuinness from Inishowen and the former Labour senator Sean Maloney from Letterkenny. This strategy improved the party's first preference vote share by just over 2%. McGuinness was marginally the stronger of the two candidates; he polled 3,914 first preferences while Maloney polled 3,723. However, the then independent Niall Blaney was 2,000 first preferences ahead of each of the Fine Gael candidates on the first count. Maloney attracted more transfers than

McGuinness but, even following McGuinness's elimination and the distribution of his votes, he was still more than 1,350 votes behind Blaney for the last seat.

The party's single candidate in this election is Senator Joe McHugh. In 2002 he was elected to Seanad Éireann on the Administrative panel and he is currently the party's spokesperson on Community, Rural, Gaeltacht and Marine Affairs in the upper house. He was a member of Donegal County Council for the Letterkenny electoral area from 1999 to 2004. Formerly a teacher and community development worker, McHugh married the Fine Gael deputy for Laois–Offaly, Olwyn Enright, in July 2005.

Labour Party: Seán Maloney's defection to Fine Gael put paid to any chance the party had of being in contention in this constituency in 2002. Their candidate in that election was Jackie McNair, a Letterkenny-based SIPTU shop steward who polled just 1,021 first preferences. Siobhan McLaughlin is the Labour candidate in this election. She has been manager of the Donegal Travellers Project for 10 years, is chair of the County Community Forum and is a member of the County Development Board. Originally from Buncrana, she is now based in Letterkenny.

Green Party: Their candidate is Frank Gallagher. He is based in Rathan, Letterkenny and has been Chairman of the Irish National Organisation for the Unemployed in Donegal.

Sinn Féin: 33-year-old Pádraig MacLochlainn is again the Sinn Féin candidate in this election. MacLochlainn polled 3,611 in the 1997 Dáil election, increasing the party vote by 2%. He has been a member of Buncrana Town Council since 2002 and was elected to Donegal County Council in the 2004 local elections, topping the poll in the Inishowen electoral area with 2,264 first preferences. Pádraig MacLochlainn is a former member of the national executive of the Irish National Organisation for the Unemployed and is a director of Action Inishowen.

Others: The former Fine Gael councillor Jimmy Harte is running as an independent, having failed to be selected as a candidate by the party. A son of Paddy Harte, who was a Fine Gael TD from 1961 to 1997, he has been a member of Donegal County Council since 1999. In the 2004 local elections he polled 1,532 first preferences in county council elections in the Letterkenny electoral area. He is also a member of Letterkenny Town Council.

A Fianna Fáil candidate in 1982, Ian McGarvey, now representing Milford as an independent on Donegal County Council, is also expected to run as an independent on a hospital ticket.

DONEGAL NORTH EAST 2007 FIGURES

Candidate	Party	1st Count	2nd Count	3rd Count	4th Count	5th Count	Later counts

YOUR PREDICTION 2007

	Candidate Elected	Party
1		
2		
3		
4		
5		

RESULT 2007

	Candidate Elected	Party
1		
2		
3		
4		
5		

NOTES/UPDATES

DONEGAL NORTH EAST 2002 FIGURES

3 seats   **Quota: 9,087**

Candidate	Party	1st	2nd	3rd	4th	5th	6th
Transfer of			McNair	McDaid's surplus	Mac Lochlann	Keaveney's surplus	McGuiness
James McDaid*	FF	**9,614**					
Cecilia Keaveney*	FF	**8,340**	+123 **8,463**	+249 **8,712**	1,012 **9,724**		
Niall Blayney	Ind FF	**6,124**	+137 **6,261**	+131 **6,392**	+1,275 **7,667**	+364 **8,031**	+758 **8,789**
Bernard McGuiness	FG	**3,914**	+187 **4,101**	+10 **4,111**	+265 **4,376**	+175 **4,551**	Elim'd
Sean Maloney	FG	**3,723**	+358 **4,081**	+100 **4,181**	+446 **4,627**	+53 **4,680**	+2,752 **7,432**
Padraig Mac Lochlainn	SF	**3,661**	+103 **3,714**	+37 **3,751**	Elim'd		
Jackie McNair	LAB	**1,021**	Elim'd				
Non-Transferable			113	0	753	45	1,041

*Outgoing Deputy

DONEGAL SOUTH WEST

Outgoing Deputies: Pat 'The Cope' Gallagher (FF), Mary Coughlan (FF), Dinny McGinley (FG).

The Constituency: This is a **three-seat** constituency which is all within the county of Donegal. The constituency stretches across an area south of the Errigal Mountains and the Finn Valley. Following the redrawing of constituency boundaries since 2002, the constituency gained an area in the Lifford-Raphoe area (2002 population 5,386) from Donegal North East.

Party	Votes 2002	Quota 2002	% Vote 2002	% Vote 1997	Swing
Fianna Fáil	14,997	1.7	42.09%	38.04%	4.05%
Fine Gael	9,058	1.0	25.42%	22.97%	2.44%
Labour	1,079	0.1	3.03%	4.20%	−1.17%
Sinn Féin	3,829%	0.4	10.75%	–	10.75%
Others	6,672	0.7	18.72%	30.58 %	−11.86%

2007 Candidates will include: Pat 'The Cope' Gallagher (FF), Mary Coughlan (FF), Dinny McGinley (FG), Seamus Rogers (Lab), Seán Ó Maolchallann (GP), Pearse Doherty (SF).

In Brief: There could be a Minister of State or ministerial casualty here if Fine Gael holds on to its seat and Sinn Féin also makes a gain, but it is unlikely that both parties can do so. Fine Gael's chances of retaining its seat have been made more difficult by the initial announcement of the retirement of their sitting deputy, Dinny McGinley, which was then reversed. Sinn Féin's Pearse Doherty, who did spectacularly well as the party candidate in the North and West constituency in the 2004 European parliament election, has a real prospect of winning a seat in this Dáil constituency. The most likely outcome is two seats for Fianna Fáil and one seat for Sinn Féin.

Fianna Fáil: This was Fianna Fáil's easiest gain in the 2002 election. Pat 'The Cope' Gallagher, who had been elected a member of the European Parliament in the 1995 European elections and had not contested the 1997 Dáil election, returned to domestic politics to contest the 2002 Dáil election. As a result the party comfortably regained the seat it lost to the TV deflector campaigner Tom Gildea in 1997.

Pat Gallagher was first elected to Dáil Éireann in 1981 and was returned on each subsequent occasion until 1997, when he did not contest the election. He was elected to the

Dáil again in 2002 and is currently the Minister of State in the Department of Transport, having held that position since January 2006. He was Minister of State at the Department of the Marine from 2004 to 2006 and Minister of State at the Department of the Environment from 2002 to 2004. He was a member of the European Parliament for the Connacht-Ulster constituency from 1994 to 2002. In the 1994 European election he polled 53,171 first preferences and in the 2004 European election he polled 66,055. He took the first seat in the European constituency on each occasion. He was previously Minister of State at the Department of Marine from 1987 to 1989, and was Minister of State at the Department of Art, Culture and the Gaeltacht from 1989 to 1994. He was a member of Donegal County Council from 1979 to 1987. He is a former fish exporter and is based in Dungloe.

The party's other candidate is the Minister for Agriculture, Mary Coughlan. She was first elected to Dáil Éireann in a by-election in 1987 and has been re-elected in each subsequent election. She has been the party's national honorary secretary since 1995. She was Minister for Social and Family Affairs from 2002 to 2004 and Minister of State at the Department of Arts, Heritage, Gaeltacht and the Islands from 2001 to 2002. Her late uncle, Clement Coughlan, was a Dáil deputy for the same constituency from 1980 to 1983 and her late father, Cathal Coughlan, was a Dáil deputy from 1983 to 1986. She is based in the Inver area.

Fine Gael: Fine Gael ran two candidates here in 2002 – the outgoing deputy Dinny McGinley and the former deputy Jim White. White was ahead of McGinley on the first count by 302 votes but McGinley did significantly better on transfers and by the eighth and final count he had 1,400 votes more than White.

In the summer of 2006 Dinny McGinley announced that he was retiring and would not contest the 2007 Dáil election. The party selected Glenties area county councillor Terence Slowey to contest the election in his stead. However, in February 2007 McGinley reversed his decision to retire and the party announced that Slowney was standing down from the ticket and that McGinley would contest after all.

Dinny McGinley was first elected to Dáil Éireann in 1982 and has held his seat in each subsequent election. Based in Bunbeg, he has never held ministerial office, at junior or senior level, during his 25 years in Dáil Éireann. He was Fine Gael's frontbench spokesperson on Arts, Heritage, Gaeltacht and the Islands and was a junior spokesperson on the Gaeltacht, emigrant welfare and youth affairs and sports at various times in the late 1980s and 1990s. He was appointed the party's spokesperson on Defence by Enda Kenny in June 2002. Formerly a teacher, he is based in Bunbeg

Labour Party: The party's candidate in this election is Seamus Rodgers. Rodgers, who has unsuccessfully contested 12 Dáil Éireann elections since 1961, polled 1,079 first preferences in 2002. He was an unsuccessful candidate in the 1999 and 2004 local elections, when he stood for Donegal County Council in the Glenties electoral area. He polled 922 in the 1999 election and 682 in the 2004 election. He was Donegal county chairman of the Gaelic Athletic Association from 1976 to 1979. He is a retired SIPTU official.

Green Party: The party's candidate is Seán Ó Maolchallann, who is a Senior Lecturer in Mathematics in Letterkenny Institute of Technology.

Sinn Féin: The party ran two candidates in 2002: Ballyboffey-based Tom Dignam and Gweedore man Pearse Doherty, who polled 1,133 and 2,696 first preference votes, respectively. Combined, that gave them just under 11% of the first preference vote in this constituency.

In this election Pearse Doherty is their only candidate. He has been a member of Donegal County Council since 2004. In the 2004 local elections he polled 1,892 first preferences in the Gweedore local electoral area. On the same day he was the party's candidate in the European elections for the North and West constituency where he did surprisingly well, polling 65,321 first preferences and increasing the party's vote share from 6.4% in 1999 to 15.5% in 2004. He is 29 years of age.

Others: The departure from the political scene of Tom Gildea in 2002 meant that there was no serious independent challenge in this constituency. In fact, Gildea's constituency assistant, Gwen Breslin, who ran in his stead, was the poorest performer in that election, polling just 951 first preference votes. Independent Fianna Fáil also ran a candidate here in 2002. Joe Kelly, a young man from Falcarragh, polled an impressive 3,091 votes. His father, Paddy Kelly, was a member of Donegal County Council at the time and had stood for Independent Fianna Fáil in the 1997 Dáil election. His organisation has since merged with Fianna Fáil so it will be interesting to see what impact the absence of an Independent Fianna Fáil candidate will have on the 2007 contest. When Joe Kelly was eliminated in 2002 he had 3,796 votes. 422 of these went to Fianna Fáil's Mary Coughlan and 779 to her party colleague, Pat 'the Cope' Gallagher, while 1,004 went to Sinn Féin's Pearse Doherty, 224 to Fine Gael's Jim White and 705 to his party colleague, Dinny McGinley, with 662 being non-transferable.

DONEGAL SOUTH WEST 2007 FIGURES

Candidate	Party	1st Count	2nd Count	3rd Count	4th Count	5th Count	Later counts

YOUR PREDICTION 2007

	Candidate Elected	Party
1		
2		
3		
4		
5		

RESULT 2007

	Candidate Elected	Party
1		
2		
3		
4		
5		

NOTES/UPDATES

DONEGAL SOUTH WEST 2002 FIGURES

3 seats   Quota: 8,909

Candidate	Party	1st	2nd	3rd	4th	5th	6th	7th	8th
Transfer of			Breslin	Dignam	Rodgers	Pringle	Kelly	Gallagher's surplus	Doherty
Pat 'The Cope' Gallagher	FF	7,740	+103 7,843	+117 7,960	+242 8,202	+300 8,502	+779 9,281		
Mary Coughlan*	FF	7,257	+123 7,380	+85 7,465	+82 7,547	+788 8,335	+422 8,757	+175 8,932	
James White	FG	4,680	+40 4,720	+20 4,740	+82 4,822	+339 5,161	+224 5,385	+17 5,402	+528 5,930
Dinny McGinley*	FG	4,378	+106 4,484	+28 4,512	+285 4,797	+419 5,216	+705 5,921	+81 6,002	+1,368 7,370
Joe Kelly	Ind FF	3,091	+83 3,174	+45 3219	+110 3,329	+467 3,796	Elim'd		
Pearse Doherty	SF	2,696	+75 2,771	+800 3,571	+149 3,720	+446 4,166	1,004 5,170	+99 5,269	Elim'd
Thomas Pringle	IND	2,630	+257 2,887	+21 2,908	+170 3,078	Elim'd			
Tom Dignam	SF	1,133	+15 1,148	Elim'd					
Seamus Rodgers	LAB	1,079	+120 1,199	+6 1,205	Elim'd				
Gwen Breslin	IND	951	Elim'd						
Non-Transferable			29	26	85	319	662	0	3,373

*Outgoing Deputy

DUBLIN CENTRAL

Outgoing Deputies: Bertie Ahern (FF), Tony Gregory (Ind), Joe Costello (Lab), Dermot Fitzpatrick (FF).

Dermot Fitzpatrick (FF) is retiring and will therefore not be contesting the 2007 election.

The Constituency: This is a **four-seat** constituency, all of which is north of the Liffey. It includes all of the City Council areas of North Inner City, Cabra and much of Drumcondra. In the redrawing of constituencies since 2002 it has lost a small area in Islandbridge (2002 population 955) to Dublin South Central.

Party	Votes 2002	Quota 2002	% Vote 2002	% Vote 1997	Swing
Fianna Fáil	13,488	2.0	39.58%	42.83%	−3.25%
Fine Gael	3,768	0.6	11.06%	14.51%	−3.45%
Labour	4,149	0.6	12.17%	8.49%	3.68%
Green Party	1,470	0.2	4.31%	3.51%	0.81%
Sinn Féin	4,979	0.7	14.61%	6.65%	7.96%
Others	6,227	0.9	18.27%	24.02	−5.75%

2007 Candidates will include: Bertie Ahern (FF), Cyprian Brady (FF), Mary Fitzpatrick (FF), Pascal Donohoe (FG), Joe Costello (Lab), Patricia McKenna (GP), Mary Lou McDonald (SF), Tony Gregory (Ind), Paul O'Loughlin (Ind), Tom Prenderville (Ind).

In Brief: The key question in this constituency will be whether the outgoing Taoiseach, Bertie Ahern, can again secure the election of a second Fianna Fáil TD. This will also be the venue for a high-profile challenge for a Dáil seat from Sinn Féin MEP Mary Lou McDonald. In 2002 Fianna Fáil's second seat was secured with just a 79 vote lead over Sinn Féin's then candidate, Nicky Kehoe. There is even a prospect that Labour's Joe Costello could lose out in the tussle among high-profile contenders, who also include the sitting independent Tony Gregory and the Green Party's candidate, Patricia McKenna, a former MEP for Dublin.

Fianna Fáil: In 2002, in his first run as outgoing Taoiseach, Bertie Ahern again topped the poll decisively. Ahern has a local constituency operation which has a reputation for unrivalled efficiency and he polled 31.5% of the total vote and almost 81% of the Fianna Fáil vote here. In 2002 Ahern's vote was down to 10,882 first preferences compared to his 1997 performance of 12,175, but this did not entirely help his running mate, Dermot Fitzpatrick. Fitzpatrick's own vote was low at 2,590 first preferences. Ahern had a surplus of 4,075 and 2,265 of these transferred to Fitzpatrick on the second count, which amounted to an internal party transfer rate of 55% – marginally lower than the national internal transfer rate but enough to give him the seat by that very narrow margin.

One of Fianna Fáil's new candidates this time out is councillor Mary Fitzpatrick, who is a daughter of the retiring deputy Dermot Fitzpatrick. In 2004 she won a seat on Dublin City Council in Cabra-Glasnevin, where she polled 1,848 first preferences in a ward where the quota was 3,027. This was an impressive performance when one considers that her opponents included the Taoiseach's brother, Maurice Ahern, and Sinn Féin's Nicky Kehoe. Like her father, she has an obvious voter base in the Navan Road end of the constituency. Her father, a local doctor, was previously a deputy from 1987 to 1989 as well as being elected again in 2002. He was nominated to the Seanad by Bertie Ahern from 1997 until his re-election.

The other Fianna Fáil contender is Senator Cyprian Brady. He has managed the Taoiseach's constituency organisation and held a key role in it for more than 15 years and was nominated by Bertie Ahern to the Seanad in 2002. His brother Royston was a member of Dublin City Council for the North Inner City area from 1999–2004, Mayor of Dublin in 2003–2004 and an unsuccessful candidate in the 2004 European elections. This is Cyprian Brady's first electoral contest.

Fine Gael: In 2002 Fine Gael's only candidate was their outgoing deputy, Jim Mitchell. Mitchell was first elected to Dáil Éireann in 1977 and followed his Ballyfermot/Inchicore base as it was redrawn into and out of several constituencies. In 2002 he polled 3,769 first preferences, 1,417 less than in 1997, and was eliminated on the fourth count. His electoral base in Dublin Central was considerably reduced in the redrawing of constituencies before the 2002 election and he faced strong opposition from several well-placed candidates. A sprained ankle also hampered him during the 2002 campaign. The party's vote in the redrawn constituency fell almost 3.5 percentage points between 1997 and 2002. Mitchell died in December 2002 at the relatively young age of 56.

The party's new candidate is councillor Paschal Donohoe, who is a member of Dublin City Council for the Cabra Glasnevin electoral area, where he polled 1,703 votes in the 2004 local elections. Originally from the Cabra area, he now lives in Phibsboro and works as a sales and marketing manager. He is chair of the Engineering and Environment Strategic Policy Committee, as well as the central area committee of Dublin City Council.

Labour Party: The party's outgoing deputy is Joe Costello. He won a seat for the party here in 1992 but lost it in the Labour collapse in 1997. He won back the seat in 2002. He was a member of the Seanad from 1989 to 1992 and from 1997 to 2002. He is a former member of Dublin City Council for the North Inner City electoral area, where his wife Emer now holds a seat. She polled 1,832 first preferences in the 2004 local elections. Joe Costello is a former teacher and a former president of the Association of Secondary Teachers of Ireland. He is also a former chairman of the Irish Prisoner Rights organisation. He was the party's spokesperson on Justice from 2002 to 2004, when he became their spokesperson on Defence. Although he was felt to be under pressure from Sinn Féin in 2002, his first preference vote of 4,136 was 1,101 votes more than he obtained in 1997.

Green Party: The Green Party has never held a seat in Dublin Central. The party's candidate in 2002 was Tommy Simpson, the party's international secretary and a trade unionist. He polled just 1,469 votes. This time, however, the party has a more high-profile candidate in Patricia

McKenna, who is a former Member of the European Parliament for the Dublin constituency. A native of Monaghan but long based in Dublin, McKenna was elected to the European Parliament at her first attempt in 1995, when she topped the poll with 40,388 votes. In 1999 she comfortably retained her seat, getting 35,659 votes but she lost it in the 2004 European elections.

McKenna was the plaintiff in the so called 'McKenna case' in which the Supreme Court found it was unconstitutional for the government to spend public money advocating a 'yes' vote in the divorce referendum. She contested Dublin Central once before, in 1992, but was eliminated on the sixth count with 927 votes. She can be expected to do much better on this occasion, however, and will be in contention for a Dáil seat.

Sinn Féin: In 2002 Sinn Féin's long-standing candidate in this constituency, Councillor Christy Burke, passed the baton to Cabra councillor Nicky Kehoe. Although Kehoe was hemmed in somewhat by Fianna Fáil's decision to run another Cabra councillor, Dermot Fitzpatrick, he still managed to poll an impressive 4,979 first preference votes. This was more than a doubling of the Sinn Féin vote. The party obtained 6.65% of the first preferences in 1997 but increased that to 14.61% in 2002. Kehoe came very close to winning the fourth seat and was beaten by Dermot Fitzpatrick by just 79 votes.

In December 2005 Mary Lou McDonald was chosen as the Sinn Féin candidate for this constituency. Originally a member of Fianna Fáil, McDonald first ran for office when she unsuccessfully contested the Dublin West constituency for Sinn Féin at the 2002 general election, polling 8.02% of first preference votes. She was elected as MEP (Sinn Féin's first in the Republic of Ireland) for the Dublin constituency in the 2004 European election with 60,395 first preferences, which represented 14.32% of the vote. She is a member of the Sinn Féin Ard Comhairle and is also currently the party's National Chairperson.

Others: Tony Gregory first won his independent seat here in 1982 and has retained it on every occasion since. He is the longest-serving independent in the Dáil. He first gained national prominence when he negotiated the famous 'Gregory deal' in return for his support for the short-lived March to November 1982 Haughey-led minority government. He is a former secondary school teacher and a former member of Dublin City Council. He was first elected to the City Council for the North Inner City ward in 1979 and repeatedly topped the poll, comfortably above the quota, in all local elections until he had to step down in 2004 because of the 'dual mandate' ban.

Although the Sinn Féin threat might have been expected to cause some erosion of Gregory's support in 2002 and might be expected to do so again in 2007, his base has been solidified by two decades of constituency work and high-profile activism on issues such as crime, drugs and deprivation in the area. In the 1997 Dáil election he polled 5,261 first preferences and that increased to 5,675 in 2002. He attracted 814 transfers from Bertie Ahern's surplus and 617 from the elimination of Green Party's Tommy Simpson, taking the second seat on the fourth count.

Paul O'Loughlin contested the 2002 general election in Dublin Central and the 2004 local elections in the North Inner City. He failed to be elected both times with 1.08% and 1.69% of the vote, respectively.

Tom Prenderville is a journalist who covers local news stories in the Dublin Central area. He has run unsuccessfully for the North Inner City in the 1999 local elections, for Dublin Central in the 2002 general election and for Dublin in the 2004 European elections.

DUBLIN CENTRAL 2007 FIGURES

Candidate	Party	1st Count	2nd Count	3rd Count	4th Count	5th Count	Later counts

YOUR PREDICTION 2007

	Candidate Elected	Party
1		
2		
3		
4		
5		

RESULT 2007

	Candidate Elected	Party
1		
2		
3		
4		
5		

NOTES/UPDATES

DUBLIN CENTRAL 2002 FIGURES

4 seats   Quota: 6,807

Candidate	Party	1st	2nd	3rd	4th	5th	6th	7th
Transfer of			Ahern's surplus	O'Loughlin Prendeville O'Donnell	Simpson	Mitchell	Costello's surplus	Gregory's surplus
Bertie Ahern*	FF	10,882						
Tony Gregory*	IND	5,664	+813 6,477	+148 6,625	+617 7,242			
Nicky Kehoe	SF	4,972	+328 5,300	+43 5,343	+144 5,487	+331 5,818	+359 6,177	+162 6,339
Joe Costello	LAB	4,136	+363 4,499	+40 4,539	+507 5,046	+2,824 7,870		
Jim Mitchell*	FG	3,769	+207 3,976	+87 4,063	+205 4,268	Elim'd		
Dermot Fitzpatrick	FF	2,590	+2,265 4,885	+113 4,968	+75 5,043	+517 5,560	+704 6,264	+154 6,418
Tommy Simpson	GP	1,469	+76 1,545	+107 1,652	Elim'd			
Paul O'Loughlin	CSP	366	+11 377	Elim'd				
Tom Prendeville	IND	97	+6 103	Elim'd				
Patrick O'Donnell	IND	89	+6 95	Elim'd				
Non-Transferable			0	37	104	596	0	119

*Outgoing Deputy

DUBLIN MID-WEST

Outgoing Deputies: John Curran (FF), Mary Harney (PD), Paul Gogarty (GP).

The Constituency: This is now a **four-seat** constituency having gained a seat in the redrawing since the 2002 election. It encompasses Saggart and Rathcoole and the area west of the M50 between the Naas Road and the Liffey, covering the Clondalkin-Ronanstown, Brittas and Lucan areas and now also the Palmerstown area, which was in Dublin West in 2002.

Party	Votes 2002	Quota 2002	% Vote 2002
Fianna Fáil	9,122	1.3	32.06%
Fine Gael	3,276	0.5	11.51%
Labour	2,563	0.4	9.01%
PDs	5,706	0.8	20.05%
Green Party	3,508	0.5	12.33%
Sinn Féin	1,855	0.3	6.52%
Others	2,426	0.3	8.53%

2007 Candidates will include: John Curran (FF), Luke Moriarty (FF), Frances Fitzgerald (FG), Mary Harney (PD), Paul Gogarty (GP), Joanne Tuffy (Lab), Joanna Spain (SF), Mick Finnegan (WP), Derek Keating (Ind).

In Brief: The presence of the former Tánaiste and current Minister for Health, Mary Harney, gives this constituency star value. It also has an extra seat on this occasion as a result of the redrawing and is now a four seater. Among those contending for that extra seat are Labour senator Joanna Tuffy, the independent Lucan-based councillor Derek Keating, Fine Gael candidate Frances Fitzgerald (the former Dublin South East deputy) and Sinn Féin's Joanna Spain. Fianna Fáil's John Curran is likely to be safe, but his running mate, Luke Moriarty, will struggle to get elected despite the extra seat. There have been suggestions that the Green Party's sitting deputy, Paul Gogarty, may not be safe and may be the casualty of the combined Sinn Féin-independent challengers in Lucan; however, he is unlikely to lose his seat.

Fianna Fáil: This would have been the logical constituency for the outgoing Lucan-based deputy Liam Lawlor if he had decided to contest the 2002 election. Lawlor had resigned from Fianna Fáil following an internal party investigation into matters raised in evidence at the Flood Tribunal in 2002. As a result, the party ran two new candidates in 2002 in a move designed to appeal to the two ends of the constituency and in an effort to win a seat in Lawlor's absence from this new constituency. Des Kelly had just failed to get elected in the Castleknock area in the 1999 local elections and did relatively well, focusing on the Lucan area in the 2002 Dáil election. He polled 3,218 first preference votes, but with just 1.3 quotas the party could win only one seat.

John Curran is a former member of South Dublin County Council. He laid the groundwork for the 2002 Dáil challenge when he topped the poll with 1,174 first preference votes in the 1999 local elections in the Clondalkin electoral area. A businessman and prominent GAA activist in the area, he polled 5,904 first preferences and took the first seat. He is currently a member of the Public Accounts Committee and the Education and Science Committee.

This is Luke Moriarty's first electoral contest. A businessman, he owns four SuperValu supermarkets, including stores in Crumlin and Palmerstown. He also owns hotels in Leixlip and Balbriggan.

Fine Gael: Following the redrawing of constituencies before the 2002 election, the former presidential candidate and Minister of State, Austin Currie, was forced to follow his Lucan base into this constituency. There were some reports that Currie, who was first elected to the Dáil in 1989, having had a lengthy career in Northern Ireland politics, might retire in 2002, but he was prevailed upon to contest the new constituency. It proved to be an unwise decision. His vote in Dublin West in 1997 was 5,256 but he polled just 2,008 in Dublin Mid-West in 2002.

Currie's running mate in 2002 was Clondalkin-based Therese Ridge, then a senator, who is a former chair of South Dublin County Council on which she represented the Clondalkin area. However, in a performance which illustrates how bad things were for Fine Gael in Dublin in 2002, she actually polled less than she had in the local election, with just 1,268 first preferences.

The party's candidate in 2007 is the former Dublin South East TD Frances Fitzgerald. Fitzgerald was a Dáil Deputy from 1992 to 2002; she is a former social worker and former high-profile chairperson of the Council for the Status of Women. She was previously the party's frontbench spokesperson on Equality Opportunity and Family Affairs from 2000 to 2001.

Labour Party: Lucan-based senator Joanna Tuffy is again the party candidate in this election. She is a daughter of former Lucan councillor Eamon Tuffy and she herself was a member of South Dublin County Council from 1999 to 2004. She polled 1,226 first preference votes in the 1999 local elections in the Lucan electoral area. A solicitor by profession, she was elected to Seanad Éireann on the Administrative Panel in 2002 and has been the party's spokesperson on Education and Science, Justice, Equality and Law Reform, and Defence in the Upper House.

Tuffy's performance in the 2002 election was below expectation with a first preference vote of just 2,563 votes where the quota was 7,115, and crucially she was almost 1,000 votes behind fellow Lucan councillor, the Green Party candidate Paul Gogarty, on the first count. Consequently the Greens won the only left-wing seat in this constituency. However, now that there are four seats there may be room for her to get elected to the Dáil this time around.

Progressive Democrats: The then Progressive Democrat leader and Tánaiste, Mary Harney, followed her base into this constituency after the redrawing before the 2002 election and comfortably won the second seat after Fianna Fáil's John Curran. Harney was Tánaiste from 1997 to September 2005 and leader of the Progressive Democrats from October 1993 to

September 2005. She had previously been appointed to the Seanad by Taoiseach Jack Lynch in 1977, having contested that year's Dáil election unsuccessfully in the Dublin South East constituency. She was first elected for the Dublin South West constituency in 1981 as a Fianna Fáil TD but left the party in 1986 and was a founder member of the Progressive Democrats.

Harney was a member of Dublin County Council from 1979 to 1991, in the latter period for the Clondalkin electoral area. She polled 4,713 first preferences in Dublin South West in the 1997 Dáil election and 5,706 first preferences in Dublin Mid-West in 2002. Harney has been Minister for Health since 2004, and was Minister for Enterprise, Trade and Employment from 1997 to 2004. She was Minister of State at the Department of the Environment from 1989 to 1992.

Green Party: Lucan-based Paul Gogarty is the party's outgoing deputy. He won the third seat when this constituency was a three-seater in 2002 and has since been the party spokesperson on Education and Science, Sports, Tourism and Arts and Youth Affairs. He was previously a journalist.

Gogarty was a candidate for the party in Dublin West in 1997, where he polled 1,732. He made a breakthrough for the party in that part of the city when he topped the poll to win a seat for the party in the 1999 local elections. In the 2002 election he actually achieved more than 12% of the vote with 3,508 first preferences and attracted considerable transfers – more than a third of the available transfers when the Sinn Féin candidate was eliminated and 275 when Austin Currie was eliminated.

Sinn Féin: The party candidate is 26-year-old Joanne Spain and this is her first election. A former journalist for *An Phoblacht*, she has also worked as a Sinn Féin press officer. She is originally from Coolock but now lives in the Clondalkin area. Sinn Féin did well in this area in the 2004 local elections, with Shane O'Connor polling 2,421 votes in Clondalkin electoral area, where he was elected on the first count.

Others: Derek Keating is an independent member of South Dublin County Council in the five-seater Lucan local electoral area. He polled 1,113 votes there in the 1999 local elections (quota 1,681) and took the last of the four seats. In the 2004 local elections he increased his vote considerably, polling 3,680 when the quota was 3, 385 and comfortably took the first seat.

Mick Finnegan is a trade union activist who has been involved in various campaigns and stood as a Workers Party candidate in Clondalkin in the 1999 local elections and for Sinn Féin in Dublin West in the 1981 general election.

DUBLIN MID-WEST 2007 FIGURES

Candidate	Party	1st Count	2nd Count	3rd Count	4th Count	5th Count	Later counts

YOUR PREDICTION 2007

	Candidate Elected	Party
1		
2		
3		
4		
5		

RESULT 2007

	Candidate Elected	Party
1		
2		
3		
4		
5		

NOTES/UPDATES

DUBLIN MID-WEST 2002 FIGURES

3 seats — Quota: 7,115

Candidate	Party	1st	2nd	3rd	4th	5th	6th	7th	8th	9th	10th
Transfer of			Callanan	O'Mara	McGrath McGuinness	Green	Ridge	Flannery	Currie	Kelly	Curran's surplus
John Curran	FF	5,904	+24 5,928	+51 5,979	+133 6,112	+180 6,292	+216 6,508	+401 6,909	+177 7,086	+2,264 9,350	
Mary Harney*	PD	5,706	+13 5,719	+13 5,732	+80 5,812	+141 5953	+243 6196	+152 6348	+576 6924	+600 7,524	
Paul Gogarty*	GP	3,508	+15 3,523	+18 3,541	+86 3,627	+243 3,870	+77 3,947	+647 4,594	+666 5,260	+385 5,645	+700 6,345
Des Kelly	FF	3,218	+14 3,232	+5 3,237	+53 3,290	+91 3,381	+53 3,434	+191 3,625	+112 3,737	Elim'd	
Joanna Tuffy	LAB	2,563	+3 2,566	+36 2,602	+142 2,744	+147 2,891	+308 3,199	+395 3,594	+901 4,495	+313 4,808	+563 5,371
Austin Currie*	FG	2,008	+9 2,017	+6 2,023	+28 2,051	+49 2,100	+473 2,573	+114 2,687	Elim'd		
Tony Flannery	SF	1,885	+6 1,861	+51 1,912	+119 2,031	+213 ,2244	+82 2,326	Elim'd			
Therese Ridge	FG	1,268	+3 1,271	+43 1,314	+105 1,419	+117 1,536	Elim'd				
David Green	IND	1,078	+14 1,092	+78 1,170	+143 1,313	Elim'd					
Colm McGrath	IND	487	+1 488	+33 521	Elim'd						
Andrew McGuinness	WP	393	+0 393	+14 407	Elim'd						
Michael O'Mara	IND	361	+1 362	Elim'd							
Colm Callanan	CSP	107	Elim'd								
Non-Transferable			4	14	39	132	84	426	255	175	972

DUBLIN NORTH

Outgoing Deputies: Trevor Sargent (GP), Seán Ryan (Lab), Jim Glennon (FF), GV Wright (FF).

Seán Ryan (Lab), Jim Glennon (FF) and GV Wright (FF) are all retiring and will therefore not be contesting the 2007 election.

The Constituency: This **four-seater** is in the north Dublin county area, including the electoral areas of Malahide and Swords, and stretches to the Louth border. In the redrawing of constituencies since 2002 it lost an area west of Dublin Airport, in the St Margarets/Killsallaghan area, to the Dublin West constituency.

Party	Votes 2002	Quota 2002	% Vote 2002	% Vote 1997	Swing
Fianna Fáil	16,803	1.9	38.24%	38.65%	−0.41%
Fine Gael	5,189	0.6	11.81%	18.98%	−7.17%
Labour	6,359	0.7	14.47%	13.64%	0.83%
PDs	–	–	–	3.48%	−3.48%
Green Party	7,294	0.8	16.60%	13.64%	2.96%
Sinn Féin	1,350	0.2	3.07%	–	3.07%
Others	1,446	0.16	3.29%	4.39%	−1.10%
Socialist Party	5,501	0.63	12.52%	7.22%	5.3%

2007 Candidates will include: Michael Kennedy (FF), Darragh O' Brien (FF), John O'Leary (FF), James Reilly (FG), Brendan Ryan (Lab), Tom Morrissey (PD), Trevor Sargent (GP), Joe Corr (GP), Matt McCormack (SF), Clare Daly (Soc).

In Brief: As well as being the constituency of the Green Party leader, this is also a key marginal between the current government and the Rainbow alternative. There will be three new TDs, since both of the sitting Fianna Fáil deputies, GV Wright and Jim Glennon, are stepping down, as is the sitting Labour deputy, Seán Ryan. Sargent is likely to hold his seat. Clare Daly of the Joe Higgins-led Socialist Party, who came close to winning a seat in 2002, has to be favoured to win a seat this time out. Fine Gael is also seeking to regain the seat lost by Nora Owen in 2002 and have selected former President of the Irish Medical Organisation James Reilly. Seán Ryan's brother Brendan will struggle to hold the seat for Labour.

Fianna Fáil: In 2002 Fianna Fáil won two seats, thereby regaining the second seat it won in 1997 but subsequently lost in the 1998 by-election caused by the resignation from the Dáil of then Foreign Affairs Minister Ray Burke. This left GV Wright, who had regained his seat in the Dáil in 1997, as the only Fianna Fáil deputy in this constituency going into the 2002 election. In the absence of Burke the party struggled to finalise its candidate selection before the 2002 election and in the end it decided to run a three-man ticket, with one candidate in each of the three strongholds of Swords, Malahide and Balbriggan/Skerries. Jim Glennon, a former Irish international rugby player, was establishing a new political base for the party in the Balbriggan/Skerries area of North Dublin. The outgoing deputy, GV Wright, operated mainly off a Malahide base and Michael Kennedy had a Swords base. The Fianna Fáil candidates were remarkably close together in first preferences with Glennon on 5,892, Wright on 5,658 and Kennedy, crucially, 405 first preferences behind at 5,253. Kennedy was unable to close this gap with transfers and when he was eliminated on the seventh count his transfers ensured the election of Glennon and Wright.

Michael Kennedy is the only one of the three re-contesting. Having been a member of Dublin County Council and later of Fingal County Council since 1991, he is currently a councillor for Swords, where he polled 2, 266 first preferences and took the second seat after the Socialist's deputy leader, Clare Daly, in 2004. Kennedy was also an unsuccessful candidate in the 1998 by-election caused by the resignation of Ray Burke. He lives in Skerries and is an insurance broker with businesses in both Swords and Portmarnock.

Darragh O'Brien is a councillor in the Malahide electoral area. He was co-opted to the Fingal County Council seat vacated by the sitting deputy GV Wright in 2004 and was re-elected to the council in the 2004 local elections. He polled 2,000 first preferences when the quota was 2,356 and took the third seat in the four-seater. He works in the life and pensions industry.

The third Fianna Fáil candidate, John O'Leary, was added in November 2006, some weeks after the surprise announcement from Jim Glennon TD that he would step down from Dáil Eireann at the 2007 election. O'Leary won All-Ireland medals with Dublin as goalkeeper in 1983 and 1995. He is a mortgage advisor based in Balbriggan.

Fine Gael: Fine Gael's long day's journey into electoral disaster in 2002 began with the announcement of the electronically counted results in this constituency in the early hours of the day after the election. Nora Owen had enjoyed a high profile as Minister for Justice and deputy leader under the Bruton leadership. She was regarded as safe going into the election. An injured ankle in the run-up to the campaign impacted on her canvassing ability and her vote fell from 5,956 in 1997 to 4,012 in 2002. Her running mate, Cathal Boland, polled only 1,177. Overall the party's vote dropped from 18.9% in 1997 to just 11.8% in 2002. The manner in which the loss of her seat was announced became one of the television moments of the count weekend and forewarned the severe losses Fine Gael suffered later that day.

Dr James Reilly is the new Fine Gael candidate in this constituency. He is a general practitioner with practises in Lusk and Donabate and is a former president of the Irish Medical Organisation. He is currently Chairman of the GP development team and the IMO representative at the World Medical Organisation.

Labour Party: The outgoing deputy, Seán Ryan, was first elected to Dáil Éireann in 1989 when he topped the poll. He topped it spectacularly again in 1992 with 14,693 votes but lost his seat in the backlash against Labour in 1997. However, he won the seat back in 1998 in the by-election caused by the resignation of Ray Burke and comfortably retained it in 2002, polling 6,359, which was a 743 vote and almost 1% increase on his 1997 performance. With Seán Ryan having announced his retirement from Dáil Éireann, his younger brother Brendan was selected as the party's candidate for this election. Although he has been an active member of the Labour Party since 1978, this is Brendan's first electoral contest. He lives in Skerries and works as an operations manager.

Progressive Democrats: Senator Tom Morrisey, who was the party's candidate in the 2002 election in the neighbouring Dublin West constituency, has transferred to Dublin North for this election. Morrissey has been a Taoiseach's nominee to Seánad Éireann since 2002 and is the party's spokerperson on transport. He was a member of Fingal County Council for the Castleknock electoral area from 1999 to 2004. In Dublin West as a Progressive Democrats candidate he polled 3,050 votes in 1997 and 2,370 votes in 2002. He twice ran for the Dáil as a Fine Gael candidate in Dublin West, in the 1992 general election and in the by-election held in that constituency in 1996. As party Transport spokesperson his advocacy of the moving of Dublin Port to Balbriggan may not make him popular in the latter area.

Green Party: In 2002 the Green Party leader, Trevor Sargent, held his seat with an increased vote. So confident are the party of Sargent being re-elected in 2007 in a scenario where he is the only sitting deputy for any party standing in this election that the Green Party is running two candidates in this constituency.

Sargent was first elected to Dáil Éireann in 1992 and has held the seat on each occasion since. His vote and his vote share have risen significantly on each election He polled 8.8% of the vote in 1992 and 13.6% in 1997 and 16.6% in 2002. His first preference vote in 1992 was 3,788, in 1997 was 5,614, in 2002 was 7,294. Sargent, a former national school principal, was elected the party's first leader in October 2001 and he is also the party spokesperson on Northern Ireland, Gaeltacht and Agriculture. He was an unsuccessful candidate in the then three-seat constituency for the Green Alliance in 1987 and for the Green Party in 1989. He also contested the 1999 European elections for the Dublin constituency. Based in Balbriggan, he was a member of Dublin County Council for that electoral area from 1991 to 1993.

The second Green Party candidate is Councillor Joe Corr. A native of Lusk, Corr is a member of Fingal County Council and was elected for the Balbriggan electoral area, where in the 2004 local elections he polled 1,460 votes, which represented 10.2% of the vote share.

Sinn Féin: Sinn Féin's candidate is Matt McCormack. He was an unsuccessful candidate in the 2004 local elections in the Swords electoral area, where he polled 995 first preferences when the quota was 2,789. Mick Davis, the party's candidate in 2002, polled just 1,350 votes. River Valley based, he is a trade union activist and employee of Eircom.

Others: The Socialist Party candidate is again Clare Daly. She put in a particularly impressive performance in 2002 when she polled 5,501 first preferences, which represented 12.5% of the vote, and she ended up fifth in this four seater. This was a significant improvement on her 1997 performance, when she polled 2,971, which was just over 7% of the vote. She was also a candidate in the 1998 by-election, polling an 8.12% share. She is an Aer Lingus shop steward. She has been a member of Fingal County Council for the Swords electoral area since 1999. She polled 1,287 first preferences in 1999 when the quota was 1,517. In the 2004 local elections she topped the poll with 2,763, when the quota was 2,789. She is prominent on local issues like the bin tax and planning issues.

DUBLIN NORTH 2007 FIGURES

Candidate	Party	1st Count	2nd Count	3rd Count	4th Count	5th Count	Later counts

YOUR PREDICTION 2007

	Candidate Elected	Party
1		
2		
3		
4		
5		

RESULT 2007

	Candidate Elected	Party
1		
2		
3		
4		
5		

NOTES/UPDATES

DUBLIN NORTH 2002 FIGURES

4 seats   Quota: 8,789

Candidate	Party	1st	2nd	3rd	4th	5th	6th	7th	8th
Transfer of			Quinn Walshe	Goulding	Boland	Davis	Owen	Sargent surplus	Kennedy
Trevor Sargent*	GP	7,294	*+86* 7,380	*+298* 7,678	*+140* 7,818	*+300* 8,118	*+1,667* 9,785		
Sean Ryan*	LAB	6,359	+48 6,407	+128 6,535	+130 6,665	+182 6,847	+1,731 8,578	+550 9,128	
Jim Glennon	FF	5,892	*+53* 5945	*+83* 6,028	*+124* 6,152	*+142* 6,294	*+217* 6,511	*+85* 6,596	*+2,044* 8,640
GV Wright*	FF	5,658	*+49* 5,707	*+32* 5,739	*+38* 5,777	*+91* 5,868	*+271* 6,139	*+110* 6,249	*+2,368* 8,617
Clare Daly	SP	5,501	*+50* 5,551	*+179* 5,730	*+66* 5,796	*+448* 6,244	*+346* 6,590	*+182* 6,772	*+751* 7,523
Michael Kenndy	FF	5,253	*+56* 5309	*+59* 5,368	*+54* 5,422	*+110* 5,532	*+200* 5732	*+69* 5801	*Elim'd*
Nora Owen*	FG	4,012	*+18* 4,030	*+102* 4,132	*+588* 4,720	*+43* 4,763	*Elim'd*		
Mick Davis	SF	1,350	*+32* 1,382	*+42* 1,424	*+16* 1,440	*Elim'd*			
Cathal Boland	FG	1,177	*+12* 1,189	*+27* 1,216	*Elim'd*				
Ciaran Goulding	IND	914	*+95* 1,009	*Elim'd*					
Eamon Quinn	IND	285	*Elim'd*						
David Walshe	CSP	247	*Elim'd*						
Non-Transferable			33	59	60	124	331	0	638

DUBLIN NORTH CENTRAL

Outgoing Deputies: Seán Haughey (FF), Ivor Callely (FF), Richard Bruton (FG), Finian McGrath (Ind).

The Constituency: This is now a **three-seat** constituency having lost a seat in the redrawing since the 2002 election. This transferred an area around Edenmore (2002 population 5,820) to Dublin North East, and the Santry River now forms most of the boundary between the two constituencies. The redrawing also transferred part of this constituency in the Beaumount and Whitehall areas (2002 population 5,020) into Dublin North West.

Party	Votes 2002	Quota 2002	% Vote 2002	% Vote 1997	Swing
Fianna Fáil	20,043	2.5	50.05%	46.44%	3.61%
Fine Gael	6,809	0.9	17.00%	26.03%	–9.03%
Labour	4,203	0.5	10.49%	9.37%*	1.13%[2]*
Green Party	2,275	0.3	5.68%	3.82%	1.86%
Sinn Féin	2,299	0.3	5.74%	–	5.74%
Others	4,419	0.6	11.03%	11.05	–0.02%

2007 Candidates will include: Ivor Callely (FF), Seán Haughey (FF), Richard Bruton (FG), Bronwen Maher (GP), Derek McDowell (Lab), Peter Lawlor (SF), Frances McCole (SF), Finian McGrath (Ind), Antoinette Keegan (Ind).

In Brief: This constituency lost a seat in the redrawing since the last election, leaving four outgoing deputies and other high-profile names fighting for the remaining three seats. It is a key marginal between Fianna Fáil and the colourful independent, Finian McGrath. Newly appointed Minister of State Seán Haughey will fight intensely in a tight electoral battle, not least with his party colleague, Ivor Callely, who was forced to resign as a Minister of State in December 2005. The Fine Gael deputy leader and party Finance spokesperson, Richard Bruton, is likely to hold his seat. Also in the mix is the former Labour TD, now senator, Derek McDowell.

Fianna Fáil: In 2002, when this was a four seater, Fianna Fáil won two seats but failed to win a third seat they had targeted. In 2002 they ran the two sitting deputies, Ivor Callely and Seán Haughey, along with the high-profile councillor, Deirdre Heney. In that election managing the Callely vote appeared to be the priority for Fianna Fáil, while media speculation about a push to replace Seán Haughey with Deirdre Heney also contributed to severe tensions between the candidates. Haughey, however, topped the poll with 7,614 first preference votes and he took the first seat. Ivor Callely, who had agreed to share some of his traditional area with the third candidate, saw his vote drop to 6,896 but was still strong enough to take the second seat comfortably. Heney was almost 1,100 votes behind the independent Finian McGrath on the last count.

Seán Haughey was a member of the Dublin City Council from 1985 to 2004, in the latter period for the Artane local electoral area. He was a candidate in neighbouring Dublin North East in the 1987 and 1989 elections, a senator from 1987 to 1992 and Lord Mayor of Dublin from 1989 to 1990, transferring to this constituency when his late father, the former Taoiseach, who was a Dáil deputy from 1957 to 1992, retired from the Dáil. Seán Haughey was first elected to Dáil Éireann in 1992 and was comfortably re-elected in 1997 and 2002, being appointed a Minister of State at the Department of Education in December 2006. He is also a former national chairman of Ógra Fianna Fáil.

Ivor Callely has always been a strong vote-getter in this constituency. He was elected to Dáil Éireann on his first attempt in 1989, when the party won three out of four seats in this constituency. He was comfortably re-elected in 1992. In the 1997 election he polled 11,190 first preferences, when the quota was 8,637, which gave him one of the highest personal votes in the country. In 2002, however, his first preference vote was 6,896 when the quota was 8,010. He is a former member of Dublin City Council, where he represented the Clontarf ward in the latter period of his tenure. He is also a former chair of the Eastern Region Health Authority.

In 2002 Callely was appointed Minister of State at the Department of Health and Children with Special Responsibility for Services for Older People, a post he held until 2004. He was then appointed Minister of State at the Department of Transport. He resigned from this office in December 2005 as a result of controversies concerning the staff turnover at his department and a decorating job at his home.

Fine Gael: Richard Bruton, the party's outgoing TD in this constituency, is their deputy leader and their sole candidate here. He was first elected to Dáil Éireann in 1982 and was a Minister of State at the Department of Industry and Commerce from 1986 to 1987. Since the early 1990s he has held a range of portfolios on the party's front bench, including Education. He was Minister for Enterprise and Employment in the 'Rainbow' government from 1994 to 1997 and is currently the party's spokesperson on Finance. Richard Bruton is a brother of the former Taoiseach and Meath deputy, John Bruton. An economist, he was also briefly a senator in 1981–1982, a member of Dublin City Council 1991–1994 and a member of Meath County Council 1979–1981.

In 2002 Richard Bruton had a new running mate in the person of Clontarf-based councillor Gerry Breen. The party's vote fell dramatically in that election, however, from 26.03% in 1997 to 17% in 2002. Bruton's own vote fell from 8,196 in 1997 to 5,159 in 2002. The transfer rate between the two Fine Gael candidates was very impressive. Of the 1,661 transfers available when Breen was eliminated, Bruton got 1,052. Bruton also attracted 40% of the transfers when Labour's then outgoing deputy, Derek McDowell, was eliminated on the fifth count. These transfers put Bruton over the quota and he took the second seat.

Labour Party: In 2002 Labour's Derek McDowell lost his seat to independent Finian McGrath. McDowell was a member of Dáil Éireann from 1992 to 2002. In 1997 he polled just 2,848 first preference votes and took the last seat after sweating through 11 counts. In 2002 he actually increased his first preference vote substantially, from 2,488 in 1997 to 4,203, and he was 422 votes ahead of the independent Finian McGrath on the first count. Going into the 2002 election he had a high profile as the party's spokesperson on Finance. However, McGrath proved better than McDowell at attracting transfers, particularly from the Green Party and Sinn Féin. McDowell is a former member of Dublin City Council for the Clontarf ward. In the 1999 local elections he polled less than half a quota in first preferences and was elected on the last count.

Green Party: Bronwen Maher is again the party's candidate. She has been campaign manager for Patricia McKenna in various European elections and worked as the MEP's personal assistant. Maher is also a former national campaign organiser for the Green Party. In 2002 she polled 2,275 first preferences. She unsuccessfully contested the local elections in the Artane ward in 1991 and the Clontarf ward in 1999. However, she won a seat in the Clontarf ward in the 2004 local elections, where she polled 1,576 first preferences. The quota in this ward was 3,432 and Maher managed to attract sufficient transfers to almost double her vote to 2,976, taking the fourth of the five seats.

Sinn Féin: Interestingly, Sinn Féin is running two candidates in this constituency. Frances McCole, a teacher in the north inner city, does not share the profile of her party colleagues in other Dublin constituencies. However, in the 2002 Dáil election when she was the only candidate, she polled 2,299 first preferences. This time McCole is joined on the ticket by Marino-based Peter Lawlor. Lawlor was an unsuccessful candidate in the Clontarf ward in the 2004 local elections. He polled 1,478 in a ward where the quota was 3,432.

Others: The outgoing independent deputy Finian McGrath cut his political teeth with Tony Gregory in the inner city campaigns of the 1980s. He had a strong performance in the Clontarf electoral ward in the 1999 local elections, where he polled 1,861 first preferences. He tapped into a left-wing and republican-minded vote and into the independent base that Seán 'Dublin Bay' Loftus used to hold in this constituency. During the 2002 election campaign he joined the loosely attached group of independent candidates campaigning on health issues under the banner name of the Health Alliance.

McGrath unsuccessfully contested the 1997 Dáil election and polled just 1,551 first preferences. In the 2002 Dáil election, however, he polled 3,781 first preferences and attracted considerable transfers from all candidates who were eliminated. He obtained more than a quarter of the Sinn Féin transfers, more than a third of the Green Party transfers and attracted nearly 40% of the Labour transfers. He attracted much publicity, and raised a lot of money for Downs Syndrome Ireland as the runner-up in the *Celebrity You're a Star* TV programme in 2005. He is a former school principal.

Antoinette Keegan is a founding member of the Stardust Victims Committee. This is her first electoral contest.

DUBLIN NORTH CENTRAL 2007 FIGURES

Candidate	Party	1st Count	2nd Count	3rd Count	4th Count	5th Count	Later counts

YOUR PREDICTION 2007

	Candidate Elected	Party
1		
2		
3		
4		
5		

RESULT 2007

	Candidate Elected	Party
1		
2		
3		
4		
5		

NOTES/UPDATES

DUBLIN NORTH CENTRAL 2002 FIGURES

4 seats   Quota: 8,010

Candidate	Party	1st	2nd	3rd	4th	5th	6th
Transfer of			Browne	Breen	McCole	Maher	McDowell
Sean Haughey*	FF	7,614	+41 7,665	+63 7,718	+310 8,028		
Ivor Callely*	FF	6,896	+41 6,937	+98 7,035	+178 7,213	+225 7,438	+395 7,833
Deirdre Heney	FF	5,533	+31 5,564	+63 5,627	+175 5,802	+299 6,101	+426 6,527
Richard Bruton*	FG	5,159	+36 5,195	+1,052 6,247	+115 6,362	+388 6,750	+2,295 9,045
Derek McDowell*	LAB	4,203	+82 4,285	+146 4,431	+288 4,719	+829 5,548	Elim'd
Finian McGrath	IND	3,781	+112 3,893	+128 4,021	+677 4698	+1,058 5,756	+1,882 7,638
Frances McCole	SF	2,299	+146 2,445	+14 2,459	Elim'd		
Bronwen Maher	GP	2,275	+128 2,403	+83 2,486	+572 3,058	Elim'd	
Gerry Breen	FG	1,650	+11 1,661	Elim'd			
Ritchie Browne	SWP	638	Elim'd				
Non-Transferable			10	14	144	259	550

*Outgoing Deputy

DUBLIN NORTH EAST

Outgoing Deputies: Michael Woods (FF), Tommy Broughan (Lab), Martin Brady (FF).

The Constituency: This is a **three-seat** constituency. It has gained an area in the Edenmore area (2002 population 5,820) from Dublin North Central. The Santry River forms most of the boundary between this constituency and Dublin North Central and the northern boundary of the constituency is aligned with the M50 and the Moines River.

Party	Votes 2002	Quota 2002	% Vote 2002	% Vote 1997	Swing
Fianna Fáil	11,761	1.6	40.12%	40.61%	−0.49%
Fine Gael	4,504	0.6	15.36%	18.90%	−3.54%
Labour	4,758	0.6	16.23%	17.25%	−4.72%[1]*
PDs	1,219	0.2	4.16%	11.50%	−3.65%
Green Party	1,656	0.2	5.65%	3.57%	2.08%
Sinn Féin	3,003	0.4	10.24%	5.93%	4.31%
Others	2,417	0.3	8.24%	2.23%	6.01%

2007 Candidates will include: Martin Brady (FF), Michael Woods (FF), Brody Sweeney (FG), Terence Flanagan (FG), Tommy Broughan (Lab), Keith Redmond (PD), David Healy (GP), Larry O'Toole (SF).

In Brief: This is a key target for Fine Gael to take a seat from Fianna Fáil. Alternatively it could be the venue for a Sinn Féin gain. The sandwich bar entrepreneur Brody Sweeney and local councillor Terence Flanagan are the Fine Gael candidates. On the Fianna Fáil side the candidate line-up is veteran deputy and former minister Michael Woods and outgoing depty Martin Brady. There is also a prospect that if Fianna Fáil loses a seat and Fine Gael fails to win one, Sinn Féin candidate councillor Larry O'Toole could be elected.

Fianna Fáil: Fianna Fáil's Michael Woods and Martin Brady impressively held their two seats here in 2002. The finalisation of the party ticket for the 2007 election was delayed until March, apparently because of uncertainty about whether their outgoing deputy, Michael Woods, would contest this election.

Michael Woods was first elected to Dáil Éireann in 1977 and has held his seat in each subsequent election. He was appointed government chief whip in 1979 and was a member of every Fianna Fáil front bench or cabinet from then until 2002. He has served as Minister for Social Welfare, Health, Agriculture, Marine and Education.

Martin Brady was first elected to Dáil Éireann in 1997 and has a particularly large electoral base in the Donaghmede area of the constituency. He was an unsuccessful candidate in the 1992 Dáil election. He was a member of Dublin City Council from 1991 to 2004 and is a former Eircom executive.

In 2002 there was a marginal increase in the Fianna Fáil vote share and the fact that the party was running two rather than three candidates meant that both the Woods and Brady vote shares were up on 1997, notwithstanding the reduction in the size of the constituency from a four-seater to a three-seater. Woods's vote grew from 5,735 in 1997 to 6,457 while Brady's vote also grew marginally, from 5,018 in 1997 to 5,304. Both won their seats comfortably.

Fine Gael: With four outgoing deputies contesting for three seats, someone had to lose out in the reduction of this constituency to a three seater in 2002. Given the national trend, it was no surprise that Fine Gael's Michael Joe Cosgrave lost the seat which he had regained in 1997, due in no small part to 3,500 transfers, 2,000 of which came from his running mate, Joan Maher. In the 2002 general election his new running mate was a young candidate, Gavin Doyle, who was based in Sutton. A former disc jockey, Doyle put in a colourful campaign.

The two candidates came in surprisingly close together. Doyle polled a respectable 2,156 first preferences while Cosgrave's vote dropped from 4,173 first preferences in 1997 to 2,349 in 2002. The overall Fine Gael vote went from 18.9% in 1997 to 15.4% in 2002 which, in the absence of any available Labour transfers, was too low to win a seat. Crucially, Doyle was 29 votes ahead of Cosgrave on the third count and, when Cosgrave was eliminated, Doyle survived to the last count. However, he was almost 2,000 votes behind Fianna Fáil's Martin Brady for the last seat.

Fine Gael has two new candidates for the 2007 election. The first to be selected was businessman Brody Sweeney, who was put into the electoral field in this constituency in 2005, although he spoke at a parliamentary party meeting in September 2004. Sweeney is the founder of the O'Brien's Sandwich Bar Group. He is also co-founder of the charity African Connections, which twins businesses in Ireland and Ethiopia and is on the board of Paddy Powers plc. This is his first electoral contest.

Concern about Sweeney's prospects of winning a seat prompted Fine Gael to add local councillor Terence Flanagan to the Dáil election ticket in late 2006. Flanagan is a member of Dublin City Council for the Artane electoral area, where he polled 2,594 in the 2004 local elections when the quota was 2,802.

Labour Party: Tommy Broughan was first elected to Dáil Éireann in 1992 when he and Seán Kenny won two seats in this constituency for the Labour Party. Broughan had also contested for the Dáil unsuccessfully in 1989. He was one of the few Labour deputies elected for the first time in 1992 who were re-elected in 1997. Broughan and Kenny were again the two candidates for that election but Kenny lost and Broughan retained his seat. In 2002 Broughan was the only candidate and he comfortably held the seat. He polled 3,447 in 1997 and 4,758 in 2002.

Broughan was a member of Dublin City Council for the Donaghmede electoral area from 1999 to 2004. He is based in Howth and is a former teacher. He is currently the party spokesperson on Communications, Marine and Natural Resources. The party had two outgoing deputies as candidates in 1997 so in 2002, when Broughan was the only candidate, the party's vote inevitably fell, in this case by five percentage points.

Progressive Democrats: The party's candidate in 1997, Mairéad Foley, received 2,911 votes.

Noelle Ryan declared very late in the run-up to the 2002 election and only polled 1,219 first preferences. This time round their candidate is Keith Redmond, a 33-year-old dentist originally from Finglas. This is his first election.

Green Party: David Healy is again the party's candidate. Healy, who comes from Howth, polled just 1,656 first preference votes in the 2002 election. He is an environmental consultant, active in the Friends of the Irish Environment. He was a member of Fingal County Council from 1991 to 1999 and was re-elected to the county council in the 2004 local elections. He polled 1,242 first preferences (quota 2,533) and managed to exceed the quota on the sixth count and take the second seat in the four seater.

Sinn Féin: In 2002 the performance of Sinn Féin's Larry O'Toole was relatively disappointing, given the party's performance in other parts of Dublin, but given the rising support which national polls suggest the party is attracting and O'Toole's performance in the 2004 local elections, he is a strong contender for a seat in this election.

Larry O'Toole has been the party's standard-bearer in this constituency for quite some time and he polled a respectable 2,212 first preferences in the 1997 general election. In the 2002 Dáil election he took fourth place on the first count, polling 3,003 first preference votes, and was the last candidate to be eliminated. He has been a member of Dublin City Council since 1999 for the Artane electoral area. In the 2004 local election he topped the poll in Artane with 4,497 first preferences, well above the quota of 2,802. O'Toole is based in Darndale.

DUBLIN NORTH EAST 2007 FIGURES

Candidate	Party	1st Count	2nd Count	3rd Count	4th Count	5th Count	Later counts

YOUR PREDICTION 2007

	Candidate Elected	Party
1		
2		
3		
4		
5		

RESULT 2007

	Candidate Elected	Party
1		
2		
3		
4		
5		

NOTES/UPDATES

DUBLIN NORTH EAST 2002 FIGURES

3 seats   Quota: 7,330

Candidate	Party	1st	2nd	3rd	4th	5th	6th
Transfer of			Ryan Jenkinson	Healy	Cosgrave	Harold	O'Toole
Michael Woods*	FF	6,457	+285 6,742	+169 6,911	+227 7,138	+414 7,552	
Martin Brady*	FF	5,304	+227 5,531	+126 5,657	+119 5,776	+279 6,055	+854 6,909
Tommy Broughan*	LAB	4,758	+173 4,931	+495 5,426	+450 5,876	+949 6,825	+1,601 8,426
Gavin Doyle	FG	2,155	+218 2,373	+202 2,575	+1,520 4,085	+563 4,648	+289 4,937
Larry O'Toole	SF	3,003	+80 3,083	+203 3,286	+87 3,373	+347 3,720	Elim'd
Michael Joe Cosgrove*	FG	2,349	+105 2,454	+92 2,546	Elim'd		
Mark Harrold	IND	2,116	+205 2,321	+485 2,806	+106 2,912	Elim'd	
David Healy	GP	1,656	+200 1,856	Elim'd			
Noelle Ryan	PD	1,219	Elim'd				
Thomas Jenkinson	IND	301	Elim'd				
Non-Transferable			27	84	47	360	976

*Outgoing Deputy

DUBLIN NORTH WEST

Outgoing Deputies: Noel Ahern (FF), Róisín Shortall (Lab), Pat Carey (FF).

The Constituency: This is a **three-seat** constituency. It embraces the Santry, Ballymun, Whitehall and Finglas communities and extends north to the M50. In the redrawing of constituencies since the 2002 election it has gained an area in the Beaumont/Whitehall area (2002 population 5,020) from Dublin North Central. It also gained an area from Dublin West (2002 population 1,106) aligning the border between the two constituencies more with the M50.

Party	Votes 2002	Quota 2002	% Vote 2002	% Vote 1997	Swing
Fianna Fáil	12,435	1.9	47.54%	47.04%	0.50%
Fine Gael	2,082	0.3	7.96%	15.60%	−7.64%
Labour	4,391	0.7	16.79%	21.21%*	−4.43%**
Green Party	607	0.1	2.32%	4.06%	−1.83%
Sinn Féin	4,781	0.7	18.28%	–	18.28%
Others	1,862	0.4	7.12%	11.99%	−4.87%

2007 Candidates will include: Noel Ahern (FF), Pat Carey (FF), Bill Tormey (FG), Róisín Shortall (Lab), Dessie Ellis (SF), John Dunne (WP), Owen Martin (WP).

In Brief: Sinn Féin's Dessie Ellis could win a seat here and this is likely to be at the expense of Fianna Fáil rather than the Labour Party. On the basis of the last election results, Fianna Fáil's high-profile backbencher Pat Carey is more vulnerable than Minister of State Noel Ahern, brother of the Taoiseach. Labour's Róisín Shortall, who struggled to hold her seat in 2002, is probably safer this time out, but her losing to Sinn Féin's Ellis cannot be completely ruled out. Fine Gael's candidate is the colourful and opinionated doctor, Bill Tormey.

Fianna Fáil: Notwithstanding the reduction of this constituency from a four seater to a three seater, Fianna Fáil held its two seats in 2002, not least because of the strength of the party's two outgoing deputies. The Fianna Fáil vote held up in the constituency: indeed, it was up a half a percentage point. With almost two quotas and the two deputies coming in close together, the party managed to hold its two seats.

Noel Ahern is the Minister of State at the Department of Environment and Local Government with special responsibility for Housing and Urban Renewal and at the Department of Community, Rural and Gaeltacht Affairs with responsibility for the National Drugs Strategy. He was first elected to the Dáil in 1992 and has held the seat since. He was a member of Dublin

City Council for the Ballymun/Whitehall ward from 1985-2002 and previously worked as an official with CIE. His brother, Taoiseach Bertie Ahern, is a deputy for the neighbouring Dublin Central constituency.

Pat Carey was an unsuccessful candidate in the 1992 election and was first elected to Dáil Éireann in 1997. In 2002 he had a first preference vote of 5,523 and took the second seat on the last count, having just exceeded the quota. He was an alternate member to the Convention on Europe which drew up the European Constitution. He was vice-chairman of the Joint Oireachtas Committee on Foreign Affairs up to November 2004, and is a member of the Joint Oireachtas Committee on European Affairs and of the Oireachtas Committee on the Scrutiny of EU Legislation. He is currently co-chair of the British-Irish Inter-parliamentary Body. He is a former school teacher and was Chairman of the Dublin county vocational education committee from 1988 to 1991. Carey was a member of Dublin City Council for the Finglas electoral area from 1985 to 2003.

Fine Gael: Even though the party ran two candidates in the 1997 general election, they failed to win any seat. In 2002 they ran just one candidate – Brendan Brady, who was based in Ballymun. Brady received 2,901 first preferences in 1997 when he ran with the then outgoing deputy Mary Flaherty. However, in 2002 the party's vote dropped 7.6% and Brady's own first preference vote, as the sole candidate, dropped to 2,082.

This time the party candidate is Dr. Bill Tormey, who is consultant pathologist at Dublin's Beaumont Hospital. He has had a chequered electoral history. He stood as an Independent Labour candidate in the 1992 election, polling 2,515, in the 1997 election polling 1,479 votes and in the 2002 election polling 1,100 first preferences. He contested the 2004 local election for Fine Gael in the Finglas electoral area, where he polled 1,743 when the quota was 2,882 and won the third of the four seats. He had run unsuccessfully as an independent in the 1999 local elections, polling 1,061 first preferences. In 1991 he contested the local elections in the same ward as a Labour Party candidate, getting 1,090 votes.

Labour Party: Róisín Shorthall was first elected to Dáil Éireann in 1992. She was one of the few deputies elected for the first time in 1992 to retain her seat in 1997. Having received 4,084 first preferences in 1997, Shortall increased that to 4,391 in 2002. Although she polled just 11% on the first count, she managed to gain sufficient transfers to win her seat. She was 390 votes behind Sinn Féin's Dessie Ellis on the first count but proved much better at attracting transfers, particularly on the last count. When the former Labour man Bill Tormey and Fine Gael's Brendan Brady were eliminated together and had 3,554 vote transfers, Shorthall received 2,017 of them, almost four times as many as Ellis. Shorthall had 1,331 votes to spare over Ellis when she won the last seat.

She won a seat on Dublin City Council in the Finglas ward in the 1990 local elections. Having received a good first preference vote of 1,571 she had to wait until the eighth count to retain her Dublin City Council seat in 1999. She is currently the party spokesperson on Transport and was previously the party spokesperson on Health and Children. She was chairperson of the Eastern Health Board from 1996 to 1998. Her political survival has been assisted by the Labour-Democratic Left merger, and in particular by the decision of the former Democratic Left leader, Prionsias de Rossa, to concentrate on the European Parliament and not to contest the 2002 Dáil election. She is a former primary school teacher at St Joseph's School for the Deaf, Cabra.

Green Party: Their first-time candidate in 2002 was Eugene O'Brien, who polled a poor 607 first preference votes. They are not running a candidate in this constituency in 2007.

Sinn Féin: Dessie Ellis was first elected to political office on Dublin City Council for the Finglas electoral area in the 1999 local elections, polling 2,278 first preference votes. In the 2002 Dáil election he polled 4,781 in the entire constituency, which was almost three-quarters of a quota and was 390 votes ahead of Labour's Róisín Shortall. However, Ellis did not do as well on transfers and he was 1,331 behind Shortall on the sixth and final count.

In the 2004 local elections he topped the poll with 4,300 first preference votes, again in the Fingal electoral area, where this time the quota was 2,882. His vote in that local election was more than twice the nearest candidate. He is the owner of a TV repair business.

Others: The Workers' Party candidate is Owen Martin who was an unsuccessful candidate for Dublin City Council in the Finglas ward, where he polled 458 votes in the 2004 local election.

DUBLIN NORTH WEST 2007 FIGURES

Candidate	Party	1st Count	2nd Count	3rd Count	4th Count	5th Count	Later counts

YOUR PREDICTION 2007

	Candidate Elected	Party
1		
2		
3		
4		
5		

RESULT 2007

	Candidate Elected	Party
1		
2		
3		
4		
5		

NOTES/UPDATES

DUBLIN NORTH WEST 2002 FIGURES

3 seats Quota: 6,540

Candidate	Party	1st	2nd	3rd	4th	5th	6th
Transfer of			Larkin	Ahern's surplus	O'Cionnaith	O'Brien	Brady Tormey
Noel Ahern *	*FF*	6,912					
Pat Carey*	*FF*	5,523	+42 5,565	+262 5,827	+79 5,906	+62 5,968	+631 6,599
Dessie Ellis	*SF*	4,781	+18 4,799	+26 4,825	+168 4,993	+105 5,098	+504 5,602
Roisin Shortall*	*LAB*	4,391	+9 4,400	+43 4,443	+186 4,629	+286 4,915	+2017 6,932
Brendan Brady	FG	2,082	+18 2,100	+20 2,120	+25 2,145	+58 2,203	Elim'd
Bill Tormey	Ind	1,100	+28 1,128	+9 1,137	+68 1,205	+146 1,351	Elim'd
Sean Ó Cionnaith	WP	608	+6 614	−6 620	Elim'd		
Eugene O' Brien	GP	607	+22 629	+6 635	+69 704	Elim'd	
Michael Larkin	CSP	154	Elim'd				
Non-Transferable			11	0	25	47	402

*Outgoing Deputy

DUBLIN SOUTH

Outgoing Deputies: Séamus Brennan (FF), Tom Kitt (FF), Liz O'Donnell (PD), Olivia Mitchell (FG), Eamon Ryan (GP).

The Constituency: This is a **five-seat** constituency. In the redrawing of constituencies since 2002 Dublin South lost a small area (2002 population 1,995) in Firhouse to the Dublin South West constituency.

Party	Votes 2002	Quota 2002	% Vote 2002	% Vote 1997	Swing
Fianna Fáil	20,250	2.2	36.64%	38.62%	−1.98%
Fine Gael	10,931	1.2	19.78%	29.09%	−9.31%
Labour	5,247	0.6	9.49%	10.60%	−1.11%
PDs	8,288	0.9	15.00%	9.39%	5.61%
Green Party	5,222	0.6	9.45%	6.10%	3.35%
Sinn Féin	2,172	0.2	3.93%	–	3.93%
Others	3,153	0.3	5.71%	6.2	−0.49%

2007 Candidates will include: Séamus Brennan (FF), Maria Corrigan (FF), Tom Kitt (FF), Olivia Mitchell (FG), Jim O'Leary (FG), Alan Shatter (FG), Aidan Culhane (Lab), Alex White (Lab), Liz O'Donnell (PD), Eamon Ryan (GP), Sorcha Nic Cormaic (SF), Shaun Tracey (SF) , Liam Ó Gógain (Ind).

In Brief: This is a key target for both Fine Gael and the Labour Party to make a gain. The Green's high-profile deputy, Eamon Ryan, should hold his seat and the two Fianna Fáil cabinet members, Séamus Brennan and Tom Kitt, should be safe. Much of the attention will therefore be on whether the Progressive Democrat deputy leader, Liz O'Donnell, can hold her seat. Fine Gael has a strong ticket which includes the incumbent party Transport spokesperson, Olivia Mitchell, and the former frontbencher, Alan Shatter. Labour hope to regain the seat won spectacularly by Eithne Fitzgerald in 1992 and lost equally spectacularly in 1997. There has been and will be intense intra-party competition between the Labour candidates, Alex White and Aidan Culhane. There are changes and surprises in Dublin South in every election and 2007 should be no different.

Fianna Fáil: In 2002 the party held its two seats comfortably. The party's senior deputy, Séamus Brennan, is the outgoing government Minister for Social, Community and Family Affairs. He was Minister for Transport from 2002 to 2004 and government chief whip from 1997 to 2002. Brennan was first elected to Dáil Éireann in 1981 and has held his seat on every occasion since, thanks mainly to a strong reputation for solid constituency work and a high national profile. In 2002 he topped the poll with 9,326 first preference votes, exceeding the quota by 115 votes on the first count. He was General Secretary of Fianna Fáil from 1973 to 1980 and, prior to his election to Dáil Éireann, had been a member of Seanad Éireann from 1977 to 1981 as a Taoiseach's nominee. He was Minister of State with responsibility for Trade and Marketing 1987–1989, Minister for Tourism and Transport from 1989 to 1991, Minister for Education from 1992 to 1993 and Minister for Commerce and Technology from 1993 to 1994. In the current Dáil he was Minister for Transport form 2002 to 2004 and is now Minister for Social, Community and Family Affairs.

The party's other outgoing deputy, now also at the cabinet table, is Tom Kitt, who was appointed government chief whip in 2004. He was first elected to Dáil Éireann in 1987 and has held his seat since, having been an unsuccessful candidate in the Dáil elections held in the 1981 to 1982 period. In 1997 he received 9,904 first preferences, outpolling his party colleague Séamus Brennan for the first time. In 2002 he polled 7,744 first preference votes and comfortably took the second seat. He was Minister of State at the Department of Foreign Affairs with responsibility for Overseas Development Assistance from 1993 to 1994 and at the Department of An Taoiseach with responsibility for European Affairs from 1992 to 1993. For a year before that he had responsibility for Women's Affairs, Arts and Culture in the same department. He was Minister of State for Labour and Consumer Affairs from 1997 to 2002. He is a former teacher. Tom is brother of the Galway East senator and former TD, Michael Kitt. Their father, Michael Kitt, was a TD for Galway East from 1948 to 1951 and from 1957 to 1975.

Fianna Fáil's third candidate in this election is again councillor Maria Corrigan. Geographically well placed in the middle-class Leopardstown end of the constituency, Corrigan polled reasonably well in 2002 with 3,180 first preferences. She has been a member of Dun Laoghaire-Rathdown County Council for the Glencullen electoral area since 1999. In the 2004 local elections Corrigan took the second seat in the three-seat Glencullen election area, where she polled 1,812 first preferences. She is a psychologist by profession.

Fine Gael: In 2002 the Fine Gael vote fell by almost a third to just 19.78% and the party did not have a large enough vote share to win two seats. Alan Shatter's vote fell from 8,094 in 1997 to 5,368 in 2002. Olivia Mitchell's vote also fell from 8,775 to 5,568. Mitchell stayed ahead of Shatter and by the seventh count she led him by 657 votes. When Shatter was then eliminated he had 6,484 votes, 4,508 of which transferred to Mitchell. She took the fourth seat on the eighth count.

Currently Fine Gael's Transport spokesperson, Olivia Mitchell was first elected to Dáil Éireann in 1997 when she polled 8,775 first preferences. She unsuccessfully contested the 1989 and 1992 Dáil elections. She was a member of Dublin County Council from 1985 to 1994 and of Dun Laoghaire-Rathdown County Council from 1994 to 2004 for the Glencullen electoral area. She was Cathoirleach of Dun Laoghaire-Rathdown for the year 1996–97.

The party's former deputy, Alan Shatter, is also contesting the 2007 election. Shatter was first elected to Dáil Éireann in 1981 and held his Dáil seat on each election from 1981 until 2002. He had been a member of most of Fine Gael's front benches in the 1980s, mainly in the areas of Justice, Health and Law Reform and was the party spokesperson on Justice and

Security before the 2002 election. He is the author of a number of private member bills which were enacted in the area of family law. A solicitor, he was a member of Dublin County Council and later of South Dublin County Council between 1979 and 1999

The third Fine Gael candidate is Jim O'Leary. O'Leary has been a member of Dun Laoghaire-Rathdown County Council since 2004. He represents the Dundrum electoral area, where he polled 1,850 first preferences, which represented just under 11% of the vote. He is a member of the Environment and Economic Development and the Planning Strategic Policy committees of the council.

Labour Party: Eithne Fitzgerald polled 17,256 first preferences when she won a seat for the party here in 1992. However, she lost the seat when she fell victim to the backlash against Labour in 1997. Her vote dropped from 28.9% in 1992 to 10.6% in 1997 and she lost her seat. She surprised many by deciding not to contest the 1999 local elections. She did contest the Dáil again in the 2002 election but polled just 9.5% of the vote with 5,247 first preference votes, which was down 900 votes on her first preference poll in 1997. Although she was ahead of the Green Party on the first count, her lead was just 25 votes. On the last count Eamon Ryan was 965 votes ahead of Fitzgerald for the last seat.

Labour has two new candidates for this election, Aidan Culhane and Alex White. When the party held its selection convention in November 2005, they tied for the one place on the ticket which the convention was called to fill. Ultimately, Culhane was chosen by drawing from a hat. Some months later, however, in June 2006, the party added Alex White to the ticket, much to the publicly stated annoyance of Culhane.

Aidan Culhane has been a member of Dun Laoghaire-Rathdown County Council for the Dundrum electoral area since 1999. He topped the poll there in the 2004 local elections with 2,216 first preferences, just short of the quota of 2,485. He is chairman of the council's Housing Strategic Policy committee, the Dundrum Area Committee, and the county development board.

Alex White is a member of South Dublin County Council in the Terenure-Rathfarnham electoral area, where he polled 2,109 first preferences in the 2004 local elections. White is a practising barrister specialising in employment and labour law and is a former RTÉ radio producer.

Progressive Democrats: The party's deputy leader, Liz O'Donnell, is the PD candidate here. She was elected to Dáil Éireann on her first attempt in 1992 and, despite frequent predictions to the contrary, has held the seat in each election since. This was one of those constituencies where the swing to the Progressive Democrats during the course of the 2002 campaign was significant. In 2002 the party's vote was up 5.6 percentage points. O'Donnell's first preferences increased from 5,444 in 1997 to 8,288 first preferences in 2002. O'Donnell was second on the first count and, with the help of Fianna Fáil transfers, she exceeded the quota and took the third seat on the sixth count.

O'Donnell was Minister of State at the Department of Foreign Affairs with special responsibility for Overseas Development Assistance and Human Rights from 1997 to 2002. She is currently the party's chief whip and was previously the party's spokesperson on Health, Social Welfare and Justice. She has been deputy leader of the party since the change of leadership from Mary Harney to Michael McDowell in September 2006. There was some surprise when O'Donnell announced, in June 2002, that for personal reasons she was would not be seeking an appointment even at junior ministerial level in the new Fianna Fáil/Progressive Democrats administration. O'Donnell was a high-profile chair of the Women's Political Association. She was also a member of Dublin City Council in the Rathmines ward, which is in the neighbouring Dublin South East Dáil constituency, from 1991 to 1994.

Green Party: In 1989 Roger Garland won the Green Party's first Dáil seat ever in Dublin South but he lost it at the next election in 1992. It was 10 years before the party won a seat here again and their sitting deputy, Eamon Ryan, looks as if he will avoid Garland's one-term fate.

Ryan is currently the party's spokesperson on Transport, Enterprise, Trade and Employment, Communications, Marine and Natural Resources. He was a member of Dublin City Council from 1998 to 2002 for the Rathmines ward, which is in the neighbouring Dublin South East constituency. Having being co-opted to the council seat to replace John Gormley, who had resigned when elected to Dáil Éireann in 1997, Ryan held the seat in the 1999 local elections, topping the poll in the Rathmines ward with 1,434 first preferences. He transferred to become the party's candidate in Dublin South for the 2002 election and polled 5,222 first preferences votes, a significant increase on their 1997 candidate, who had polled just 3,539 first preferences. Ryan is a former managing director of Irish Cycling Safaris, a leisure holiday company.

Sinn Féin: In 2002 the Sinn Féin candidate was Deirdre Whelan, who polled 2,172 first preference votes and was eliminated on the fourth count.

This time the party is running two candidates. Sorcha Nic Cormac was an unsuccessful candidate in the Dundrum electoral area in the 2004 local elections, where she polled 1,876 first preference votes, which represented 6.5% of the vote. She works as a primary school teacher in Dundrum and is a former member of Sinn Féin Ard Comhairle.

Shaun Tracey is a 26-year-old former plumber who began working for the party full time in 1994. He is currently a press officer for the party's five Dáil deputies based in Leinster House.

Others: Liam Ó Gógain has previously contested both Louth and Meath in general elections, stood for the Seanad in the NUI panel and contested the East constituency in the 2004 European elections, all on his parental equality platform.

DUBLIN SOUTH 2007 FIGURES

Candidate	Party	1st Count	2nd Count	3rd Count	4th Count	5th Count	Later counts

YOUR PREDICTION 2007

	Candidate Elected	Party
1		
2		
3		
4		
5		

RESULT 2007

	Candidate Elected	Party
1		
2		
3		
4		
5		

NOTES/UPDATES

DUBLIN SOUTH 2002 FIGURES

4 seats — Quota: 9,211

Candidate	Party	1st	2nd	3rd	4th	5th	6th	7th	8th	9th
Transfer of			Maher	Brennan's surplus	Canning	Whelan	Corrigan	Kitt's surplus	Shatter	Mitchell's surplus
Seamus Brennan*	FF	**9,326**								
Liz O'Donnell*	PD		+56	+12	+291	+169	+499			
		8,288	**8,344**	**8,356**	**8,647**	**8,816**	**9,315**			
Tom Kitt*	FF		+113	+60	+200	+379	+2,430			
		7,744	**7,857**	**7,917**	**8,117**	**8,496**	**10,926**			
Olivia Mitchell*	FG		+61	+4	+211	+84	+214	+398	+4,508	−1,837
		5,568	**5,629**	**5,633**	**5,844**	**5,928**	**6,142**	**6,540**	**11,048**	**9,211**
Alan Shatter*	FG		+47	+3	+155	+85	+40	+140		
		5,363	**5,410**	**5,413**	**5568**	**5,653**	**5,693**	**5,833**	Elim'd	
Eithne Fitzgerald	LAB		+153	+4	+319	+354	+155	+251	+625	+1,155
		5,247	**5,400**	**5,404**	**5,723**	**6,077**	**6,232**	**6,483**	**7,108**	**8,263**
Eamon Ryan	GP		+260	+3	+676	+963	+195	+700	+527	+682
		5,222	**5,482**	**5,485**	**6,161**	**7,124**	**7,319**	**8,019**	**8,546**	**9,228**
Maria Corrigan	FF		+40	+25	+173	+230				
		3,180	**3,220**	**3,245**	**3,418**	**3,648**	Elim'd			
Deirdre Whelan	SF		+173	+2	+127					
		2,172	**2,345**	**2,347**	**2,474**	Elim'd				
Karen Canning	IND		+117	+2						
		2,090	**2,207**	**2,209**	Elim'd					
Lisa Maher	SP	**1,063**	Elim'd							
Non-Transferable			43	0	57	210	115	226	173	

*Outgoing Deputy

DUBLIN SOUTH CENTRAL

Outgoing Deputies: Gay Mitchell (FG), Seán Ardagh (FF), Michael Mulcahy (FF), Aengus Ó Snodaigh (SF), Mary Upton (Lab).

The Constituency: This constituency is a **five-seater**. It includes the local electoral areas of Crumlin and Drimnagh, part of the electoral area of Rathfarnham, and the communities of Ballyfermot, Inchicore, Bluebell and Kilmainham. In the redrawing of constituencies since 2002 it has gained a small area (with a population in the 2002 census of 995) from Dublin Central.

Party	Votes 2002	Quota 2002	% Vote 2002	% Vote 1997	Swing
Fianna Fáil	15,106	2.1	34.32%	34.43%	−0.11%
Fine Gael	7,456	1.0	16.94%	24.95%	−8.01%
Labour	8,679	1.2	19.72%	21.91%*	−1.99%*
PDs	1,377	0.2	3.13%	5.01%	−1.88%
Green Party	2,299	0.3	5.22%	3.95%	1.27%
Sinn Féin	5,591	0.8	12.70%	4.77%	7.93%
Others	3,508	0.5	7.97%	5.18	2.79%

2007 Candidates will include: Seán Ardagh (FF), Michael Mulcahy (FF), Catherine Byrne (FG), Anne Marie Martin (FG), Mary Upton (Lab), Eric Byrne (Lab), Tony McDermott (GP), Aengus Ó Snodaigh (SF), Andrew McGuinness (WP), Brendan Phelan (WP), Brid Smith (SW).

In Brief: Labour has a strong prospect of making a gain here, where they hope the former Democratic Left deputy, Eric Byrne, will join their incumbent, Mary Upton. They had the same hopes in 2002 which were thwarted when Sinn Féin won a seat. The fact that long-time Fine Gael deputy Gay Mitchell, who was elected to the European Parliament in 2004, is not contesting this Dáil election creates more space for Eric Byrne to return to Dáil Éireann. Much will depend on the performance of Fine Gael's ticket in the absence of Mitchell. Fianna Fáil's Seán Ardagh and Michael Mulcahy should hold their seats. So too should Sinn Féin's Aengus Ó Snodaigh, although that is not guaranteed.

Fianna Fáil: In 2002, Fianna Fáil retained its two seats comfortably, notwithstanding the retirement of its long-time deputy, Ben Briscoe. The party ran three candidates – the outgoing deputy Seán Ardagh, then councillor Michael Mulcahy and Marian McGennis, who had followed her Ballyfermot base into this constituency from Dublin Central. Mulcahy was 1,400 votes ahead of McGennis on the first count and went on to take a seat for the party alongside Ardagh. In 2007 the party is adopting a two-candidate strategy and running just the two incumbents.

Seán Ardagh was first elected to Dáil Éireann in 1997. Despite being hampered by illness in the lead-up to the election, he topped the poll in 2002 with 6,031 first preference votes and took the second seat. Ardagh is currently the chairman of the Dáil Committee on Justice, Equality and Women's Rights. He was chairman of the subcommittee on the Dublin and Monaghan bombings and, previously, of the ill-fated subcommittee enquiring into the shooting of John Carthy at Abbeylara in April 2000. Ardagh was a member of South Dublin County Council from 1985 to 1999. In 1999 he moved his local authority base from the Walkinstown South Dublin County Council area to the Crumlin Dublin City Council area in order to consolidate his support in this redrawn constituency. He was a member of Dublin City Council from 1999 to 2004. He is a chartered accountant. His son, Charlie, was co-opted to Seán's seat in Dublin City Council when he stepped down on the introduction of the prohibition on the dual mandate. Charlie polled 2,459 votes in the 2004 local elections. Seán Ardagh's wife Máire has been a member of Dublin South County Council since 1999 for the Terenure-Rathfarnham electoral area, where she polled 2,161 in the 2004 local elections.

Michael Mulcahy was first elected to Dáil Éireann in 2002 having unsuccessfully contested the 1997 general election and the 1994 and 1999 by-elections. He came close to winning a seat in 1997 with 4,574 first preferences. He is a barrister and was a Taoiseach's nominee to Seanad Éireann, where he was the party spokesperson on Justice, from 1994 to 1997. He was a member of Dublin City Council from 1985 to 2004, initially for the South Inner City and in the latter period for the Crumlin ward. He was Lord Mayor of Dublin for the year 1996–97.

Fine Gael: Fine Gael's chances of retaining its seat here have perhaps been dealt a fatal blow by the decision of their outgoing deputy, Gay Mitchell, to retire from the Dáil. Instead Mitchell will concentrate on his new role in the European Parliament, to which he was elected in the 2004 European elections. Mitchell has been a deputy in this constituency since 1981 and had a unique Fine Gael possession – a safe Dáil seat in Dublin.

The party's candidates for this election are Catherine Byrne and Anne Marie Martin. Catherine Byrne was an unsuccessful candidate in the 2002 general election, when she received 2,012 first preferences. She was also the party's candidate in the 1999 by-election in this constituency. Byrne has been a member of Dublin City Council since 1999 representing the South West inner city area. In the 2004 local elections she topped the poll with 1,971 first preferences, which was 22.64% of the vote, and took the second seat.

Anne Marie Martin has been a member of Dublin City Council since 2003, when she was co-opted to replace Gay Mitchell in the Crumlin/Kimmage area. In the 2004 local elections she polled 1,617 first preference votes, taking the fifth and final seat on the ninth count.

Labour Party: In 2002 the Labour Party had one of its strongest tickets in the country in this constituency with sitting deputy Mary Upton and former deputy Eric Byrne. The two candidates were close on the first count. Mary Upton polled 4,520 first preferences while Eric Byrne polled 4,159 first preferences. However, this gave them only 1.2 quotas between them and therefore only one could win a seat. Although he was not eliminated, Byrne was more than 1,300 votes behind Upton for the last seat.

Mary Upton was first elected here in October 1999 in a by-election caused by the death of her brother Pat, who had been a Dáil deputy for this constituency since 1992. She held the seat comfortably in the 2002 Dáil election. A microbiologist and formerly a lecturer in University College Dublin, she is the party spokesperson on Agriculture and Food Safety. She is a former chairperson of the Radiological Protection Institute of Ireland.

Eric Byrne was a Democratic Left member of Dáil Éireann from 1989 to 1992. He narrowly lost his seat after a marathon recount against Ben Briscoe in 1997. Under the terms of the Labour and Democratic Left merger pact he contested the seat for the Labour Party alongside Mary Upton in the 2002 election. He has been a member of Dublin City Council for the Crumlin area since 1985. He topped the poll in the Crumlin/Kimmage electoral area in the 2004 local elections with 4,045 first preferences, where the quota was 3,359. He was deputy Lord Mayor of Dublin for the year 2001–2002.

Sinn Féin: The party's vote has risen dramatically here. It was 2% in 1992, 5% in 1997 and 12.7% when Aengus Ó Snodaigh won Sinn Féin's first ever seat in this part of the city in the 2002 election. He was an unsuccessful candidate in the 1999 by-election in this constituency, polling just 1,686 first preferences on that occasion. He was also unsuccessful in the neighbouring Dublin South East constituency in the 1987 election. Ó Snodaigh had been a full-time activist in the south west inner city area of Dublin South Central for a considerable period before the 2002 election. In that election, he increased the party vote by almost 8 percentage points, polling 5,591 first preference votes. He took the fourth seat comfortably. Ó Snodaigh is currently the party's chief whip and spokesperson on Justice and Equality, Culture, Gaeilge, an Gaeltacht, International Affairs and Defence. He previously worked as a journalist with *An Phoblacht* and as an officer with Bórd na Gaeilge.

Green Party: The party candidate in 2002, Kristine McElroy, although polling 9.5% in the south west inner city ward in the 1999 local elections, failed to win a seat. Based in Drimnagh, she polled 2,299 votes. The party's candidate in 2007 is Tony McDermott. McDermott has been a member of South Dublin County Council since 2004. He stood in the Terenure/Rathfarnham area in the 2004 local elections, where he polled 2,045, which was four-fifths of a quota, taking the last of the five seats. He is currently chairman of the Environment Strategic Policy Committee of South Dublin County Council.

Progressive Democrats: The party ran a candidate here in 2002, Bob Quinn, who polled only 1,377, but is not running a candidate on this occasion.

Others: Bríd Smith is the Socialist Workers Party candidate. She also ran in the 1997 and 2002 elections but made no impact. She did, however, come close to a seat in the 2004 local elections in the Ballyfermot ward, where she polled 11.7% of the vote and came fourth in the three seater.

The Workers Party ran the same two candidates here in 1992, 1997 and 2002 – Linda Kavanagh and Shay Kelly. In 2002 Kavanagh polled 553 votes and Kelly polled 270 votes. This time round the candidates are Andrew McGuinness and Brendan Phelan. Andrew McGuinness received 393 first preference votes when he stood in the Dublin Mid-West Constituency in 2002 and 188 votes as a candidate for Ballyfermot in the 2002 local elections. Brendan Phelan polled 341 votes in Crumlin/Kimmage in the same elections.

DUBLIN SOUTH CENTRAL 2007 FIGURES

Candidate	Party	1st Count	2nd Count	3rd Count	4th Count	5th Count	Later counts

YOUR PREDICTION 2007

	Candidate Elected	Party
1		
2		
3		
4		
5		

RESULT 2007

	Candidate Elected	Party
1		
2		
3		
4		
5		

NOTES/UPDATES

DUBLIN SOUTH CENTRAL 1997 FIGURES

5 seats **Quota: 7,337**

Candidate	Party	1st	2nd	3rd	4th	5th	6th	7th	8th	9th	10th	11th
Transfer of			Kelly	Smith	Kavanagh	Ni Chonaill	Jackson	Quinn	Byrne C.	McElroy	McGennis	Ardagh's surplus
Seán Ardagh*	FF	6,031	+2 6,033	+14 6,047	+19 6,066	+65 6,131	+71 6,202	+197 6,399	+73 6,472	+123 6,595	+1,612 8,207	
Aengus Ó Snodaigh	SF	5,591	+28 5,619	+140 5,759	+120 5,879	+220 6,099	+277 6,376	+55 6,431	+91 6,522	+370 6,892	+390 7,282	+241 7,523
Gay Mitchell*	FG	5,444	+12 5,456	+13 5,469	+38 5,507	+105 5,612	+96 5,708	+233 5,941	+1,339 7,280	+429 7,709		
Michael Mulcahy	FF	4,990	+4 4,994	+13 5,007	+17 5,024	+78 5,102	+63 5,165	+177 5,342	+49 5,391	+106 5,497	+1,867 7,364	
Mary Upton*	LAB	4,520	+9 4,529	+64 4,593	+84 4,677	+72 4,749	+114 4,863	+247 5,110	+222 5,332	+954 6,286	+389 6,675	+288 6,923
Eric Byrne	LAB	4,159	+29 4,188	+77 4,265	+100 4,365	+71 4,436	+132 4,568	+91 4,659	+180 4,839	+599 5,438	+220 5,658	+186 5,844
Marian McGennis*	FG	4,085	+0 40,85	+25 4,110	+50 4,160	+39 4,199	+224 4,423	+158 4,581	+95 4,676	+151 4,827 Elim'd		
Kristina McElroy	GP	2,299	+12 2,311	+89 2,400	+91 2,491	+84 2,575	+196 2,771	+203 2,974	+141 3,115 Elim'd			
Catherine Byrne	FG	2,012	+3 2,015	+10 2,025	+34 2,059	+32 2,091	+55 2,146	+113 2,259 Elim'd				
Bob Quinn	PD	1,377	+4 1,381	+14 1,395	+10 1,405	+67 1,472	+62 1534 Elim'd					
Vincent Jackson	Ind	1,142	+5 1,147	+56 1,203	+120 1,323	+88 1,411 Elim'd						
Ainé Ni Chonaill	Ind	926	+4 930	+19 949	+17 966 Elim'd							
Bríd Smith	SWP	617	+16 633 Elim'd									
Linda Kavanagh	WP	553	+139 692	+90 782 Elim'd								
Shay Kell	WP	270 Elim'd										
Non-Transferable			3	9	82	45	121	60	69	383	349	155

DUBLIN SOUTH EAST

Outgoing Deputies: John Gormley (GP), Michael McDowell (PD), Eoin Ryan (FF) Ruairi Quinn (Lab).

Eoin Ryan (FF) was elected to the European Parliament in 2004 and is not contesting the 2007 Dáil election.

The Constituency: This is a **four-seat** constituency and includes much of the postal districts of Dublin 2 and Dublin 4 and parts of Dublin 6. It includes the local electoral areas of South East Inner City, Pembroke and most of Rathmines. The boundaries of this constituency are unchanged since 2002.

Party	Votes 2002	Quota 2002	% Vote 2002	% Vote 1997	Swing
Fianna Fáil	8,767	1.4	27.03%	25.79%	1.25%
Fine Gael	5,210	0.8	16.06%	27.38%	−11.32%
Labour	4,032	0.6	12.43%	16.67%	−4.24%
PDs	6,093	0.9	18.79%	10.97%	7.82%
Green Party	5,264	0.8	16.23%	11.71%	4.52%
Sinn Féin	2,398	0.4	7.39%	–	7.39%
Others	669	0.1	2.06%	7.47	−5.41%

2007 Candidates will include: Chris Andrews (FF), Jim O'Callaghan (FF) Lucinda Creighton (FG), Ruairi Quinn (Lab), Michael McDowell (PD), John Gormley (GP), Daithí Doolan (SF), Rory Hearne (Ind).

In Brief: The fact that this is the constituency of Tánaiste and Progressive Democrats leader Michael McDowell makes this constituency newsworthy in itself. With two other high-profile deputies contesting the election here, Fianna Fáil at risk of losing its seat and Fine Gael trying to win one, it will be one of the most dramatic contests in the country. Fianna Fáil's sitting Dáil deputy and member of the European Parliament, Eoin Ryan, is not contesting and there are no guarantees that even one of the party's two candidates, Chris Andrews and Jim O'Callaghan, can win a seat. Fine Gael's new candidate, Lucinda Creighton, is hoping to win back their seat in this one-time Fine Gael heartland. The fortunes of former Labour leader Ruairi Quinn, who came within 500 votes of losing his seat in 2002, will also attract interest, although he should be safer this time out. Sinn Féin's candidate, Daithí Doolan, is also high profile but is unlikely to be in the frame for a seat. Both McDowell and the Green Party's John Gormley appear to be safe on the published polls, but anything can happen in this constituency between now and polling day.

Fianna Fáil: Eoin Ryan, the party's outgoing deputy, was first elected to Dáil Éireann in 1992 and held the seat comfortably in 1997 and 2002. He was elected to the European Parliament for the Dublin constituency in June 2004 and is therefore not contesting the 2007 Dáil election.

Ryan's running mate in 2002 was Chris Andrews, who is again contesting in 2007. Some months before the 2002 election, published opinion polls suggested that Andrews would displace Eoin Ryan and win a Dáil seat, but in the election itself Ryan was almost 2,000 votes ahead of him on the first count. Fianna Fáil's vote in this constituency has been the lowest in the country for the last couple of elections. In 2002 it was 27.3% which was up only marginally on the 1997 result, notwithstanding an 11.3% drop in the Fine Gael vote.

Chris Andrews was a member of Dublin City Council for the Pembroke electoral area from 1999 to 2004. He polled 1,225 first preferences in the 1999 local election and took the first of the three seats. However, in the 2004 local elections, although his vote was up to 1,538, he lost his council seat. In late 2005 he was co-opted back on to the council to fill a vacancy in the South West Inner City ward caused by the resignation of Gary Keegan. Chris Andrews' recently deceased father, Niall Andrews, was a member of the European Parliament for the Dublin constituency from 1984 to 2004, and before that was a Dáil deputy for the neighbouring Dublin South constituency. Chris Andrews is also a cousin of the party's Dun Laoghaire deputy, Barry Andrews, and nephew of former deputy and Minister for Foreign Affairs, David Andrews.

The other Fianna Fáil candidate is Jim O'Callaghan. O'Callaghan was an unsuccessful candidate for Dublin City Council in the 2004 local elections where he contested in the Rathmines ward and polled 902 when the quota was 2,205. He also contested the 2002 Seanad election as an independent candidate on the NUI panel, polling 1,239 first preferences. O'Callaghan is a barrister and gained rugby caps for Ireland at under-21 level.

Fine Gael: This was the constituency of former leaders John A. Costello and Garret FitzGerald and has traditionally been a Fine Gael stronghold. FitzGerald was a deputy here from 1969 to 1992.

Fine Gael's vote collapsed here in the 2002 election. Frances Fitzgerald's own vote went from 5,501 in 1997 to just 3,337 in 2002. In 1997 her running mate, the former deputy Joe Doyle, polled 4,541 first preferences. However, her 2002 running mate, the barrister and environmental campaigner Colm MacEochaidh, although high profile, polled just 1,873 first preferences. The party had just 0.8 of a quota from the two candidates combined and Fitzgerald lost her seat by 605 votes on the last count. Fitzgerald was a deputy for this constituency from 1992 to 2002 and is contesting the 2007 election in the Dublin Mid-West constituency.

The party's new candidate for the 2007 election is Lucinda Creighton. A *Magill* magazine's 'Politician to Watch' winner in 2006, she has been a member of Dublin City Council for the Pembroke ward since 2004 when she polled 1,567 first preferences, when the quota was 2,380, and took the first of the three seats. A Trinity College Dublin law graduate, she qualified as an attorney in the state of New York and was recently called to the Irish bar. She has worked both on Democratic Party campaigns in New York and as a political advisor in Dáil Éireann.

Labour Party: This was one of those constituencies where it might have been expected that the decline of the Fine Gael vote would have led to an improvement in the Labour Party's vote. However, in 2002 Labour's deputy Ruairi Quinn struggled to keep his seat, proving again that Labour leaders do not automatically get a bounce in their own constituencies during elections. Notwithstanding the collapse of the Fine Gael vote, the Labour Party vote in this constituency also decreased by more than 4 percentage points.

Ruairi Quinn was first elected to Dáil Éireann in 1977, lost his seat in 1981, regained it in 1982 and has retained it at every election since. He was the party's deputy leader from 1990 to 1998 and leader from 1997 to 2002. He was a Minister of State at the Department of Environment from 1982 to 1983, Minister for Labour from 1984 to 1987, Minister for Enterprise, Trade and Employment from 1993 to 1994 and Minister for Finance from 1994 to 1997. From 1976 to 1977 and again from 1981 to 1982 he was a member of Seanad Éireann and he was a member of Dublin City Council for the Pembroke ward from 1974 to 1977. He is currently the party's spokesperson on Enterprise, Trade and Employment.

Progressive Democrats: The party's leader, Tánaiste and Minister for Justice, Equality and Law Reform, Michael McDowell, is their outgoing deputy in this constituency. He was first elected to Dáil Éireann in 1987, lost his seat in 1989, regained it in 1992 and lost it again in 1997. The loss in 1997 came after a week-long recount in which the Green Party's John Gormley took the last seat at the expense of McDowell by just 27 votes. Following this defeat, McDowell allowed his membership of the party to lapse. However, he was appointed Attorney General in 1999 and in January 2002 rejoined the Progressive Democrats, was appointed party president by Mary Harney and agreed to contest the 2002 election. McDowell had polled 4,022 first preferences in 1997 and increased this to 6,093 first preferences in 2002, topping the poll and winning the second seat just after Gormley.

He has been leader of the party and Tánaiste since September 2006. He was chairman of the party from 1989 to 1992 and has also been the party's spokesperson on Foreign Affairs and Northern Ireland, Trade Tourism and Finance. He is a senior counsel, was Attorney General from 1999 to 2002 and has been Minister for Justice, Equality and Law Reform since June 2002.

Green Party: The party chairman, John Gormley, is their outgoing deputy in this constituency. He is also currently the party's spokesperson on Foreign Affairs, Defence and on Health and Children. Gormley was first elected to Dáil Éireann in 1997 after the long recount with the Progressive Democrat's Michael McDowell. In 2002 he held on to his seat with surprising ease. He was second on the first count, with 1,000 more first preferences than he had polled in 1997 and he took the first of the four seats. He was an unsuccessful candidate in the 1989 and 1992 Dáil elections. As a member of Dublin City Council from 1991 to 1997 he represented the Rathmines ward but now resides in the Ringsend end of the constituency. He was Lord Mayor of Dublin for the year 1994–95.

Sinn Féin: The party's candidate is again Daithí Doolan. In the 2002 Dáil elections he polled 2,398 first preferences which represented 7.39% of the vote. He was eliminated on the third count. He has since been elected to Dublin City Council on which he represents the South East Inner City. In the 2004 local elections he polled 1,921 first preferences, coming in just 59 votes behind the Labour Party's Kevin Humphreys, who topped the poll. Doolan took the second of the three seats in the ward on the second count.

Others: Other candidates in 2002 included Tom Crilly of the Workers Party, who polled just 284 votes, Shay Ryan of the Socialist Workers Party, who polled 286 votes, and independent candidate Norman Gray, who received only 99 votes.

Running this time is TCD graduate student Rory Hearne. He has been particularly involved in the campaign against an incinerator at Poolbeg, the anti-bin tax campaign, the Socialist Workers Party and the anti-war movement. He was president of Trinity College Students' Union in 2000. He is running as an independent but for the People before Profit Alliance.

DUBLIN SOUTH EAST 2007 FIGURES

Candidate	Party	1st Count	2nd Count	3rd Count	4th Count	5th Count	Later counts

YOUR PREDICTION 2007

	Candidate Elected	Party
1		
2		
3		
4		
5		

RESULT 2007

	Candidate Elected	Party
1		
2		
3		
4		
5		

NOTES/UPDATES

DUBLIN SOUTH EAST 2002 FIGURES

4 seats   Quota: 6,487

Candidate	Party	1st	2nd	3rd	4th	5th	6th
Transfer of			Gray Crilly S. Ryan	Mac Eochaidh	Doolan	Andrews	E. Ryan's surplus
John Gormley*	GP	5,264	*+219* 5,483	*+310* 5,793	*+1,051* 6,844		
Michael McDowell	PD	6,093	*28* 6,121	*+297* 6,418	*+91* 6,509		
Eoin Ryan*	FF	5,318	*54* 5.372	*36* 5,408	*415* 5,823	*2,819* 8,642	
Ruairi Quinn*	LAB	4,032	*+95* 4,127	*+191* 4,318	*+356* 4,674	*+477* 5,151	*+709* 5,860
Frances Fitzgerald*	FG	3,337	*+21* 3,358	*+1,013* 4,371	*+72* 4,443	*+225* 4,668	*+587* 5,255
Chris Andrews	FF	3,449	*+24* 3,473	*+27* 3,500	*+324* 3,824	Elim'd	
Daithí Doolan	SF	2,398	*+157* 2,555	*+23* 2,578	*Elim'd*		
Com Mac Eochaidh	FG	1,873	*+32* 1,905	*Elim'd*			
Tom Crilly	WP	284	*Elim'd*				
Norman Gray	Ind	99	*Elim'd*				
Non-Transferable		39		8	269	303	859

*Outgoing Deputy

DUBLIN SOUTH WEST

Outgoing Deputies: Seán Crowe (SF), Charlie O'Connor (FF), Conor Lenihan (FF), Pat Rabbitte (Lab).

The Constituency: This constituency has **four seats**. It now includes Tallaght and Firhouse. To the east it is bounded largely by the M50, Greenhills Road and Templeville Road. In the redrawing since 2002 it gained a small area in Firhouse (2002 population 1,995) from Dublin South.

Party	Votes 2002	Quota 2002	% Vote 2002	% Vote 1997	Swing
Fianna Fáil	14,235	1.9	38.68%	29.94%	8.74%
Fine Gael	4,654	0.6	12.65%	15.50%	−2.85%
Labour	7,285	1.0	19.80%	21.89%	−2.10%
PDs	–	–	–	13.64%	−13.64%
Green	1,157	0.2	3.14%	3.14%	0.00%
Sinn Féin	7,466	1.0	20.29%	8.90%	11.39%
Others	2,005	0.3	5.45%	6.995	−1.54%

2007 Candidates will include: Conor Lenihan (FF), Charlie O'Connor (FF), Brian Hayes (FG), Pat Rabbitte (Lab), Elizabeth Davidson (GP), Seán Crowe (SF), Mick Murphy (SP).

In Brief: This is essentially the constituency of Tallaght and is a key target for a Fine Gael gain from Fianna Fáil. Fine Gael's candidate is the former deputy and current leader in the Seanad, Brian Hayes, who topped the poll in his first attempt in 1997 but lost his seat in 2002. If he regains the seat it is more likely to be at the expense of Fianna Fáil backbencher Charlie O'Connor than of the Minister of State Conor Lenihan, although a Lenihan win is not guaranteed. Labour leader Pat Rabitte should hold his seat comfortably.

Fianna Fáil: Despite the effect of the reduction of the constituency from five seats in 1997 to four seats in 2002, the resignation of then outgoing deputy Chris Flood and the emergence of a strong Sinn Féin candidate, Fianna Fáil retained its two seats with some ease in 2002. The Fianna Fáil vote increased by a striking 8.74%, the highest vote swing to the party in the country, and the party's two candidates came in very close together, with just 75 votes between them on the first count, both being within 300 votes of a quota.

Conor Lenihan was first elected to Dáil Éireann in 1997 on his first attempt and he was re-elected in 2002. He was appointed Minister of State at the Department of Foreign Affairs with special responsibilities for overseas development and human rights in September 2004. A former political correspondent with the Dublin radio station 98 FM and programme manager with ESAT digifone, he is brother of the Dublin West deputy and Minister of State Brian Lenihan. Their father was the late Tánaiste and Minister, Brian Lenihan, and their aunt is the party former deputy leader and candidate for this election in Westmeath, Mary O'Rourke.

Charlie O'Connor was first elected to Dáil Éireann in 2002. He was a member of Dublin County Council, then South Dublin County Council, from 1991 to 2004, in the latter period for the Tallaght South local electoral area and he was chair of South Dublin County Council for the year 1999–2000. Prominent for decades in many Tallaght community organisations, he is a member of the board of Tallaght Hospital. In the first count in 2002 he was second to Sinn Féin's Seán Crowe.

Fine Gael: Although the Fine Gael vote was down just 2.85% in the 2002 election, with one less seat in the constituency, Brian Hayes lost his seat. He had been elected to the Dáil in 1997, when he topped the poll on his first attempt, but in 2002, in a dramatic turnaround in his fortunes, his first preference vote dropped from 6,487 to 4,654. He was subsequently elected to the Seanad, where he was appointed leader by Enda Kenny. He is also the party's spokesperson on Dublin. He was previously a schoolteacher and also worked as Fine Gael National Youth and Education Officer.

Labour Party: In the 1992 general election Labour won two seats in this constituency and Democratic Left another. The 1997 general election, however, saw Democratic Left's Pat Rabbitte take a single seat for the left, while Labour's Eamonn Walsh lost out. The two of them ran for the merged Labour Party in 2002. There was never any prospect of two Labour seats and, indeed, polls in advance of the election implied Rabbitte's seat might be in danger because of the Sinn Féin challenge. However, in 2002 Rabbitte had one of his best electoral performances ever. He polled 6,314, a significant improvement on his 1997 performance of 5,094 votes. In 2002 he took the last seat with more than 2,500 votes to spare over Brian Hayes.

Rabbitte has held a Dáil seat since 1989, when he was elected as a deputy for the Workers Party. He was re-elected as a Democratic Left deputy in 1994 and joined the Labour Party on the merger of the two parties in 1999. From 1994 to 1997 he was a Minister of State to the government and at the Department of Enterprise, Trade and Employment with responsibility for Commerce, Science and Technology.

Rabbitte was first elected to local government in 1991 for the Tallaght/Oldbawn area as a Worker's Party candidate and was a member of Dublin County Council for Tallaght South from 1999 to 2004. He is a former President of the Union of Students in Ireland and a former National Secretary of the Irish Transport and General Workers Union. He has been leader of the Labour Party and its spokesperson on Northern Ireland since 24 October 2002.

Sinn Féin: Sinn Féin winning a seat here in the 2002 election may not have been a surprise, having been predicted in the many media polls published in advance of the election, but it was a significant achievement nonetheless.

Although Seán Crowe was elected in 2002 at the top of the poll, he had been unsuccessful in 1989, 1992 and 1997. He polled 3,725 first preferences in 1997, but almost doubled that to 7,446 in 2002. He was a member of Dublin South County Council for the Tallaght South electoral area from 1999 to 2004.

In the 1999 local elections the party won seats in both the Tallaght South and Tallaght

Central local electoral areas. In that election Crowe polled 5,045 first preferences in Tallaght and was elected on the first count. In the 2002 Dáil election Crowe's stunning poll-topping vote of 7,466, which put him 100 votes over the quota on the first count. In the 1999 European election he was the party's candidate in the Dublin constituency, where he polled 18,633 first preferences.

Green Party: Elizabeth Davidson is a former art teacher and is prominent locally in a number of campaigns, including the Friends of Massey Woods, which is campaigning for the development of the Woods as an amenity for south west Dublin. She is originally from Limerick but has lived in Tallaght for most of her adult life. This is her first electoral contest. In 2002 Patrick Quinn, the Green Party candidate, polled 1,157 first preference votes, a 3.14% share.

Other: The Socialist Party candidate here is Mick Murphy, who is a member of South Dublin County Council for the Tallaght Central electoral area, where he polled 2,505 first preferences in the 2004 local elections when the quota was 2,593. In the 1997 Dáil election he polled 2,026 votes but won just 954 votes in the 2002 Dáil election. He is prominent in the campaign against water and refuse charges and was previously the national organiser of the Motor Justice Action Group, campaigning for reductions in insurance charges for young people. He is a senior engineer for C&C's bottling plant in Kylemore, Dublin.

DUBLIN SOUTH WEST 2007 FIGURES

Candidate	Party	1st Count	2nd Count	3rd Count	4th Count	5th Count	Later counts

YOUR PREDICTION 2007

	Candidate Elected	Party
1		
2		
3		
4		
5		

RESULT 2007

	Candidate Elected	Party
1		
2		
3		
4		
5		

NOTES/UPDATES

DUBLIN SOUTH WEST 2002 FIGURES

4 seats — **Quota: 7,361**

Candidate	Party	1st	2nd	3rd	4th	5th	6th
Transfer of			Kelly	O'Reilly	Crowe's surplus	Walsh	Murphy
Seán Crowe	SF	**7,466**					
Charlie O'Connor	FF	**7,155**	+34 / **7,189**	+153 / **7,342**	+19 / **7,361**		
Conor Lenihan*	FF	**7,080**	+36 / **7,116**	+116 / **7,232**	+18 / **7,250**	+111 / **7,361**	
Pat Rabbitte*	LAB	**6,314**	+50 / **6,364**	+135 / **6,499**	+24 / **6,523**	+667 / **7,190**	+458 / **7,648**
Brian Hayes*	FG	**4,654**	+27 / **4,681**	+122 / **4,803**	+12 / **4,815**	+95 / **4,910**	+174 / **5,084**
Patrick Quinn	GP	**1,157**	+57 / **1,214**	+120 / **1,334**	+14 / **1,348**	+60 / **1,408**	+279 / **1,687**
Mick Murphy	SP	**954**	+40 / **994**	+61 / **1,055**	+14 / **1,069**	+35 / **1,104**	Elim'd
Eamonn Walsh	LAB	**971**	+13 / **984**	+20 / **1,004**	+4 / **1,008**	Elim'd	
Darragh O'Reilly	CSP	**760**	+19 / **779**	−19 / Elim'd			
Ray Kelly	IND	**291**	Elim'd				
Non-Transferable			15	52		40	193

*Outgoing Deputy

DUBLIN WEST

The Outgoing Deputies: Brian Lenihan (FF), Joe Higgins (Ind), Joan Burton (Lab).

The Constituency: This **three-seat** constituency embraces Blanchardstown and Castleknock, stretching from Ballycoolin Road to the Liffey and including Quarryvale. In the redrawing of constituencies since 2002 it lost the Palmerstown area on the south side to the Dublin Mid West constituency but gained an area (2002 population 3,927) in the St Margarets/Killsallaghan area west of Dublin Airport from Dublin North.

Party	Votes 2002	Quota 2002	% Vote 2002	% Vote 1997	Swing
Fianna Fáil	10,386	1.4	34.63%	33.19%	1.45%
Fine Gael	3,694	0.5	12.32%	16.94%	–4.62%
Labour	3,810	0.5	12.71	12.11%	0.59%
PDs	2,370	0.3	7.90%	7.61%	0.29%
Green Party	748		2.49%	4.32%	–1.83%
Sinn Féin	2,404	0.3	8.02%	5.00%	3.02%
Others	134	0.02	0.45%	–	0.45%
Socialist Party	6,442	0.86	21.48%	16.21%	5.27%

2007 Candidates will include: Brian Lenihan (FF), Gerry Lynam (FF), Leo Varadkar (FG), Joan Burton (Lab), Roderic O'Gorman (GP), Felix Gallagher (SF), Joe Higgins (Soc).

In Brief: A Fine Gael gain is in prospect here and is likely to be at the expense of Labour. It will therefore not affect the Ahern-Kenny vote for Taoiseach. However, if Fine Gael took the seat of the Socialist Party leader Joe Higgins, this would give an additional definite vote for Kenny. Fine Gael's candidate in the 2007 Dáil election, Leo Varadkar, polled 3,550 votes in the Castleknock ward in the 2004 local election, albeit in the absence of big national names. If Varadkar wins a seat, Labour's Finance spokesperson, Joan Burton, although likely to be high profile in the national campaign, may lose her seat. Fianna Fáil's Brian Lenihan, who will also be high profile during the campaign, is safe.

Fianna Fáil: The party's outgoing deputy is the Minister of State with responsibility for Children, Brian Lenihan. Lenihan was first elected to the Dáil in the 1996 by-election caused by the death of his father, also Brian, who had been a TD for this constituency since 1977, and a former Tánaiste and Minister. Brian Junior was comfortably re-elected in both the 1997 election and the 2002 election. A senior counsel and former lecturer in law at Trinity College, he is a brother to the Dublin South West candidate and Minister of State, Conor Lenihan, and nephew of the Westmeath candidate Mary O'Rourke. He was chairman of the All-Party Committee on the Constitution. In 1997 he topped the poll with 6,842 first preferences. In 2002 he again topped the poll and his vote increased to 8,086 votes, which was 1,500 votes above the quota.

The party's second candidate in 2002 was Lucan–based councillor Deidre Doherty-Ryan. Doherty-Ryan had been elected to South Dublin County Council in the 1999 local elections. However, because of the redraw only half of that council remained in the Dublin West constituency. Her first preference vote was just 2,300.

On this occasion Lenihan's running mate will be Gerry Lynam, who is a former independent member of Fingal County Council, where he represented the Mulhuddart ward from 1999 to 2004, when he polled sixth in the four-seater area. He is Chairman of the Dublin 15 Project, which will provide a new hospice and hospice outpatient care for North West Dublin.

Fine Gael: In 2002 the party's sitting Dublin West deputy, Austin Currie, decided to follow his Lucan base into the new constituency of Dublin Mid-West, so Sheila Terry, a former Progressive Democrat county councillor and general election candidate, was the Fine Gael candidate here. Under the Fine Gael banner she polled 3,694 first preferences in 2002. This put her only 168 votes behind Labour's Joan Burton on the first count, but Burton did better on transfers and, as a result, Terry was 631 votes behind Burton for the last seat on the last count.

This time round, the party is running Leo Varadkar. He is a former member of the National Executive of Young Fine Gael. He is a member of Fingal County Council for the Castleknock electoral area. He was co-opted to replace Senator Sheila Terry in 2003. He retained the seat in spectacular fashion in the 2004 local election, when he topped the poll with a remarkable 4,894 first preferences, which was just under two quotas. Varadkar is a doctor, working at Blanchardstown Hospital.

Labour Party: Outgoing deputy Joan Burton is currently Labour's spokesperson on Finance. She was first elected to Dáil Éireann in 1992, but lost her seat in 1997, when her vote share was almost halved to 12.1% from 22.6% in 1992. As a result of the redrawing of constituencies and the decision of Austin Currie to move to Dublin Mid West, she regained her seat in 2002, polling 3,810 first preferences and being 631 votes ahead of Fine Gael's Sheila Terry for the third seat on the last count.

Burton was a member of Dublin County Council from 1995 to 1999 for the Mulhuddart electoral area and of Fingal County Council from 1999 to 2004 for the Castleknock electoral area. She was Minister of State at the Department of Social Welfare from 1992 to 1994 and then at the Department of Foreign Affairs with responsibility for Overseas Development from 1995 to 1997. She is a former lecturer in finance at the Dublin Institute of Technology. She was an unsuccessful candidate for the Labour Party leadership in October 2002.

Progressive Democrats: Tom Morrisey, who was the party's candidate in 1997 and 2002, has transferred to Dublin North. The party's candidate in this election is Mags Murray who is a member of Fingal County Council representing the Castleknock ward. She was elected to the council on her first attempt in 2004, polling 1,288 first preferences and securing the seat previously held by Tom Morrissey.

Green Party: Robert Bonnie from Mulhuddart polled a disappointing 748 first preference votes in 2002, following the decision of Paul Gogarty to run in Dublin Mid-West. The Green Party vote in this constituency was 4.5% in 1997 and 2.49% in 2002.

Roderic O'Gorman, also from Mulhuddart, is the party's candidate in the upcoming election. He was an unsuccessful candidate in the Castleknock electoral area in the 2004 local elections, when he polled 666 votes. He was recently re-elected as deputy chair of the Green Party National Council.

Sinn Féin: In 2002, 32-year-old first-time candidate Mary Lou McDonald received an impressive 2,404 votes. This time round, she is contesting in Dublin Central and the candidate in this constituency is Felix Gallagher. Gallagher is a councillor who was co-opted when their Mulhuddart councillor, Martin Christie, resigned shortly after the 2004 local elections, having polled 1,910 in that election. Gallagher has written for *An Phoblacht* and *Republican News* and currently works as a community development officer in Blanchardstown.

Others: Socialist Party leader Joe Higgins represents this constituency. Higgins was an unsuccessful candidate in the 1992 general election and was runner-up in the 1996 by-election, when he polled 6,742 first preferences. He was first elected to Dáil Éireann in 1997 and easily held the seat in 2002. He is a strong Dáil performer and gets an outing in one of every three Dáil sitting days as the nominee of the Technical Group. Higgins represented the Mulhuddart electoral area from 1991 to 2004, first on Dublin County Council and then on Fingal County Council. Fingal County Council's decision to reintroduce service charges in the run-up to the general election and his prominence in the campaign opposing the measure probably contributed to his re-election in 2002. His first preference vote in that election was up marginally, even though the size of the constituency was reduced. He is a former member of the Labour Party. Joe Higgins is chairman of the Federation of Dublin Anti-Water Charges.

DUBLIN WEST 2007 FIGURES

Candidate	Party	1st Count	2nd Count	3rd Count	4th Count	5th Count	Later counts

YOUR PREDICTION 2007

	Candidate Elected	Party
1		
2		
3		
4		
5		

RESULT 2007

	Candidate Elected	Party
1		
2		
3		
4		
5		

NOTES/UPDATES

DUBLIN WEST 2002 FIGURES

3 seats   Quota: 7,498

Candidate Transfer of	Party	1st	2nd Bonnie Smith	3rd Lenihan's surplus	4th McDonald	5th Morrisey	6th Doherty- Ryan
Brian Lenihan*	FF	8,086					
Joe Higgins*	SP	6,442	+218 6,660	+71 6,731	+1,122 7,853		
Joan Burton	LAB	3,810	+210 4,020	+59 4,079	+296 4,375	+750 5,125	+1,175 6,300
Sheila Terry	FG	3,694	+89 3,783	+46 3829	+153 3,982	+881 4,863	+806 5,669
Mary Lou McDonald	SF	2404	+94 2,498	+26 2,524	Elim'd		
Tom Morrissey	PD	2,370	+110 2,480	+74 2,554	+108 2,662	Elim'd	
Deirdre Doherty Ryan	FF	2,300	+86 2,368	+312 2,698	+358 3,056	+672 3,728	Elim'd
Robert Bonnie	GP	748	Elim'd				
John Smyth	CSP	134	Elim'd				
Non-Transferable			75	0	487	359	1,747

*Outgoing Deputy

DUN LAOGHAIRE

Outgoing Deputies: Mary Hanafin (FF), Eamon Gilmore (Lab), Fiona O'Malley (PD), Barry Andrews (FF), Ciarán Cuffe (GP).

The Constituency: This is a **five-seater**. It covers almost all the administrative area of Dun Laoghaire-Rathdown council, including the communities of Dun Laoghaire, Balckrock, Booterstown, Loughlinstown and much of Glencullen. The boundaries of this constituency are unchanged since 2002.

Party	Votes 2002	Quota 2002	% Vote 2002	% Vote 1997	Swing
Fianna Fáil	16,243	1.8	30.29%	25.83%	4.46%
Fine Gael	8,069	0.9	15.04%	30.96%	−15.92%
Labour	12,164	1.4	22.68%	21.52	0.13%*
PDs	7,166	0.8	13.36%	8.55%	4.82%
Green Party	5,002	0.6	9.33%	5.09%	4.24%
Sinn Féin	2,159	0.2	4.03%	–	4.03%
Others	2,830	0.9	5.28%	7.03	−1.75%

2007 Candidates will include: Barry Andrews (FF), Mary Hanafin (FF), John Bailey (FG), Sean Barrett (FG), Eugene Regan (FG), Eamon Gilmore (Lab), Oisín Quinn (Lab), Fiona O'Malley (PD), Ciarán Cuffe (GP), Richard Boyd Barrett (SW).

In Brief: The Progressive Democrats' Fiona O'Malley and the Greens' Ciaran Cuffe hold the most vulnerable seats here. Fine Gael, which once had three seats in this constituency, lost their two seats in 2002. The return of former Minister Sean Barrett to the fray alongside former Dublin GAA chairman Sean Bailey and Eugene Regan SC positions them well to win at least one seat. If Fine Gael does not win two then Labour, who are running Oisín Quinn (nephew of Ruairi) with their frontbencher Eamon Gilmore, could win a second. Education Minister Mary Hanafin should be safe, as should her Fianna Fáil running mate, Barry Andrews, although given the likely intensity of the contest here the latter's seat is not guaranteed.

Fianna Fáil: The party's senior deputy is Minister for Education Mary Hanafin. She was first elected to Dáil Éireann in 1997. She was government chief whip from 2002 to September 2004 and Minister of State at the Departments of Education, Justice and Health with responsibility for children's issues from 2000 to 2002. In 2002 she topped the poll, with 8,818 first preference votes, over 3,000 more votes than her 1997 performance of 5,079. A former national treasurer of the party, she was an unsuccessful candidate in the Dublin South East constituency in the 1989 Dáil election. She was a member of Dublin City Council for the Rathmines electoral area from 1985 to 1991. Previously a secondary school teacher, she is daughter of former Senator Des Hanafin and a brother of current Senator John Hanafin.

The party's other outgoing deputy, Barry Andrews, was elected for the first time in 2002. He is a son of David Andrews, former Minister for Foreign Affairs, and TD for this constituency from 1965 to 2002. Barry Andrews was a member of Dun Laoghaire-Rathdown County Council for the Blackrock electoral area from 1999 to 2004. In the 2002 Dáil election he polled 7,425 first preferences and took the third seat on the fourth count. He is a barrister and formerly worked as a secondary school teacher.

Fine Gael: Before the 2002 election Fine Gael thought that they would have a struggle to hold on to their two seats in this constituency, which has traditionally been a strong base for them. Nobody could have imagined that they would lose both. In 1997 the party received 25.8% of the vote and won two seats with ease when Seán Barrett topped the poll and Monica Barnes was also elected comfortably. The decisions by both Barrett and Barnes to retire from politics threw the party into a candidate selection crisis in the lead-in to 2002. Long-standing senator and former Dáil deputy Liam Cosgrave, the son and grandson of former Taoisigh, was selected to lead the party ticket. The second slot went to Senator Helen Keogh, who had defected from the Progressive Democrats in 2000. Based in Dun Laoghaire itself, Keogh had been a Progressive Democrat deputy from 1992 to 1997.

Days before the election was called the party added John Bailey, then chairman of the Dublin GAA county board, to the ticket. The weakness of their ticket and an upsurge in Progressive Democrat support in the last week of the campaign gave rise to a collapse in the Fine Gael vote, which plummeted to just 15%. The fact that this 15% was divided, albeit unevenly, between three candidates prevented any one candidate from being in a position to win a seat.

Seán Barrett held a seat here for Fine Gael from 1981 to 2002. He decided not to contest the last election and announced his retirement. This has been short-lived and he has returned to the electoral fray this time. Barrett was government chief whip and Minister of State for Sport from 1982 to 1987. He was Minister for Defence and Marine 1994 to 1997. He spent 11 years as a member of various local councils, being chairman of Dublin County Council for the year 1981 to 1982.

John Bailey will again run on behalf of Fine Gael in 2002. He was elected to Dun Laoghaire-Rathdown County Council for the Dun Laoghaire local electoral area in 2004, topping the poll with 2,189 first preferences when the quota was 2,589. On the same day his daughter Maria won a seat in the neighbouring Ballybrack ward with 2,055 where the quota was 2,418. As well as having been chairman of the county GAA board for 10 years, John is a former managing director of Brendan Tours Limited and former managing director of Budget Rent-A-Car. He is also a former publican in the constituency and was a registered Irish racehorse trainer.

The third Fine Gael candidate is Eugene Regan. Like Bailey, he has been a member of the Dun Laoghaire-Rathdown Council for the Dun Laoghaire local electoral area since 2004. In that election he polled 1,957 first preferences. He is currently the Cathaoirleach of the council. He is a senior counsel.

Labour Party: In 2002 the Labour Party, which had merged with the Democratic Left since the previous election, ran a very strong ticket here with the former Labour Minister for Education Niamh Bhreathnach, who had lost her seat in 1997, running with the former Democratic Left deputy, Eamon Gilmore. On paper the Labour/Democratic Left merger should have put the party in a position to win two seats. In 1997 they had a combined vote of 22.5%. In 2002 the merged Labour Party vote held up at 22.7%. However, the gap between Gilmore's 8,271 first preference votes and Niamh Bhreathnach's 3,893 first preference votes was too wide and the party won only one seat. Gilmore took the second seat on the eighth count while Bhreathnach was eliminated on the tenth.

Eamon Gilmore has always been a strong vote-getter having been first elected to the Dáil as a Workers Party deputy in 1989. He was a co-founder of the Democratic Left in March 1992 and became a member of the Labour Party following the merger. He was a member of Dublin County Council and then of Dun Laoghaire-Rathdown County Council from 1991 to 1995 for the Ballybrack ward and from 1999 to 2004 for the Dun Laoghaire ward. He combines a high media profile with a strong reputation for hard work in this constituency, which has large working-class pockets. In particular, he is well supported in the Dun Laoghaire electoral area where he won 2,500 votes the last time he contested a local election in 1999.

Oisín Quinn will be contesting in this constituency for the Labour Party, along with Gilmore. He is a nephew of Dublin South East TD and former party leader Ruairi Quinn and was elected to Dublin City Council for the Rathmines electoral area at his first attempt in the 2004 elections, polling 1,478 first preference votes, a 13% share. He is a practising barrister specialising in employment law. He is currently a member of the Environment Policy Committee of Dublin City Council and he is also on the board of Crumlin Children's Hospital.

Progressive Democrats: Fiona O'Malley was elected to Dáil Éireann on her first attempt in 2002. She polled 7,166 first preferences and picked up enough transfers to take the third of the five seats. A colourful deputy, with the benefit of a well-known political name, she also benefited from the swing to the party in the last weeks of the campaign. She was elected to Dun Laoghaire-Rathdown County Council for the Stillorgan ward in the 1999 local elections and resigned from the council in 2004 owing to the dual mandate ban. She previously worked as an arts administrator. She is a daughter of the former Progressive Democrat leader and government minister Desmond O'Malley, who was a TD for Limerick East from 1969 to 1997 and a cousin of Tim O'Malley TD, Minister of State at the Department of Health with special responsibility for mental health and disability services, a candidate for this election in the Limerick East constituency.

Green Party: The outgoing Green Party deputy is Ciarán Cuffe. A long-time Green Party and planning activist, Cuffe transferred his electoral base from inner city Dublin to Dun Laoghaire in order to be the party's new candidate for the 2002 Dáil election. Like many of the Green Party candidates in the city, he attracted votes from both working and middle-class areas. His first preference vote of 5,002 was impressive and almost doubled the party's vote in this constituency. His ability to attract transfers from across the political spectrum was also impressive. He was 1,040 ahead of Fine Gael's Liam Cosgrave for the last seat.

Cuffe is the party's spokesperson on Justice, Equality and Law Reform, Environment and Local Government. He had previously been a member of Dublin City Council for the South Inner City ward from 1991 to 2002. He formerly worked as a lecturer in urban planning.

He was an unsuccessful candidate in the Dublin Central constituency in the 1997 Dáil election.

Sinn Féin: The Sinn Féin candidate here is Eoin Ó Broin. He has worked full time for Sinn Féin for 11 years. He was the national organiser for Ógra Sinn Féin from 1997 to 1999. He represented the Old Park electoral district on Belfast City Council from 2001 to 2004. Since 2004 Eoin has held the position of Director of European Affairs within the party and he is also a member of the party's Ard Comhairle. A native of Cabinteely and Blackrock, he moved to Belfast in 1995 but recently returned to live in Dun Laoghaire.

Others: Richard Boyd Barrett is the Socialist Workers Party candidate and a native of the Dun Laoghaire area. He is the chair of the Dun Laoghaire/Rathdown Campaign against the Bin Tax and convener of the Save Our Seafront group, which is campaigning against developments at Dun Laoghaire Baths and the Carlisle Pier. Barrett is also chairperson of the Irish Anti War Movement. He was a candidate in the 2002 election when he polled 878 first preferences votes, which was 1.63% of the vote. In the 2004 local elections he ran for Dun Laoghaire-Rathdown County Council in the Dun Laoghaire local electoral area, polling 1,439 votes, which at 8% of the vote was impressive but still not enough to win a seat.

DUN LAOGHAIRE 2007 FIGURES

Candidate	Party	1st Count	2nd Count	3rd Count	4th Count	5th Count	Later counts

YOUR PREDICTION 2007

	Candidate Elected	Party
1		
2		
3		
4		
5		

RESULT 2007

	Candidate Elected	Party
1		
2		
3		
4		
5		

NOTES/UPDATES

DUN LAOGHAIRE 2002 FIGURES

5 seats Quota: 8,939

Candidate	Party	1st	2nd	3rd	4th	5th	6th	7th	8th	9th	10th	11th
Transfer of			Hyland	Redmond	Williams	O'Buachalla	Mc Dowell	O'Keefe	Bailey	O'Brien	Keogh	Bhreathnach
Mary Hanafin*	FF	8,818	+9 8,827	+93 8,920	+30 8,950							
Eamon Gilmore*	LAB	8,271	+13 8,284	+13 8,297	+46 8,343	+32 8,375	39 8,414	+348 8,762	+180 8,942			
Barry Andrews	FF	7,425	+6 7,431	+18 7,449	+10 7,459	+24 7,483	+36 7,519	+157 7,676	+66 7,742	+547 8,289	+78 8,367	+551 8,918
Fiona O' Malley	PD	7,166	+5 7,171	+17 7,188	29 7,217	+43 7,260	+49 7,309	+189 7,498	+79 7,577	+130 7,707	552 8,259	+1,005 9,264
Ciaran Cuffe	GP	5,002	+10 5,012	+21 5,033	+75 5,108	+69 5,177	+129 5,306	+389 5,695	+104 5,799	+800 6,599	+319 6,918	+1,752 8670
Niamh Bhreathnach	LAB	3,893	+6 3,899	+1 3,900	+35 3,935	+35 3,970	+32 4,002	+100 4,102	+145 4,247	+303 4,550	+540 5,090	
Helen Keogh	FG	3,229	+1 3,230	+3 3,233	+19 3,252	+20 3,272	+16 3,288	+54 3,342	+527 3,869	+47 3,916		
Liam T Cosgrave	FG	3,135	+2 3,137	+16 3,153	+14 3,167	+14 3181	+24 3,205	+67 3,272	+639 3,911	+85 3,996	+2330 6,326	+1,204 7530
Michael O' Brien	SF	2,159	+1 2,160	+13 2,173	+3 2,176	+16 2,192	+13 2,205	+200 2,405	+16 2,421			
John Bailey	FG	1,705	+1 1,706	+6 1,712	+8 1,720	+15 1,735	+10 1,745	+50 1,795	Elim'd			
Richard Boyd Barret	SWP	876	+2 878	+2 880	+10 890	+26 916	+16 932	Elim'd				
Patrick O Keefe	IND	593	+3 596	+18 614	+14 628	+56 684	+40 724	Elim'd				
Denis O Buachalla	IND	346	+7 353	+8 361	+19 380	Elim'd						
Vincent McDowell	IND	345	+9 354	+15 369	+25 394	+24 418	Elim'd					
Heather Williams	IND	319	+4 323	+15 338	Elim'd							
Michael Redmond	CSP	265	+2 267	Elim'd								
Barbara Hyland	IND	86	Elim'd									
Non-Transferable			5	8	1	6	14	102	39	509	97	

GALWAY EAST

Outgoing Deputies: Paul Connaughton (FG), Joe Callanan (FF), Paddy McHugh (Ind), Noel Treacy (FF).

The Constituency: This **four-seat constituency** is entirely within the county of Galway. The boundaries of this constituency are unchanged since 2002.

Party	Votes 2002	Quota 2002	% Vote 2002	% Vote 1997	Swing
Fianna Fáil	23,117	2.3	46.77%	48.60%	−1.83%
Fine Gael	15,576	1.6	31.52%	31.17%	0.35%
Labour	–	–	–	7.92%	−7.92%
PDs	–	–	–	7.41%	−7.41%
Green Party	1,022	0.1	2.07%	–	2.07%
Sinn Féin	1,828	0.2	3.70%	–	3.70%
Others	7,879	0.8	15.94%	4.89	11.05%

2007 Candidates will include: Joe Callanan (FF), Michael Kitt (FF), Noel Treacy (FF), John Barton (FG), Ulick Burke (FG), Paul Connaughton (FG), Tom McHugh (FG), Colm Keaveney (Lab), Jason Devlin (SF), Paddy McHugh (Ind), Ciaran Cannon (PD).

In Brief: This is a key Fine Gael target for a seat gain at the expense of either Fianna Fáil or the Independent Paddy McHugh. Fine Gael is running a four-person ticket with the incumbent Paul Connaughton and former deputy Ulick Burke likely to be the two strongest candidates. Even if Fianna Fáil holds its two seats, there is also a prospect of a change of personnel on the Fianna Fáil side, with Michael Kitt returning to Dáil Éireann, perhaps at the expense of Minister of State Noel Treacy.

Fianna Fáil: Fianna Fáil is running the same three candidates it ran here in 2002 and 1997 – Joe Callanan, Noel Treacy and Michael Kitt.

Joe Callanan was the strongest of the three in 2002. He came very close to winning a seat in 1997, when, with a quota of 8,584, he polled 6,221 first preferences and was only 338 votes behind Noel Treacy for the last seat. In 2002 the quota was 9,885 and Callanan improved his first preference vote to 7,898 to take the second seat. Joe Callanan was a member of Galway County Council from 1992 to 2004, representing the Loughrea electoral area. He is also a farmer.

The other outgoing deputy is Noel Treacy, who is based in the Ballinasloe end of the constituency. Treacy was first elected to Dáil Éireann in a May 1982 by-election, which was the last time Fianna Fáil won a by-election in government. Treacy has retained his seat in every election since. Having previously held office as the first Minister for Heritage Affairs and in the departments of Health, Finance (with special responsibility for the OPW), Transport, Energy and Communications (with special responsibility for Energy), Enterprise, Trade and Employment (with special responsibility for Science, Technology and Commerce) and Agriculture and Food (with special responsibility for Food and Horticulture), he is currently Minister of State at the Departments of An Taoiseach and Foreign Affairs with special responsibility for European Affairs. He was a member of Galway County Council from 1985 to 1991 for the Ballinasloe electoral area and was chairman of the council for the year 1986–87. He was also an unsuccessful candidate in the European elections in 1999 for the Connacht/Ulster constituency, where he polled 47,933 votes, a 14.97% share, and was eliminated on the fourth count.

The other candidate is the former deputy and current senator, Michael Kitt. He was first elected to Dáil Éireann in 1975 in a by-election caused by the death of his father. He lost the seat in 1977 but regained it in 1981 and held it until 2002. He was a Minister of State at the Department of An Taoiseach from November 1991 to February 1992. Michael Kitt was a member of Galway County Council for the Ballinasloe electoral area from 1975 to 1991. He was previously a senator from 1977 to 1981 and has been a Taoiseach's nominee to Seanad Éireann since 2002. He formerly worked as a teacher and is based in Castleblakeney. His father, Michael F. Kitt, was a member of Dáil Éireann from 1948 to 1951 and again from 1957 to 1975. His brother, Tom Kitt, is the Fianna Fáil chief whip and deputy for Dublin South, and his sister, Áine, who contested the 2005 Kildare North by-election, is again running in that constituency in 2007.

Fine Gael: Paul Connaughton has been on the Fine Gael ticket here in every Dáil election since 1972. Ulick Burke has been on the same ticket in all but one of them. In 1997 a well-managed vote strategy meant that both of them were elected. In 2002 the Fine Gael vote was actually up marginally here, but the gap between them was much wider than it had been in 1997 and the presence of former Fianna Fáil councillor Paddy McHugh, running as an independent, meant that Burke lost his seat. This time they are running four candidates, which may be an unwise strategy when trying to win two seats in a four-seater.

Paul Connaughton was an unsuccessful candidate in the 1973 Galway North East Dáil by-election and in the 1977 Galway East general election. He was first elected to Dáil Éireann for this constituency in 1981 and has been re-elected on each subsequent occasion. Connaughton was a Minister for State at the Department of Agriculture with responsibility for Land Structure and Western Development from 1982 to 1987. He is currently the party spokesperson on Regional Development and Emigrant Affairs, having previously been the frontbench spokesperson on Marine and Natural Resources and on Agriculture. He was a member of Seanad Éireann from 1977 to 1981 and a member of Galway County Council for the Ballinasloe electoral area from 1977 to 1981.

Ulick Burke was an unsuccessful candidate in the Dáil election in 1981, February 1982, November 1982, 1987 and 1989 and a member of Dáil Éireann from 1997 to 2002, but unsuccessful in 2002. He has been a member of Seanad Éireann on the Agriculture Panel since 2002, having previously been in the Seanad from 1981 to 1982 and from 1983 to 1987. A former teacher, he was a member of Galway County Council from 1974 to 2004 for the

Loughrea electoral area. He is a member of the Joint Oireachtas Committee on Education and Science and is the Fine Gael Seanad spokesperson on Education and Science.

Tom McHugh has been a member of Galway County Council for the Tuam electoral area since 1999. In the 2004 local elections he polled 1,557 first preferences when the quota was 2,265, taking the sixth of the seven seats. He is a building contractor and shop owner.

John Barton is a consultant physician/cardiologist in Portiuncula Hospital in Ballinasloe, Co. Galway. He is chairman of the Health Services Action Group or HSAG, set up to fight for the retention of services in smaller hospitals. This is his first electoral contest.

Labour Party: Colm Keaveney is a member of Galway County Council for the Tuam electoral area, where he polled 1,923 first preferences in the 2004 local elections, when the quota was 2,265, taking the second of the seven seats. He is a SIPTU trade union official and a former president of the Union of Students in Ireland. The party ran no candidate here in 2002.

Progressive Democrats: The party ran no candidate here in 2002 but in 1997 Joe Burke polled 4,182 first preferences. This time the PDs are running councillor Ciaran Cannon, who has been a member of Galway County Council since 2004 and represents the Loughrea electoral area. The 2004 local election was his first electoral contest and he polled 1,307 first preferences to take the seventh seat. He is currently chair of the Planning and Strategic Policy Committee of the council and lives in Athenry.

Sinn Féin: The party candidate in 2002 was Daithí Mac an Bhaird, who polled 1,828 first preferences and was eliminated on the first count. This time their candidate is Jason Devlin, a native of Ballinasloe. He is a trade union shop steward at Portiuncula Hospital, where he works as a porter. Devlin is chair of the party's organisation in this constituency. He is also an active member of the Ireland Palestine Group.

Others: Paddy McHugh was elected to Dáil Éireann on his first attempt in 2002. His election owed much to local controversy about the Tuam hospital. He is a former Fianna Fáil councillor and councillors' representative on the party's Ard Comhairle. He ran as an independent in 2002 after failing to secure a Fianna Fáil nomination. He was a member of Galway County Council for the Tuam electoral area from 1985 to 2004 and is also former member of Tuam Town Council. He formerly worked as an architect.

GALWAY EAST 2007 FIGURES

Candidate	Party	1st Count	2nd Count	3rd Count	4th Count	5th Count	Later counts

YOUR PREDICTION 2007

	Candidate Elected	Party
1		
2		
3		
4		
5		

RESULT 2007

	Candidate Elected	Party
1		
2		
3		
4		
5		

NOTES/UPDATES

GALWAY EAST 2002 FIGURES

4 Seats   Quota 9,885

Candidate	Party	1st	2nd	3rd	4th	5th
Transfer of			Ni Bhroin MacMeanmain	Mac an Bhaird	Burke	Connaughton's surplus
Paul Connaughton*	FG	8,635	+131 8,766	+218 8,984	+4,987 13,971	
Joe Callanan	FF	7,898	+65 7,963	+352 8,315	+1,099 9,414	+952 10,366
Paddy McHugh	IND	7,786	+256 8,042	+539 8,581	+244 8,825	+1,056 9,881
Noel Treacy*	FF	7,765	+82 7,847	+244 8,091	+635 8,726	+537 9,251
Michael Kitt	FF	7,454	+59 7,513	+198 7,711	+239 7,950	+293 8,243
Ulick Burke*	FG	6,941	+211 7,152	+293 7,445	Elim'd	
Daothí Mac An Bhaird	SF	1.828	+240 2,068	Elim'd		
Úna Ni Bhroin	GP	1,022	Elim'd			
Manus Mac Meanmain	CSP	93	Elim'd			
Non-Transferable			71	224	241	1,258

*Outgoing Deputy

GALWAY WEST

Outgoing Deputies: Eamon Ó Cuiv (FF), Frank Fahey (FF), Pádraic McCormack (FG), Michael D. Higgins (Lab), Noel Grealish (PD).

The Constituency: This is a **five-seat** constituency. It includes the city of Galway and the western part of County Galway. The boundaries of this constituency are unchanged since 2002.

Party	Votes 2002	Quota 2002	% Vote 2002	% Vote 1997	Swing
Fianna Fáil	20,442	2.5	41.33%	45.94%	– 4.62%
Fine Gael	8,359	1.0	16.90%	22.21%	– 5.32%
Labour	5,213	0.6	10.54%	10.07%	+ 0.47%
PDs	6,192	0.8	12.52%	12.27%	+ 0.25
Green Party	2,193	0.2	4.43%	3.44%	+ 0.99%
Sinn Féin	2,779	0.3	5.62%	2.51%	+ 3.11%
Others	4,288	0.5	8.67%	1.14%	+ 7.53%

2007 Candidates will include: Eamon Ó Cuiv (FF), Frank Fahey (FF), Michael Crowe (FF), Pádraic McCormack (FG), Fidelma Healy Eames (FG), Seán Kyne (FG), Michael D. Higgins (Lab), Noel Grealish (PD), Ann Marie Carroll (SF), Niall Ó Brolcháin (GP), Catherine Connolly (Ind).

In Brief: This will be a very interesting five-seater. It is a realistic prospect for a Green gain with the current Mayor of Galway, Niall Ó Brolcháin, in contention for a seat, probably at the expense of either the Progressive Democrats or Fine Gael. It is also a Fianna Fáil target for a seat gain but less realistically. Internal tensions in Fianna Fáil over the selection of the candidates have not helped the party's prospects. Although the former Labour councillor Catherine Costelloe is running as an independent, the published constituency polls suggest Michael D. Higgins is still safe. The move by the Fine Gael incumbent Pádraic McCormack to reverse his earlier decision to retire strengthens that party's prospects of holding onto its seat.

Fianna Fáil: A row between party headquarters and the local organisation in this constituency over the number of candidates to be selected led to the election convention being abandoned and instead the three candidates, outgoing deputies Eamon Ó Cuiv and Frank Fahey and the formerly independent city councillor Michael Crowe being nominated by the party nationally.

Eamon Ó Cuiv was first elected to Dáil Éireann in 1992 and has held the seat since. He was an unsuccessful candidate in the 1989 election. He has been Minister for Arts, Culture,

Heritage and the Islands since 2002. He was previously a Minister of State at the Department of Agriculture with responsibility for rural and western development from 2001 to 2002 and Minister of State at the Department of Arts, Culture and the Gaeltacht from 1997 to 2001. He was a member of Seanad Éireann from 1989 to 1992. He formerly worked as the manager of a Gaeltacht co-operative in Corr Na Móna and was a member of Galway County Council for the Connemara electoral area from 1991 to 1997. He is a grandson of former President and former Taoiseach Eamon de Valera and a cousin of Sile de Valera, the outgoing deputy for the Clare constituency who is retiring at this election.

Frank Fahey was first elected to Dáil Éireann in February 1982, re-elected in 1987 and 1989 but lost his seat in 1992. He was a member of Seanad Éireann on the Labour panel from 1993 to 1997. He is currently Minister of State at the Department of Justice, Equality and Law Reform with responsibility for Equality. He was Minister of State at the Department of Enterprise, Trade and Employment from 2002 to September 2004. He was Minister for Marine and Natural Resources from 2000 to 2002. He was Minister of State with responsibility for Children from 1997 to 2000 and previously a Minister of State at the Department of Education and at the Department of Tourism, Transport and Communications from 1987 to 1992.

The party's new candidate is Michael Crowe, who has been a member of Galway City Council since 2004. He ran as an independent candidate in that election and topped the poll in the Galway No.1 ward in the 2004 local elections with 1,027 first preferences, when the quota was 1,223. He joined Fianna Fáil in March 2006.

Fine Gael: Fine Gael's vote dropped 5.3% in the 2002 election but they still held onto their one seat.

Pádraic McCormack has been the party's deputy here since 1989 and has been relatively comfortably re-elected on each occasion. He was also an unsuccessful candidate in the 1977 and 1981 and February 1982 Dáil elections. He was a member of Seanad Éireann on the Agricultural panel from 1987 to 1989. He held the position of chairman of Fine Gael's parliamentary party from 2001 to July 2002. He was a member of Galway County Council from 1974 to 2004 and a member of Galway City Council from 1985 to 2002. He was Mayor of Galway for the year 1992–1993.

Fidelma Healy Eames is a member of Galway County Council for the Oranmore electoral area. She polled 1,632 first preferences in that electoral area in the 2004 local elections when the quota was 2,365. She is formerly a national school teacher in Athenry and Tuam. She now lectures in education in Mary Immaculate College Limerick. She was one of the party's three candidates in the 2002 Dáil election and polled 1,320 first preferences.

The party's new candidate is Seán Kyne, who is a 32-year-old Moycullen-based agricultural consultant. He has been a member of Galway County Council since 2004 when he polled 864 first preferences and took the sixth seat in the Connemara local electoral area. He is also a member of the Moycullen Community Development Association.

Labour Party: Michael D. Higgins is the party's outgoing deputy. He was first elected to Dáil Éireann in 1981. He was re-elected in February 1982 but lost his seat in the November 1982 election. He regained his seat in 1987 and has held it since. He was also a Dáil candidate in 1969, 1973 and 1977. He was a member of Seanad Éireann for the National University of Ireland constituency from 1982 to 1987 and previously as a Taoiseach's nominee from 1973 to 1977. He was also the party candidate in Connacht Ulster in the 1979 and 1984 European elections. He was chairman of the parliamentary Labour Party and also a party spokesperson at various times on international affairs, overseas development, education and the Gaeltacht. He has been party spokesperson on Foreign Affairs since 1997 and president of the party since May 2003. He was Minister for Arts, Culture and the Gaeltacht from 1993 to 1997. He is the author of several books, including books of poetry, and is a former university lecturer. He was a member of Galway City Council from 1985 to 1993, and Mayor of Galway twice in 1981–83 and 1991–92.

Progressive Democrats: Noel Grealish was elected on his first attempt in 2002. He took the seat which had previously been held by Bobby Molloy for over 30 years, firstly for Fianna Fáil and then for the Progressive Democrats. He was a member of Galway County Council for the Oranmore electoral area from 1999 to 2004. He is the Progressive Democrat spokesman on Rural Planning and has served as the chairman of the parliamentary party. Based in Oranmore itself, he is also a company director.

Green Party: Niall Ó Brolcháin is again the party's candidate. In 2002 he polled 2,193 first preferences. He has since been elected to Galway City Council. In the 2004 local elections he polled 881 first preferences in the Galway No.3 ward and took the fourth of the four seats. He is currently the Mayor of Galway. He works as a computer consultant.

Sinn Féin: Colm Ó Ceanabháin was originally selected to represent the party in this constituency but withdrew in December 2006. Ann Marie Carroll is now the candidate. She unsuccessfully contested the 2004 local election polling 738 votes in the Galway No.2 ward.

Others: The strongest independent will be Catherine Connolly, who is a member of Galway County Council. She was formerly a Labour Party member but left the party having failed to get a nomination for this election. Catherine Connolly polled 1,265 first preferences as a Labour Party candidate in the Galway No.3 ward in the 2004 local election, having transferred from the No.2 ward where she had held a seat from 1999 to 2004. Her sister, Collette Connolly, ran in her stead in the No.2 ward in the 2004 local elections as a Labour Party candidate. However, she too has since left the party. Catherine, who is a barrister, was Mayor of Galway for the year 2004–05.

The last-minute declaration of independent MEP and former presidential candidate Dana Rosemary Scallan in the days before the 2002 election was called, although newsworthy, had no impact in the constituency. She polled disappointingly and was eliminated on the eighth count. Her transfers were distributed on an almost pro rata basis among the other parties and candidates.

GALWAY WEST 2007 FIGURES

Candidate	Party	1st Count	2nd Count	3rd Count	4th Count	5th Count	Later counts

YOUR PREDICTION 2007

	Candidate Elected	Party
1		
2		
3		
4		
5		

RESULT 2007

	Candidate Elected	Party
1		
2		
3		
4		
5		

NOTES/UPDATES

GALWAY WEST 2002 FIGURES

5 seats   Quota: 8,245

Candidate / Transfer of		1st	2nd ÓCuiv surplus	3rd Manning Nulty	4th Healy-Eames	5th Ac Coistealbha	6th McDonnell	7th Scallon	8th Callannan	9th Fahey	10th Lyons	11th Mc Donagh	12th Walsh	13th Mc Cormack	14th Brolchan	15th O Higgins surplus
Eamon Ó Cuív*	FF	9.947														
Frank Fahey*	FF	7,226	+676 7,902	+2 7,904	+89 7,993	+127 8,120	+198 8,318									
Padraic McCormack*	FG	4,760	+90 4,850	+9 4,859	+401 5,260	+58 5,318	+184 5,502	+363 5,865	+136 6,001	+11 6,012	+273 6,285	+1,338 7,623	+797 8,420			
Michael D Higgins*	LAB	5,213	+102 5,315	+28 5,343	+167 5,510	+136 5,646	+126 5,772	+323 6,095	+569 6,664	+18 6,682	+489 7,171	+327 7,498	+653 8,151	+93 8,244	+2,336 10,580	
Margaret Cox	FF	3,269	+428 3,697	+7 3,704	+48 3,752	+49 3,801	+69 3,870	+212 4,082	+215 4,297	+17 4,314	+309 4,623	+159 4,782	+462 5,244	+29 5,273	+312 5,585	+321 5,906
Noel Grealish	PD	2,735	+52 2,787	+4 2,791	+67 2,858	+18 2,876	+245 3,121	+112 3,233	+82 3,315	+8 3,323	+1,221 4,544	+554 5,098	+227 5,325	+27 5,352	+332 5,684	+531 6,215
Niall Ó Brolcháin	GP	2,193	+23 2,216	+25 2,241	+67 2,308	+108 2,416	+34 2,450	+201 2,651	457 3,108	+3 3,111	+156 3,267	+124 3,391	+358 3,749	+26 3,775	Elim'd	
Seamus Walsh	IND	2,439	+120 2,559	+29 2,588	+38 2,626	+116 2,742	+32 2,774	+170 2,944	+210 3,154	+1 3,155	+79 3,234	+94 3,328				
Michael McDonagh	FG	2,279	+21 2,300	+6 2,306	+313 2,619	+13 2,632	+38 2,670	+78 2,748	+60 2,808	+4 2,812	+76 2,888	Elim'd				
Donal Lyon	PD	1,995	+22 2,017	+9 2,026	+32 2,058	+10 2,068	+477 2,545	+168 2,713	+74 2,787	+11 2,798	Elim'd					
Daniel Callanan	SF	1,468	+17 1,485	+13 1,498	+11 1,509	+657 2,166	+34 2,200	+106 2,306	Elim'd							
Dana R Scallon	IND	1,677	+50 1,727	+13 1740	+72 1812	+60 1872	+48 1,920	Elim'd								
Declan McDonnell	PD	1,462	+17 1,479	+5 1484	+15 1499	+7 1506	Elim'd									
Sean Ac Coistealbha	SF	1,311	+62 1,373	+10 1383	+14 1397	Elim'd										
Fidelema Healy Eames	FG	1,320	+20 1,340	+7 1,347	Elim'd											
Eileen Manning	IND	96	+1 97	Elim'd												
Joseph Nulty	IND	76	+1 77	Elim'd												
Non-Transferable					7	13	38	21	187	503		195	292	831		795

KERRY NORTH

Outgoing Deputies: Tom McEllistrim (FF), Martin Ferris (SF), Jimmy Deenihan (FG).

The Constituency: This is a **three-seat** constituency made up of the local electoral areas of Tralee and Listowel. In the redrawing of constituencies since 2002 an area west of Tralee on the northern side of the Dingle Peninsula (2002 population 1,235) was transferred from Kerry South into this constituency.

Party	Votes 2002	Quota 2002	% Vote 2002	% Vote 1997	Swing
Fianna Fáil	11,811	1.2	30.15%	26.31%	3.84%
Fine Gael	8,652	0.9	22.09%	24.29%	−2.20%
Labour	8,773	0.9	22.40%	29.90%	−7.52%
Sinn Féin	9,496	1.0	24.24%	15.91%	8.34%
Others	441	0.04	1.13%	3.6	−2.47%

2007 Candidates will include: Norma Foley (FF), Tom McEllistrim (FF), Jimmy Deenihan (FG), Terry O'Brien (Lab), Martin Ferris (SF), David Grey (GP), Morgan Stack (Ind).

In Brief: Fianna Fáil, Fine Gael and Sinn Féin currently have one seat each in this constituency. Labour have hopes of regaining the seat they lost here to Sinn Féin's Martin Ferris in 2002 while the competition between the McEllistrim and Foley sides of the Fianna Fáil ticket will again be intense. Both of the party's candidates, the sitting deputy Tom McEllistrim and Norma Foley, a daughter of former deputy Denis Foley, are based at the Tralee end of the constituency. Fine Gael's Jimmy Deenihan should be the safest of the sitting deputies, with Martin Ferris probably the next most secure. However, with Labour's new candidate, Terry O'Brien, likely to do very well, none of the sitting deputies is guaranteed re-election.

Fianna Fáil: Against many predictions the Fianna Fáil vote was actually up 3.5% in this constituency in 2002 and the party's new young candidate, Tom McEllistrim, took the seat. The controversy surrounding outgoing deputy Denis Foley on his retirement, as well as the Sinn Féin challenge, were expected to cost Fianna Fáil a seat. Colourful Listowel-Tarbert-based Senator Dan Kiely, who had been a Dáil candidate three times in the 1980s, was the party's other candidate in 2002 and the one favoured by party headquarters, and by most pundits, to win.

Tom McEllistrim was elected to Dáil Éireann for the first time in 2002, having been unsuccessful in 1997, when he polled 4,036 first preference votes, 1,340 votes behind the then outgoing deputy, Denis Foley. McEllistrim is Ballymacelligot based and formerly worked as a secondary school teacher. He was a member of Kerry County Council for the Tralee electoral area from 1999 to 2004. His sister, Anne McEllistrim, ran in his stead in the 2004 local elections and comfortably retained the county council seat, polling 2,385, only 16 votes behind the poll topper, Labour's Terry O'Brien, and just 22 votes short of the quota. They are the third generation of public representatives in their family, following their father, Tom McEllistrim, a TD from 1969 to 1992 and their grandfather, Tom McEllistrim, a Dáil deputy from 1923 to 1969.

Norma Foley has been a member of Kerry County Council for the Tralee electoral area since 2002, when she was co-opted to the seat previously held by her father, Denis Foley. She retained the seat in the 2004, polling 1,471 first preferences and taking the fourth of the seven seats. She has also been a member of Tralee Town Council since 1994 and is a fomer chair of the council. She is a teacher. Her father, Denis Foley, was a member of Dáil Eireann from 1981 to 1989 and from 1992 to 2002 and a member of Seanad Éireann from 1989 to 1992.

Fine Gael: Given the intense competition here and the national drop in Fine Gael's support, the party's vote held up relatively well, down only 2.2 percentage points on 1997. Their candidate is again outgoing deputy Jimmy Deenihan.

Deenihan's base is in the Listowel end of the constituency. He was first elected to Dáil Éireann in 1987 and has retained the seat in each subsequent election. His vote has been fairly consistent across recent elections. He polled 8,689 first preferences in 1997 and 8,652 in 2002. He was a Minister of State at the Department of Agriculture and Forestry from 1994 to 1997 and has been the party's spokesperson on Arts, Sports, and Tourism since June 2002, having previously been spokesperson on Northern Ireland policy, Environmental Protection and Public Works, Tourism and Trade, and Youth and Sport. Jimmy Deenihan was a Taoiseach's nominee to Seanad Éireann from 1982 to 1987. He was a member of Kerry County Council for the Listowel electoral area from 1985 to 1994 and from 1999 to 2004. Deenihan formerly worked as a teacher and holds four All-Ireland inter-county football medals.

Labour Party: Labour suffered a severe electoral trauma here in 2002, when the former party leader and three-time Tánaiste, Dick Spring, lost his seat. While the party's vote share was down more than 7.5 percentage points at 22.4%, it was still one of their best vote shares in the country. However, the intense competition in the constituency meant even that was not enough to hold the seat. Spring has now retired from politics and the party's new candidate is Terry O'Brien. O'Brien has been a member of Kerry County Council for the Tralee electoral area since 2004. In the 2004 local elections he topped the poll with 2,401 first preferences, just six short of the quota. He has been a member of Tralee Town Council since 1999. A wheelchair user himself, O'Brien is a community development officer with the Irish Wheelchair Association.

Sinn Féin: Sinn Féin's Martin Ferris topped the poll in 2002. He was also a candidate in the 1997 Dáil election, when he polled 5,691 votes, and he increased that to 9,496 first preferences in 2002. He was the party's candidate in the Munster constituency in the 1999 European elections, polling 29,060 first preferences. Based in Ardfert, he was a member of Kerry County Council for the Tralee electoral area from 1999 to 2004. He was also a member of Tralee Town

Council from 1999 to 2004. His daughter Toireasa was co-opted to his county council seat and in the 2004 local election she polled 2,343 first preference votes and took the first seat. Martin Ferris was a member of the Forum for Peace and Reconcilaition. He served a sentence of imprisonment in Portlaoise Prison from 1984 to 1994.

Green Party: The party candidate is David Grey, who is a chief instructor in the disability sector. He is a founder of GM Free Kerry and Fair Trade Tralee. He was an unsucessful candidate for Kerry County Council in the 2004 local elections. He polled 561 first preferences in the Tralee local electoral area.

Others: Morgan Stack, a former lecturer at UCC, is running on the platform that 9/11 was an intelligence operation planned and conducted by very senior elements in the current Bush administration.

KERRY NORTH 2007 FIGURES

Candidate	Party	1st Count	2nd Count	3rd Count	4th Count	5th Count	Later counts

YOUR PREDICTION 2007

	Candidate Elected	Party
1		
2		
3		
4		
5		

RESULT 2007

	Candidate Elected	Party
1		
2		
3		
4		
5		

NOTES/UPDATES

KERRY NORTH 2002 FIGURES

146

3 Seats   Quota: 9,794

Candidate	Party	1st	2nd	3rd
Transfer of			Kiely Kennedy O Connor	McEllistrim's surplus
Martin Ferris	SF	9,496	+520 10,016	
Dick Spring*	LAB	8,773	+393 9,166	+187 9,353
Jimmy Deenihan*	FG	8,652	+886 9,538	+304 9,842
Tom McElistrim	FF	7,884	+2,401 10,285	
Dan Kiely	FF	3,927	*Elim'd*	
James Kennedy	IND	233	*Elim'd*	
Anthony O' Connor	IND	208	*Elim'd*	
Non-Transferable			168	

*Outgoing Deputy

KERRY SOUTH

> **Outgoing Deputies**: John O'Donoghue (FF), Breeda Moynihan-Cronin (Lab), Jackie Healy Rac (Ind).

> **The Constituency**: This is a **three-seat** constituency. It is entirely within the county of Kerry and covers most of the local electoral area of Dingle and all of the local electoral areas of Killarney and Killorglin. In the redrawing of constituencies since 2002, an area west of Tralee on the northern side of the Dingle Peninsula (2002 population 1,235) has been transferred from this constituency to Kerry North.

Party	Votes 2002	Quota 2002	% Vote 2002	% Vote 1997	Swing
Fianna Fáil	16,357	1.8	44.64%	31.79%	12.85%
Fine Gael	6,473	0.7	17.66%	13.77%	3.89%
Labour	5,307	0.6	14.48%	14.05%	0.43%
Others	8,509	0.9	23.22%	40.39	−17.17%

> **2007 Candidates will include**: Tom Fleming (FF), John O'Donoghue (FF), Seamus Cosaí Fitzgerald (FG), Tom Sheahan (FG), Breeda Moynihan-Cronin (Lab), Jackie Healy Rae (Ind).

In Brief: In 2002 this constituency again returned one Fianna Fáil, one Labour and one independent. Fine Gael, somewhat unrealistically, has cited this as a target for a gain, at the expense of Labour or the independent. However, if there is any change here it is likely to be a gain for Fianna Fáil, perhaps their only gain in the country. Now that Labour's sitting deputy, Breda Moynihan-Cronin, has reversed her decision to retire, the party should hold its seat here. Fianna Fáil will win one seat comfortably and if the Healy Rae seat, which Jackie came close to losing in 2002, is vulnerable this time out then Fianna Fáil's Tom Fleming could win a second seat for his party.

Fianna Fáil: In 1997 the retirement of Killarney-based deputy John O'Leary and internal Fianna Fáil divisions about his replacement created both the circumstance and opportunity for Jackie Healy Rae to win a seat at Fianna Fáil's expense. Another Fianna Fáil breakaway councillor, Brendan Mac Gearailt, also contested that election as an independent, polling 4,172 first preferences. Mac Gearailt rejoined the party in the interim and this facilitated the reintegration of a large chunk of the Fianna Fáil vote, particularly on the Dingle Peninsula. Although Mac Gearailt did not seek the Fianna Fáil nomination in 2002, his decision to rejoin was an important factor in the almost 13 percentage points growth of the Fianna Fáil vote in the 2002 election. Their ticket of John O'Donoghue and Tom Fleming came within 203 votes of winning two seats. The party is running the same two candidates in 2007.

The party's outgoing deputy is the Minister for Arts, Culture and the Gaeltacht, John O'Donoghue. O'Donoghue was first elected to Dáil Éireann in 1987 and has held the seat on each occasion since. In 2002 John O'Donoghue was just over the quota on the first count. He was briefly Minister of State at the Department of Finance with responsibility for Public Works from November 1991 to February 1992, party frontbench spokesperson on Justice from 1995 to 1997 and Minister for Justice, Equality and Law Reform from 1997 to 2002. He was a member of Kerry County Council for the Killorglan electoral area from 1985 to 1991 and again from 1993 to 1997, being chairman of the council from 1990 to 1991. His brother, Paul O'Donoghue, was elected to Kerry County Council, also for Killorglin area, in the 2004 local elections with 1,829 first preferences – the quota was 2,176.

This is Tom Fleming's second time contesting a Dáil election. In the 2002 Dáil election Fleming had the second highest first preference vote, albeit 2,500 votes behind O'Donoghue. He is a member of Kerry County Council for the Killarney electoral area and was chairman from 2000 to 2001. In the 2004 local elections he polled 3,038 votes, which was 560 votes over the quota.

Fine Gael: Fine Gael has had no seat in this constituency since 1992. In 2002 they ran two candidates, one from each end of the constituency – Killarney-based councillor Sheila Casey and her council colleague from Dingle, Seamus Cosaí Fitzgerald. Interestingly, given the party's national slide, the Fine Gael vote was up almost 4%, from a combined vote of 13.77% of the first preference vote in 1997 to 18% in 2002. In the same elections Breeda Moynihan-Cronin polled 14.05% and 14.5%, respectively. Nonetheless the seat once again went to Labour. Fine Gael is again running two candidates in 2007, although Cosaí Fitzgerald has a new running mate.

Seamus Cosaí Fitzgerald is a member of Údarás na Gaeltachta and has been a member of Kerry County Council since 1999. On the council he represents the Dingle electoral area where, in the 2004 local elections, he polled 1,565 first preferences, when the quota was 2,265. He got 4,539 first preferences (quota 9,162) in the 2002 general election. He is a farmer.

Fine Gael's new candidate is Thomas Sheahan, who has been a member of Kerry County Council for the Killarney electoral area since 2004. In those local elections he polled 1,349 votes when the quota was 2,478 and he took the last of the six seats. He is Rathmore based and is a company director.

Labour Party: In 2002 the party's vote increased marginally. Crucially, Breda Moynihan-Cronin was again ahead of both of the Fine Gael candidates on the first count, and, as in 1997, when the Fine Gael candidates went out she attracted more than two-thirds of the Fine Gael transfer.

Moynihan-Cronin was first elected to Dáil Éireann in 1992 and has held her seat in each subsequent election. In 1992, benefiting from the national Labour trend, she increased the party's vote to 24%, polling 7,537 first preferences. In 1997 her vote dropped to 14% and she polled 4,988 first preferences. In 2002 her 14.5% represented 5,307 first preferences. Moynihan-Cronin had announced her retirement from the Dáil due to ill health, but in late 2006 announced that she is able to contest the election after all. She was appointed party spokesperson on Justice, Equality and Law Reform from 1997 to 1998, on Social Community and Family Affairs from 1998 to 1999, on Tourism and Recreation from 1999 to 2002 and was spokesperson on Social and Family Affairs from 2002 to 2003. She was a member of Kerry County Council from 1991 to 2004 for the Killarney electoral area.

Others: In 2002 Jackie Healy Rae's first preference vote was down by almost 1,000 votes and he was fourth on the first count. Crucially, he benefited from transfers from the smaller independents and particularly from those of the two Fine Gael candidates when they were eliminated. When the last Fine Gael candidate, Seamus Fitzgerald, was eliminated, Healy Rae got twice as many transfers as Fianna Fáil's Tom Fleming.

The colourful Jackie Healy Rae was first elected here in 1997. He is a former Fianna Fáil local director of elections and councillor, but left the party in the lead-in to the 1997 election, having failed to get a party nomination. Based in Kilgarvan he was one of four independent deputies on whose support the Ahern-led Fianna Fáil/Progressive Democrats government relied between 1997 and 2002. He was a Fianna Fáil member of Kerry County Council from 1974 to 1997 and an independent member from 1997 to 2004.

Healy Rae's son, Danny, was co-opted to his seat on the county council in preparation for the introduction of the dual mandate ban and contested the 2004 local elections in the Killarney electoral area, where he polled 1,811 first preferences when the quota was 2,478. Another son, Michael Healy Rae, has been a member of Kerry County Council for the Killorglan electoral area since 1999. In the 2004 election he polled 1,973 votes when the quota was 2,176. He is as colourful as his father and a likely political heir as a Dáil candidate, perhaps even in this election, since Jackie Healy Rae is now 77 years of age.

KERRY SOUTH 2007 FIGURES

Candidate	Party	1st Count	2nd Count	3rd Count	4th Count	5th Count	Later counts

YOUR PREDICTION 2007

	Candidate Elected	Party
1		
2		
3		
4		
5		

RESULT 2007

	Candidate Elected	Party
1		
2		
3		
4		
5		

NOTES/UPDATES

KERRY SOUTH 2002 FIGURES

3 seats   Quota: 9,162

Candidate	Party	1st	2nd	3rd	4th	5th	6th	7th
Transfer of			Barry	Grady	O'Donaghue's surplus	Casey	Fitzgerald	Moynihan Cronin's surplus
John O'Donoghue*	FF	9,445						
Tom Fleming	FF	6,912	+83 6,995	+260 7,255	+152 7,407	+186 7,593	+683 8,276	+105 8,381
Jackie Healy-Rae*	IND	6,229	+226 6,455	+364 6,819	+74 6,893	+254 7,147	+1,262 8,409	+175 8,584
Breeda Moynihan Cronin*	LAB	5,307	5,480	+173 5,946	+466 5,979	+33 6,432	+453 9,442	+3,010
Seamus Fitzgerald	FG	4,539	+193 4,732	+59 4,791	+20 4,811	+1,272 6,083	Elim'd	
Sheila Casey	FG	1,934	+99 2,033	+183 2,216	+4 2,220	Elim'd		
Donal Grady	IND	1,346	+103 1,449	Elim'd				
Donal Barry	IND	934	Elim'd					
Non-Transferable			+57	+117		55	1,128	1,357

*Outgoing Deputy

KILDARE NORTH

Outgoing Deputies: Emmet Stagg (Lab), Bernard Durkan (FG), Catherine Murphy (Ind).

Catherine Murphy was elected in the March 2005 by-election caused by the resignation of Charlie McCreevy (FF) following his appointment to the European Commission.

The Constituency: This is now a **four-seat** constituency, having gained an additional seat as a result of the redrawing of constituencies since 2002. It is entirely within the administrative county of Kildare and is in the main an urban constituency, including Naas, Celbridge, Maynooth and Kilcock and their hinterlands. In the redrawing, part of an area in the north west of the county (2002 population 9,554) was transferred from Kildare South into this constituency.

Party	Votes 2002	Quota 2002	% Vote 2002	% Vote 1997	Swing
Fianna Fáil	14,250	1.7	43.21%	34.86%	8.35%
Fine Gael	5,786	0.7	17.54%	26.19%	−8.64%
Labour	7,051	0.9	21.38%	19.00%	−6.41%
DL				8.80%	
PDs	3,919	0.5	11.88%	6.69%	5.19%
Green Party	1,974	0.2	5.99%	4.44%	1.52%
Others	–	–	–	–	–

2007 Candidates will include: Áine Kitt-Brady (FF), Michael Fitzpatrick (FF), Bernard Durkan (FG), Darren Scully (FG), Emmet Stagg (Lab), Christine McCauley (SF), Shane Fitzgerald (GP), Catherine Murphy (Ind).

In Brief: The rapid population growth in this constituency means it has been given an additional seat since 2002 and is now a four-seater. Fianna Fáil has had no seat in this constituency since the party lost its seat in the 2005 by-election caused by Charlie McCreevy's move to the European Commission. Both Fianna Fáil and Fine Gael have hopes of winning two seats this time out, but neither is likely to do so. The most probable outcome is one seat each for Fianna Fáil, Fine Gael, the Labour Party and the independent Catherine Murphy.

Fianna Fáil: In 2002 Fianna Fáil came extremely close to winning two out of three seats in this constituency. The party ran the same two candidates, Finance Minister Charlie McCreevy and Leixlip-based solicitor Paul Kelly, in both 1997 and 2002. McCreevy topped the poll on both occasions and was comfortably elected. Kelly ended up fourth in 1997 and 2002 but came a lot closer to winning a seat in the latter election. He was just 35 votes behind Bernard Durkan for the last seat. This time the party has an all-new ticket

Áine Kitt-Brady was the party's candidate in the 2005 by-election caused by Charlie McCreevy's resignation from Dáil Éireann to take up his appointment as European Commissioner. She polled 6,201 first preferences, which was just under a quarter of the vote. She is married to Jerry Brady, who was a member of Dáil Éireann from February to November 1982. She is a sister of two other candidates in the election, the party's chief whip, Tom Kitt, who is the outgoing deputy in Dublin South, and Senator Michael Kitt, who is a former deputy in Galway West, where he is contesting this Dáil election.

Michael Fitzpatrick has been a member of Kildare County Council for the Clane electoral area since 1999. In the 2004 local elections he polled 1,652 first preferences. He was a full-time special advisor and constituency manager for Charlie McCreevy for 15 years, having previously been a member of An Garda Síochána from 1961 to 1972 and subsequently an insurance agent and an auctioneer.

Fine Gael: Fine Gael polled 26.19% of the first preferences in 1997 and that fell to 17.5% in the 2002 election, when the party came extremely close to losing its one seat.

Bernard Durkan is the party's outgoing deputy. He was first elected to Dáil Éireann in 1981, lost his seat in February 1982, regained it in November of that year and has held it in each election since. He served as a Minister of State in the Department of Social Welfare with responsibility for Information and Consumer Services from 1994 to 1997, was the party's chief whip from June 2002 to October 2004 and is currently the party spokesperson on Communications and Natural Resources. Durkan was a member of Kildare County Council for the Celbridge electoral area from 1976 to 1994 and was chairman of the council for the year 1986–87. He was a member of Seanad Éireann from February to November 2002 and formerly worked as an agricultural contractor.

The party's other candidate is Darren Scully, who was the party's candidate in the 2005 by-election, in which he polled 4,630 first preferences, which was 18% of the vote. In the 2004 local elections Scully was an unsuccessful candidate for a place on Kildare County Council in the Naas local electoral area, polling 732 votes. The quota there was 934. He was, however, elected to the Naas Town Council in the same year. Darren Scully is currently chairperson of the Naas garda liason committee. He works as an engineering surveyor.

Labour Party: In 2002 the Labour vote was down on the combined Labour/Democratic Left vote of 1997. However, Emmett Stagg had just under a quota and he comfortably took the second seat on the fourth count.

Stagg was a candidate in the 1981 Dáil election, was first elected to Dáil Éireann in 1987 for the old five-seater Kildare constituency and has held a Dáil seat ever since. He was a Minister of State at the Department of Environment with special responsibility for Housing and Urban Renewal from 1993 to 1994 and was Minister of State at the Department of Transport, Energy and Communication with responsibility for Nuclear Safety, Renewable Energy, Gas and the Oil Industry from 1994 to 1997. He was chairman of the Labour Party from 1987 to 1989. He is currently the party's chief whip and spokesperson on Nuclear Safety. He was a member of Kildare County Council for the Celbridge electoral area from 1978 to 1993 and was chairman of the council for the year 1981–82. He is based in Straffan.

Progressive Democrats: The party candidate in 2002 was Senator Kate Walsh. Walsh was elected as an independent candidate to Kildare County Council in the Celbridge electoral area in the 1999 local elections, mainly on a platform focused on planning issues. She polled an amazing 43% of the first preference vote – 2,167 votes – in that area in the 1999 local elections. In January 2002 she joined the Progressive Democrats and was announced as their candidate in this constituency in that year's election. In 2002 she polled 3,919 first preferences and was eliminated on the fourth count. The party has not yet selected a candidate for this election.

Green Party: In 1997 the Green Party candidate, Seán English, polled 4.5%. Their candidate in 2002, Anne Kelly-McCormack, increased that slightly to 6%. This time round their candidate is Shane Fitzgerald. A native of county Mayo, 31-year-old Fitzgerald has been a member of Leixlip Town Council since 2004. On the same day he was an unsuccessful candidate for Kildare County Council; he polled 815 first preferences in the Leixip local electoral area where the quota was 2,101. He was national co-coordinator of the Green Party national executive for two years from 2000 to 2002 and was assistant to the Green Party director of elections during the 2002 general election. He is a horticulturalist and owns his own business.

Sinn Féin: Cristin McCauley was an unsuccessful candidate for Kildare County Council in the Naas electoral area in the 2004 local elections, where she polled 484 first preferences (quota 2,374).

Others: The outgoing independent TD, Catherine Murphy, was elected to Dáil Éireann in the 2005 by-election. She polled 5,985 first preferences, which represented 23.64% of the vote, and attracted more transfers from all the eliminated candidates to win the seat. Murphy is a former member of the Workers Party, Democratic Left and the Labour Party. She was a member of the Kildare County Council from 1991 to 2005 when she had to step down, having won a Dáil seat. She ran in the Leixlip electoral area for Kildare County Council in the 2004 local elections as an independent candidate, topping the poll with 2,101 first preferences. She was also a member of Leixlip Town Council from 1994 to 2004.

KILDARE NORTH 2007 FIGURES

Candidate	Party	1st Count	2nd Count	3rd Count	4th Count	5th Count	Later counts

YOUR PREDICTION 2007

	Candidate Elected	Party
1		
2		
3		
4		
5		

RESULT 2007

	Candidate Elected	Party
1		
2		
3		
4		
5		

NOTES/UPDATES

KILDARE NORTH 2002 FIGURES

3 Seats   Quota 8,246

Candidate Transfer of	Party	1st	2nd McCreevy's surplus	3rd Kelly- McCormack	4th Walsh	5th Stagg's surplus
Charlie McCreevy*	FF	9,082				
Emmet Stagg*	LAB	7,051	+117 7,168	+837 8,005	+1,467 9,472	
Bernard Durkan*	FG	5,786	+73 5,859	+318 6,177	+1,164 7,341	+684 8,025
Paul Kelly	FF	5,168	+513 5,681	+242 5,923	+1,459 7,382	+508 7,890
Kate Walsh	PD	3,919	+108 4,027	+446 4,473	Elim'd	
Anne Kelly-McCormack	GP	1,974	+25 1,999	Elim'd		
Non-Transferable			0	156	383	34

*Outgoing Deputy

KILDARE SOUTH

Outgoing Deputies: Seán Ó Fearghail (FF), Seán Power (FF), Jack Wall (Lab).

The Constituency: This is a **three-seat** constituency. In the redrawing of constituencies since 2002 an area in the north west of the county (2002 population 9,554) was transferred from Kildare South into this constituency.

Party	Votes 2002	Quota 2002	% Vote 2002	% Vote 1997	Swing
Fianna Fáil	15,152	1.9	46.43%	37.59%	8.84%
Fine Gael	5,795	0.7	17.76%	26.49%	−8.73%
Labour	6,043	0.7	18.52%	20.25%	−1.73%
PDs	3,887	0.5	11.91%	13.52%	−1.61%
Green Party	1,208	0.2	3.70%	–	3.70%
Others	546	0.0	1.67%	2.14	−0.47%

2007 Candidates will include: Seán Ó Fearghail (FF), Seán Power (FF), Alan Gillis (FG), Richard Daly (FG), Jack Wall (Lab), JJ Power (GP), Threasa Bennitt (SF).

In Brief: This is a key marginal between Fianna Fáil and Fine Gael. In 2002 Fianna Fáil were very lucky to win two seats and they will find it hard to repeat this. Fine Gael has no seat here. Their former leader, Alan Dukes, lost his seat in 2002. Seán Ó Fearghail is likely to be the stronger of the two Fianna Fáil incumbents, so if Fine Gael does regain its seat, it is likely to be a Minister of State casualty here. Labour's Jack Wall is probably safe.

Fianna Fáil: Fianna Fáil came close to winning two out of three seats here in 1997. Seán Power and Seán Ó Fearghail were also the candidates on that occasion. At the last minute before nominations closed, the party added local radio personality Christy Wall to the ticket, but he polled only 662 votes. The party's combined vote in 1997 was 38% but Labour's Jack Wall did very well on transfers and held his seat. In 2002, Fianna Fáil ran only Ó Fearghail and Power. Power topped the poll with a dramatic increase in his vote and Ó Fearghail was just 412 votes behind him. They held the two top spots and took the first two seats together on the fourth count, both exceeding the quota. The Fianna Fáil vote rose by 8.84% between 1997 and 2002.

Seán Power was first elected to Dáil Éireann for the then five-seater Kildare constituency in 1989, and he has held his Dáil seat on every occasion since. He was assistant chief whip from 1992 to 2002 and was appointed a Minister of State at the Department of Health and Children in September 2004. Power represented the Naas electoral area on Kildare County Council from 1985 to 2004. Based in Caragh, near Naas, he is also a publican. His brother JJ is also running in this constituency as a Green Party candidate. Their father Paddy Power, the former Minister, was a member of Dáil Éireann for Kildare from 1969 to 1989.

Seán Ó Fearghail unsuccessfully contested the 1987, 1989 and 1992 Dáil elections and came very close to winning a seat in 1997, when he was just 439 votes behind Labour's Jack Wall on the last count. He was elected to Dáil Éireann for the first time in 2002. Ó Fearghail enjoys a strong base in Kildare town. He was a member of Kildare County Council for the Kildare electoral area from 1999 to 2004. He was elected to Seanad Éireann in a by-election in June 2000 and served in the upper house until he was elected to Dáil Éireann in 2002.

Fine Gael: This was the scene of one of Fine Gael's biggest and most surprising losses in 2002, when former leader and outgoing frontbencher Alan Dukes lost his seat. The party's vote dropped by 9% between 1997 and 2002. Duke's own vote was down almost 1,300 first preferences and he was more than 1,000 votes behind Labour's Jack Wall on the first count. He narrowed the gap with the help of transfers from his running mate Rainsford Hendy, who polled just 828 votes, and with some transfers on the elimination of the Progressive Democrats' John Dardis, but Wall was still 187 votes ahead of Dukes on the last count.

Fine Gael has two new candidates for this election. Alan Gillis was a member of the European Parliament for the Leinster constituency from 1994 to 1999. He contested the European election again in 1999 but failed to retain his seat. He was president of the Irish Farmers' Association from 1990 to 1994 and has been a member of the board of management at Tallaght Hospital since 1999, having been its chairman since 2002. He was chairman of European Movement Ireland from 1999 to 2002.

The party's other candidate is Richard Daly. He was an unsuccessful candidate for Kildare County Council in the 2004 local elections. He polled 928 first preferences in the Athy electoral area and was elected to Athy Town Council in the same year. He has recently been the cathaoirleach of the council. He is a former president of Athy Chamber of Commerce and a former national president of Young Fine Gael. He is a secondary school principal.

Labour Party: Jack Wall contested the 1992 general election with Emmet Stagg in the old Kildare five-seat constituency. He was first elected to Dáil Éireann in 1997 when this new three-seater was created. Wall is based in Athy and is a former chairman of Kildare Gaelic Athletic Association. He was a Taoiseach's nominee to Seanad Éireann from 1993 to 1997. Although the Labour vote was down almost two percentage points in 2002, Wall managed to hold the seat. He is the party's spokesperson on Arts, Sports and Tourism. Jack Wall was a member of Kildare County Council from 1999 to 2004 for the Athy electoral area and is also a former member of Athy urban district council. He formerly worked as an electrician.

Progressive Democrats: The party's leader in Seanad Éireann, John Dardis, polled 7% of the first preference vote in the five-seat Kildare constituency in 1992. In 1997 he polled 13.5% in the new three-seater. His vote here fell to 12% in 2002, making this one of the few constituencies in which the Progressive Democrats ran a candidate in that election where its vote dropped. However, this was probably attributable to the strength of the two Fianna Fáil candidates. He is not contesting the 2007 election.

Green Party: JJ Power has been a member of Kildare County Council for the Naas electoral area since 2004. In the 2004 local elections he polled 1,213 first preferences. He was also elected on the same day to Naas Town Council. He was also the party's Dáil candidate in the election in 2002, polling 1,208 first preferences, and the party's candidate in the 2005 by-election in North Kildare, when he polled 1,547 first preferences, which was 6% of the vote. He is a former telecoms engineer. He is a brother of the outgoing Fianna Fáil TD in this constituency, Seán Power, and a son of Paddy Power, who was a member of Dáil Éireann for Kildare from 1969 to 1989.

Sinn Féin: Threasa Bennitt will be the Sinn Féin candidate in Kildare South.

CONSTITUENCY BY CONSTITUENCY

KILDARE SOUTH 2007 FIGURES

Candidate	Party	1st Count	2nd Count	3rd Count	4th Count	5th Count	Later counts

YOUR PREDICTION 2007

	Candidate Elected	Party
1		
2		
3		
4		
5		

RESULT 2007

	Candidate Elected	Party
1		
2		
3		
4		
5		

NOTES/UPDATES

KILDARE SOUTH 2002 FIGURES

3 seats   Quota: 8,158

Candidate	Party	1st	2nd	3rd	4th	5th	6th
Transfer of			Fitzgibbon	Hendy	Dardis JJ Power	Seán Power's surplus	Ó Feargháil
Seán Power*	FF	7,782	+35 7,817	+43 7,860	+1,309 9,169		
Seán Ó Feargháil	FF	7,370	+88 7,458	+43 7501	+925 8,426	8,426	
Jack Wall*	LAB	6,043	+105 6,148	+116 6264	+1,179 7,443	+406 7,849	+128 7,977
Alan Dukes*	FG	4,967	+73 5,040	+506 5,546	+1,624 7,170	+480 7,650	+140 7,790
John Dardis	PD	3,887	+59 3,946	+112 4,058	Elim'd		
JJ Power	GP	1,028	+127 1,335	+16 1,351	Elim'd		
Rainsford Hendy	FG	828	+22 850	Elim'd			
Ger Fitzgibbon	IND	546	Elim'd				
Non-Transferable			+37	+14	+372	+125	

*Outgoing Deputy

LAOIS–OFFALY

Outgoing Deputies: Brian Cowen (FF), Tom Parlon (PD), Olwyn Enright (FG), John Moloney (FF), Seán Fleming (FF).

The Constituency: This **five-seater** constituency incorporates all of the counties of Laois and Offaly. The boundaries of this constituency are unchanged since 2002.

Party	Votes 2002	Quota 2002	% Vote 2002	% Vote 1997	Swing
Fianna Fáil	32,432	3.1	51.30%	49.85%	1.46%
Fine Gael	14,553	1.4	23.02%	28.38%	–5.36%
Labour	1,600	0.2	2.53%	11.61%	–9.08%
PDs	9,088	0.9	14.38%	6.51%	7.87%
Green Party	520	0.0	0.82%	–	0.82%
Sinn Féin	2,600	0.2	4.11%	–	4.11%
Others	2,424	0.2	3.83%	3.66	0.17%

2007 Candidates will include: Brian Cowen (FF), Seán Fleming (FF), John Moloney (FF), John Foley (FF), Olwyn Enright (FG), Charles Flanagan (FG), Molly Buckley (FG), David Whelan (Lab), Jim O'Brien (Lab), Tom Parlon (PD), Marie McKay (GP), Brian Stanley (SF).

In Brief: This is a key Fine Gael target for a gain from one of the current government parties. Minister for Finance Brian Cowen will top the poll and the party's Laois incumbent, John Moloney, is likely to be the second strongest of the Fianna Fáil candidates, so a Fine Gael gain will see the return of Charles Flanagan to the Dáil at the expense of Tom Parlon or Fianna Fáil's Sean Fleming. If Fine Gael does not make a gain there is an outside chance that the party's Education spokesperson, Olwyn Enright, will lose her seat to Flanagan.

Fianna Fáil: In both 1997 and 2002 the party ran the same four-man ticket. In 1997 Fianna Fáil got three seats from their 48.7% of the first preference votes. Their vote grew to 51.3% in 2002 and they had more than 2,847 votes to spare over Fine Gael for the last seat. Brian Cowen again topped the poll and was almost 2,000 votes over the quota. John Moloney was more than 1,000 votes ahead of Seán Fleming on the first count. Two-thirds of Cowen's surplus transferred to his Fianna Fáil running mates, with his one Offaly running mate gaining more than his two Laois running mates combined. When the party's fourth candidate, Gerard Killaly, was eliminated his transfer rate to his party colleagues across the county boundary was very impressive, with Fleming and Moloney getting an almost equal share so that they were both elected.

The party's outgoing deputy in Offaly is the deputy leader and Minister for Finance, Brian Cowen. He was first elected to the Dáil in 1984 in a by-election caused by the death of his father, Bernard Cowen. He was appointed Minister for Finance in September 2004, having previously been Minister for Labour from February 1992 to January 1993, Minister for Transport, Energy and Communications from 1993 to 1994, Minister for Health and Children from 1997 to 2000 and Minister for Foreign Affairs from 2000 to 2004. He was a member of Offaly County Council for the Tullamore electoral area from 1984 to 1992. His brother Barry Cowen is currently a member of the council for that area and polled 1,169 first preferences there in the 2004 local elections.

John Moloney was elected to Dáil Éireann in 1997 having been an unsuccessful candidate in the 1992 election. He was a member of Laois County Council from 1981, when he was co-opted on the death of his father, and he held this seat until the dual mandate ban was introduced in 2004. He represented the Mountmellick electoral area. He was formerly a publican and undertaker. He is a member of the Joint Oireachtas Committees on Family, Community and Social Affairs; Education and Science; and Tourism, Sport and Recreation. John Moloney is based in Mountmelllick, where the family has an undertaking business and public house.

Seán Fleming, who is based in Castletown, was first elected to Dáil Éireann in 1997 on his first attempt. He has been chairman of the Oireachtas Committee on Finance and the Public Service since 2002. He was a member of Laois County Council for the Borris-in-Ossory area from 1999 to 2004. He formerly worked as an accountant and was employed as finance director of Fianna Fáil at party headquarters

John Foley has been a member of Edenderry Town Council since 1999, having taken the first seat with a vote share of 37.12% (3.7 quotas) in 2002. He is currently the mayor of Edenderry.

Fine Gael: In 2002 it surprised many when the winning of a seat by the Progressive Democrats' Tom Parlon came at the ultimate expense of Fine Gael's outgoing Laois deputy, Charles Flanagan. With Tom Enright retiring, his daughter Olwyn, then a 27-year-old solicitor practising in Birr, took his place on the Fine Gael ticket. She polled very well, getting more than 8,000 first preferences to give her third place on the first count. Flanagan was nearly 1,500 votes behind her in sixth place. In the 2007 election the party is running Flanagan and Enright again and has added the formerly independent councillor Molly Buckley

Olwyn Enright was elected to Dáil Éireann on her first attempt in 2002. Shortly after her election she was appointed the party's frontbench spokesperson on Education. She married party colleague, Senator Joe McHugh, who is contesting this Dáil election in Donegal North East, in July 2005. Her father, Tom Enright, was a Dáil deputy from 1969 to 1992 and again from 1997 to 2002. Olwyn Enright is a former member of Offaly County Council for the Birr electoral area.

Charles Flanagan was first elected to Dáil Éireann in 1987 and held his seat until he lost it in 2002. He was a member of Laois County Council from 1984 to 2004, originally in the Tinnahinch electoral area and then, from 1999, in the Portlaoise electoral area. He did not contest the 2004 local election. From 2002 to 2004 he was the party's frontbench spokesperson on Enterprise, Trade and Employment and Local Development. He has also been opposition chief whip. He is currently a member of the National Forum for Europe. His father, Oliver J Flanagan, was a member of Dáil Éireann from 1943 to 1987,

Molly Buckley was an independent candidate in the 2002 Dáil election and was part of the Independent Health Alliance, a loose association of independent candidates formed during that election campaign. Buckley had been a long-standing member of Fine Gael but when denied a place on the party ticket for the 1999 local elections ran as an independent in the Tullamore electoral area, where she was elected on a health services ticket. She contested the 2004 local election, again as an independent, and polled 1,314 first preferences on the first count, which was just 140 votes below the quota. She is a public health nurse by profession.

Labour Party: The party last held a seat here in 1992, when Pat Gallagher was elected to Dáil Éireann on the back of the 'Spring Tide' and, although he had developed a strong local base, he lost out for the fifth seat in 1997. In the 2007 election, Labour is running two candidates.

David Whelan has been a member of the Labour Party since 2004 and was recently appointed chairperson of the Tullamore branch. He lives in Clara and has worked for the health service since 2001 as a planner in disability services. This is his first election.

Jim O'Brien works as a freelance journalist and writer and was editor of the magazine section of the *Farmers Journal* from 2002 to 2004. He also writes with comedian Pat Shortt and was involved in the first series of the TV show *Killinascully*. He lives in Rossnalis, Co. Laois. This is also his first election.

Progressive Democrats: Laois–Offaly had been a target seat for the Progressive Democrats since the party's inception. Former Senator Cathy Honan, who was based in Portarlington, was the party's unsuccessful candidate in the 1989, 1992 and 1997 elections, but before the 1999 local election she announced her decision to retire from politics. The party found an ideal high-profile candidate for the 2002 election in the former IFA leader, Tom Parlon. Parlon put in an impressive campaign in 2002 and polled a stunning 9,088 first preferences, second only to Cowen, to take the second seat. However, published constituency opinion polls have indicated that his seat may be in jeopardy in this election.

Parlon has been president of the Progressive Democrats since September 2005. He has been Minister of State at the Department of Finance with responsibility for public works since 2002. He was president of the Irish Farmers' Association from 1998 to 2002. Based in Coolderry, he is also a farmer.

Sinn Féin: The party candidate, Brian Stanley, polled 2,600 first preferences in the 2002 election, which was just over 4% of the vote. Stanley has been a member of Portlaoise County Council since 2004. He polled 1,020 in the Portlaoise local electoral area and took the second seat. He is chairperson of Laois Offaly Sinn Féin and has served on the party's Ard Comhairle.

Green Party: Marie McKay is a native of Scotland who has lived in Tullamore for 23 years. She is a former teacher. This is her first election.

LAOIS–OFFALY 2007 FIGURES

Candidate	Party	1st Count	2nd Count	3rd Count	4th Count	5th Count	Later counts

YOUR PREDICTION 2007

	Candidate Elected	Party
1		
2		
3		
4		
5		

RESULT 2007

	Candidate Elected	Party
1		
2		
3		
4		
5		

NOTES/UPDATES

LAOIS–OFFALY 2002 FIGURES

5 seats   **Quota: 10,537**

Candidate	Party	1st	2nd	3rd	4th	5th	6th
				Fettes McCormack Kelly Redmond	Dwyer	Buckley Stanley	Killally
			Cowen surplus				
Brian Cowen*	FF	12,529					
Tom Parlon	PD	9,088	+270 9,358	173 9,531	+158 9,689	+883 10,572	
Olwyn Enright	FG	8,053	+202 8,255	+148 8,403	+494 8,897	+1,308 10,205	+800 11,005
John Moloney*	FF	8,093	+167 8,260	+83 8,343	+41 8,384	+464 8,848	+2,124 10,972
Sean Fleming*	FF	7,091	+439 7,530	+112 7,642	+86 7,728	+633 8,361	+2,092 10,453
Charles Flanagan*	FG	6,500	+30 6,530	+116 6,646	+219 6,865	+519 7,384	+222 7,606
Ger Killaly	FF	4,719	+668 5,387	+50 5,437	+93 5,530	+532 6,062	
Brian Stanley	SF	2,600	+39 2,639	+181 2,820	+197 3,017	Elim'd	
Molly Buckley	IND	1,695	+88 1,783	+183 1,966	+390 2,356	Elim'd	
John Dwyer	LAB	1600	+75 1675	+134 1809	Elim'd		
Christopher Fettes	GP	520	+9 529	Elim'd			
Joe McCormack	IND	351	+1 353	Elim'd			
John Kelly	IND	236	+1 237	Elim'd			
Michael Redmond	CSP	146	+2 144	Elim'd			
Non-Transferable			83	83	131	1,034	824

*Outgoing Deputy

LIMERICK EAST

Outgoing Deputies: Willie O'Dea (FF), Michael Noonan (FG), Peter Power (FF), Jan O'Sullivan (Lab), Tim O'Malley (PD).

The Constituency: This **five-seater** constituency includes all of the administrative area of Limerick City Council together with the Castletroy-Cappaghmore Limerick County Council local electoral area. In the redrawing of constituencies since 2002, the constituency gained a small area around Ballyglass (with a population in the 2002 census of 1,025) from Clare but lost an area around Bruff, Knockainy and Knocklong (2002 population 3,228) to Limerick West.

Party	Votes 2002	Quota 2002	% Vote 2002	% Vote 1997	Swing
Fianna Fáil	19,973	2.4	39.95%	39.72%	0.23%
Fine Gael	13,919	1.7	27.84%	26.51%	1.33%
Labour	4,629	0.6	9.26%	15.94%	−6.78%
PDs	4,885	0.6	9.77%	12.42%	−2.65%
Green Party	917	0.1	1.83%	1.61	0.22%
Others	5,677	0.7	11.35%	3.69	7.66%

2007 Candidates will include: Willie O'Dea (FF), Peter Power (FF), Noreen Ryan (FF), Michael Noonan (FG), Kieran O'Donnell (FG), Jan O'Sullivan (Lab), Tim O'Malley (PD), Patricia Forde Brennan (GP), Maurice Quinlivan (SF).

In Brief: Fine Gael has designs on a second seat in this constituency but they are unlikely to make the gain. Willie O'Dea, now a Minister, will again top the poll comfortably and the other outgoing Fianna Fáil deputy, Peter Power, is likely to be stronger than their new candidate, Noreen Ryan. Former leader Michael Noonan is joined on the Fine Gael ticket by first-timer Kieran O'Donnell. If Fine Gael do make the gain, it is more likely to be at the expense of the Progressive Democrats Minister of State, Tim O'Malley, or Labour's Jan O'Sullivan than Fianna Fáil's Peter Power.

Fianna Fáil: Willie O'Dea was an unsuccessful candidate in the 1981 Dáil election but since he was first elected to Dáil Éireann in February 1982 he has comfortably held his seat in every election. He topped the poll dramatically again in 2002 – more than one in four electors in the constituency voted for him. He had nearly 5,000 votes above the quota and polled 3,723 first preferences, more than the then Fine Gael leader, Michael Noonan. O'Dea was appointed Minister for Defence in September 2004, having previously been a Minister of State at the

Department of Education, Science and Technology from 1997 to 2002 and at the Department of Justice, Equality and Law Reform with responsibility for Equality from 2002 to 2005. He was also previously a Minister of State at the Department of Justice from 1992 to 1993 and in the Departments of Justice and Health from 1993 to 1994. Willie O'Dea was formerly an accountant and college lecturer.

Peter Power was an unsuccessful candidate in the 1997 general election but won a seat in 2002 at the expense of his party colleague, Eddie Wade. Power was 963 votes ahead of Wade on the first count and doubled his lead when Willie O'Dea's surplus was transferred. He is a former solicitor and was a member of Limerick Corporation from 1999 to 2004, having been mayor of Limerick for the year 2002–01. He is chairman of the Joint Oireachtas Committee on Child Protection, established after the statutory rape controversy in the summer of 2006, which published its report in November 2006.

Noreen Ryan is the new Fianna Fáil candidate on this occasion. She has been a member of Limerick County Council for the Castleconnell electoral area since 1999 and polled 1,163 (quota 1,815) in the 2004 local elections. She is a member of the Irish delegation to the Committee of the Regions of the European Union and a former member of the Council of Europe. She played senior camogie for Limerick as full back.

Fine Gael: This is a key Fine Gael target for a gain in this election. It was also a key target in 2002 when their sitting deputy, Michael Noonan, was party leader. The party vote was up marginally at 28% and on the first count Noonan was more than 5,000 votes ahead of Jackman. The latter is not contesting in this election and the party has a new candidate, Kieran O'Donnell.

Michael Noonan was first elected to Dáil Éireann in 1981 and has held the seat on each occasion since. He was leader of the party from February 2001 until he resigned the leadership on the evening of the election count in June 2002. He was Minister for Justice from 1982 to 1986, Minister for Industry and Commerce from 1986 to 1987, Minister for Health from 1994 to 1997 and Minister for Energy from January to March 1997. He was a member of Limerick County Council from 1974 to 1981 and from 1991 to 1994. Michael Noonan is currently chairman of the Dáil Public Accounts Committee. He is a former secondary school teacher.

Kieran O'Donnell is a member of Limerick County Council for the Castleconnell electoral area, where in the 2004 local elections he polled 1,1,63 first preferences. He took the fourth of the seven seats in that election. He is also a member of the Mid-West Regional Authority and Limerick Market Trustees. He is a chartered accountant and lives in Monaleen. He is a nephew of Tom O'Donnell, who was a member of Dáil Éireann for this constituency from 1961 to 1987, and was also a government Minister and a member of the European Parliament.

Labour Party: The outgoing deputy, Jan O'Sullivan, is the party's only candidate in this election. She was an unsuccessful candidate in the Dáil elections of 1992 and 1997 and first won a seat here in the by-election caused by the death of Jim Kemmy in March 1998. She held her seat, although not comfortably, in the 2002 election. She was spokesperson on Equality and Law Reform from 1997 to 2002 and has been the party spokesperson on Education since 2002. O'Sullivan had been a member of the late Jim Kemmy's Limerick-based Democratic Socialist Party and joined Labour when the two parties merged in 1991. She was a member of Seanad Éireann from 1993 to 1997 and was leader of the Labour group in the upper house for that term.

A member of Limerick City Council from 1985 to 2001, she formerly worked as a pre-school teacher.

Progressive Democrats: Councillor Tim O'Malley surprised many by holding onto the party's seat in this constituency. The party founder, Dessie O'Malley, had been a deputy here, from 1969 to 2002, first as a Fianna Fáil TD and then for the Progressive Democrats. Indeed this is the only constituency where the Progressive Democrats had two seats, with Peader Clohessy and O'Malley in place from 1987 to 1997. Although the party's share of the first preference vote was down 2.6%, Tim O'Malley attracted a lot of transfers, particularly from O'Dea's surplus, and he took the fourth seat.

O'Malley is Minister of State at the Department of Health and Children with special responsibility for Disability and Mental Health Service. He was a member of Limerick County Council from 1991 to 2002 for the Bruff electoral area and was the party candidate in the 1998 by-election caused by the death of Labour's Jim Kemmy. In that by-election he got 4,287 first preferences, which was 10% of the vote. O'Malley is a former president of the Irish Pharmaceutical Union and worked previously in the family pharmacy business in Dooradoyle.

Green Party: The party candidate here, Patricia (Trish) Forde Brennan, is a former chair of the National Parents Council and is currently public relations officer for the National Parents Associations for Vocational Schools and Community Colleges. She is also a member of Limerick county vocational educational committee. She was an unsuccessful candidate for Limerick County Council in the 2004 local elections in the Castleconnell electoral area, where she polled 539 first preferences and was eliminated on the seventh count. Originally from Westmeath, she lives in Monaleen. She is a former secondary school teacher.

Sinn Féin: The Sinn Féin candidate is Maurice Quinlivan. In the 2004 local elections Quinlivan was an unsuccessful candidate for Limerick City Council in the Limerick No.1 ward where he polled 568 first preferences when the quota was 1,092. He has served as secretary of the party's Munster executive and was a member of the Sinn Féin Ard Comhairle. Originally from Ballynanty Beg, he now lives in the Thomondgate area of Limerick City. He is the manager of a travel agency.

Others: In 2002 Fine Gael Councillor Pat Kennedy ran as an independent having failed to get a party nomination. Although he never came close to winning a seat, he polled 2,092 first preferences and attracted considerable transfers. His total vote was 3,379, almost a third of which was non transferable. Of the other two-thirds, Fine Gael got just a fifth.

LIMERICK EAST 2007 FIGURES

Candidate	Party	1st Count	2nd Count	3rd Count	4th Count	5th Count	Later counts

YOUR PREDICTION 2007

	Candidate Elected	Party
1		
2		
3		
4		
5		

RESULT 2007

	Candidate Elected	Party
1		
2		
3		
4		
5		

NOTES/UPDATES

LIMERICK EAST 2002 FIGURES

5 seats Quota: 8,334

Candidate	Party	1st	2nd	3rd	4th	5th	6th	7th	8th	9th	10th	11th
Transfer of			O'Dea's surplus	Noonan's surplus	Bennis O Donoghue A.Ryan	Kelly	Hourigan	T.Ryan	Gilligan	Kennedy	Wade	Power's surplus
Willie O'Dea*	FF	13,174	−4,840 8,334	8,334	8,334	8,334	8,334	8,334	8,334	8,334	8,334	8,334
Michael Noonan*	FG	9,451	9,451	−1,117 8,334	8,334	8,334	8,334	8,334	8,334	8,334	8,334	8,334
Peter Power	FF	3,881	+1,957 5838	+41 5879	+90 5969	+38 6007	+73 6080	+173 6253	+172 6425	+426 6851	+2,640 9491	−1,157 8334
Tim O'Malley	PD	4,885	+442 5,327	+88 5,415	+75 5,490	+16 5,506	+125 5,631	+151 5,782	+90 5,872	+452 6,324	+629 6,953	+770 7,723
Jan O Sullivan*	LAB	4,629	+419 5,048	+145 5,193	+62 5,255	+101 5,356	+359 5,715	+212 5,927	+396 6323	+635 6,958	+298 7,256	+211 7,467
Mary Jackman	FG	4,468	+244 4,712	+697 5,409	+88 5,497	+32 5,529	+128 5,657	+185 5,842	+137 5,979	+590 6,569	+417 6,986	+176 7,162
Eddie Wade*	FF	2,918	+1111 4,029	+13 4,042	+42 4,084	+21 4,105	+29 4,134	+132 4,266	+57 4,323	+206 4,529	Elim'd	
Pat Kennedy	IND	2,092	+221 2,313	+53 2,366	+68 2,434	+133 2567	+83 2,650	+190 2,840	+539 3,379	Elim'd		
John Gilligan	IND	1,176	+139 1,315	+18 1,333	+46 1,379	+197 1,576	+104 1,680	+240 1,920	Elim'd			
Tom Ryan	IND	1,148	+121 1,269	+20 1,289	+72 1,361	+44 1,405	+73 1,478	Elim'd				
Timothy Hourigan	GP	917	+53 970	+15 985	+68 1,053	+24 1,077	Elim'd					
Michael Kelly	IND	677	+59 736	+15 751	+13 764	Elim'd						
Nora Bennis	IND	479	+57 536	+9 545	Elim'd							
Conor O'Donoghue	CSP	86	+9 95	+1 96	Elim'd							
Aidan Ryan	IND	19	+8 27	+2 29	Elim'd							
Non-Transferable			0	0	46	158	103	195	529	1,070	545	2,646

LIMERICK WEST

Outgoing Deputies: John Cregan (FF), Michael Collins (FF), Dan Neville (FG).

Michael Collins resigned from the Fianna Fáil parliamentary party in 2003. He is retiring and will not be contesting the 2007 election.

The Constituency: This **three-seater** constituency is within the administrative county of Limerick. In the redrawing of constituencies since 2002, the constituency gained an area around Bruff, Knockainy and Knocklong (2002 population 3,228) from Limerick East.

Party	Votes 2002	Quota 2002	% Vote 2002	% Vote 1997	Swing
Fianna Fáil	19,059	2.1	53.43%	32.44%	20.99%
Fine Gael	14,856	1.7	41.65%	37.19%	4.46%
Labour	–	–	–	4.22%	–4.22%
PDs	–	–	–	4.18%	–4.18%
Green Party	948	0.3	2.66%	–	2.66%
Others	806	0.2	2.26%	21.96	–19.70

2007 Candidates will include: Niall Collins (FF), John Cregan (FF), Michael Finucane (FG), Dan Neville (FG), Michael Brennan (PD).

In Brief: This is a key Fine Gael target for a gain from Fianna Fáil. The party has a strong two-man ticket which is made up of Senator, and former deputy, Michael Finucane and the party's outgoing deputy, Dan Neville. The outgoing deputy, Michael Collins, who resigned the Fianna Fáil whip in 2003, is not contesting, but his nephew, Niall Collins, is running for Fianna Fáil. The party's outgoing deputy, John Cregan, should be the stronger of the party's two candidates, so a Fine Gael gain, if it happens, is likely to be at the expense of the Collins seat.

Fianna Fáil: Party in-fighting cost Fianna Fáil dearly here in 1997. Between 1997 and 2002 the party managed to reintegrate the dissident elements and regained the seat it lost in 1997. The Fianna Fáil newcomer in that 2002 election was John Cregan, who topped the poll with one of the highest personal votes in the country. The outgoing deputy, Michael Collins, also held onto his seat.

Michael Collins was elected to Dáil Éireann on his first attempt in 2002, replacing his brother Gerard who had opted to concentrate on his role as a member of the European Parliament. In 2002 he again polled well, coming in second on the first count, just 682 votes off the quota. He took the second seat comfortably.

John Cregan was elected to Dáil Éireann on his first attempt in 2002. He was elected to Seanad Éireann in a by-election in 1998 and was a member on the Labour panel until 2002. He was a member of Limerick County Council from 1991 to 2004 for the Newcastle West electoral area. He is a former Telecom Éireann employee.

Niall Collins has been a member of Limerick County Council for the Bruff electoral area since 2004. In the 2004 local elections he polled 1,600 first preferences. His uncle, Gerry Collins, was a Minister in various departments, a member of Dáil Éireann from 1967 to 1997 and a member of the European Parliament from 1994 to 2004. Another of his uncles, Michael Collins, was a Dáil deputy from 1997 to 2002. Niall's grandfather, James J Collins, was a member of Dáil Éireann from 1948 to 1967.

In the 2002 election Fianna Fáil's vote increased by almost 21 percentage points on 1997. In fact it was even up considerably on the 47.41% obtained in 1992. In 2002 John Cregan topped the poll with 10,823 first preferences – 1,005 to spare above the quota. He received 30.34% of the first preferences, nearly one in three of all votes cast.

Fine Gael: Fine Gael lost a seat here in 2002 and the competition between their two outgoing deputies, Dan Neville and Michael Finucane, was extremely close. In 2002 the party vote was up 4.5% on 1997 but because of the reintegration of the Fianna Fáil support, Fine Gael was left with just one seat. On the first count Neville and Finucane were only 36 votes apart with Neville ahead, but by the last count Neville was ahead by just one vote.

Michael Finucane was a member of Dáil Éireann from 1989 to 2002. He has been a member of Seanad Éireann since 2002 and is the party's deputy leader in the upper house. He is also vice-chairperson of the Oireachtas All-Party Committee on the Constitution. He was chairman of the Dáil Public Accounts Committee from 2001 to 2002. He was the Fine Gael frontbench spokesperson on Marine and Natural Resources from 1997 to 2001 and on Defence from 2000 to 2001. He has also been the spokesperson on Marine and Natural Resources, Commerce and Technology and Taxation. He was a member of Limerick County Council from 1999 to 2004 for the Newcastle electoral area and was formerly a shipping agency manager.

Deputy Dan Neville was an unsuccessful candidate in the 1987 and 1992 Dáil elections, who was first elected to Dáil Éireann in 1997 and held the seat very narrowly in 2002. Having previously been the party spokesperson on areas such as Health, and Justice and Law Reform, he was appointed deputy spokesperson on Health in June 2002 and has special responsibility for Children and Mental Health. He is Fine Gael's assistant chief whip. Dan Neville was a member of Seanad Éireann on the Labour panel from 1989 to 1997 and a member of the Limerick County Council from 1985 to 2004 for the Rathkeale electoral area. He is a leading campaigner on the issue of suicide prevention.

Labour Party: Former senator Mary Kelly was the party candidate in 1997 and 1992. In 1997 her vote was half that secured in 1992. The party ran no candidate in the 2002 election. As of March 2007, the party has not selected a candidate but will be contesting here.

Progressive Democrats: Senator Michael Brennan, who is based in Adare, is the Progressive Democrats candidate in this election. Michael Brennan was a Fianna Fáil councillor in the Bruff electoral area before he first resigned from Fianna Fáil in 1997. He had failed to get a Fianna Fáil nomination to contest that electioon and instead stood as an independent, polling 3,661 votes. He subsequently rejoined Fianna Fáil in advance of the 2002 election, but did not seek a party nomination for that election. He was nominated by An Taoiseach Bertie Ahern to Seanad Éireann in 2002 and was a member of the Fianna Fáil parliamentary party. However, in the lead-in to the 2004 local elections he resigned from Fianna Fáil because of a row over whether his wife could contest the 2004 local elections, since he, as a senator, could not contest because of the dual mandate ban. Michael Brennan was a member of Limerick County Council for the Bruff electoral area from 1983 to 2004. His wife, Rose Brennan, was elected to Limerick County Council in the Bruff electoral area in the 2004 local election, polling 904 first preferences where the quota was 1,741.

In 1997 the Progressive Democrats' candidate here was Jeanette McDonnell, whose vote, at 7.36%, was a drop of more than 5% on that obtained for the party by their candidate, Seán Liston, in 1992. The party ran no candidate in 2002.

LIMERICK WEST 2007 FIGURES

Candidate	Party	1st Count	2nd Count	3rd Count	4th Count	5th Count	Later counts

YOUR PREDICTION 2007

	Candidate Elected	Party
1		
2		
3		
4		
5		

RESULT 2007

	Candidate Elected	Party
1		
2		
3		
4		
5		

NOTES/UPDATES

LIMERICK WEST 2002 FIGURES

3 Seats   Quota 8,918

Candidate	Party	1st	2nd	3rd	4th
Transfer of			Cregan's surplus	Collins' surplus	Briody MacDomhnaill O'Riordan
John Cregan	**FF**	**10,823**			
Michael Collins*	**FF**	**8,236**	*+1290* **9,526**		
Dan Neville*	**FG**	**7,446**	*+232* **7,678**	*+184* **7,862**	*+702* **8,564**
Michael Finucane	FG	**7,410**	*+274* **7,684**	*+183* **7,867**	*+696* **8,563**
Marcus Briody	GP	**948**	*+54* **1,002**	*+136* **1,138**	*Elim'd*
Mike MacDomhnaill	IND	**662**	*+48* **710**	*+79* **789**	*Elim'd*
Patrick O'Riordan	CSP	**144**	*+7* **151**	*+26* **177**	*Elim'd*
Non-Transferable			0	0	706

*Outgoing Deputy

LONGFORD–WESTMEATH

Outgoing Deputies: Willie Penrose (Lab), Donie Cassidy (FF), Paul McGrath (FG), Peter Kelly (FF), Mae Sexton (PD).

In 2002 Willie Penrose (Lab), Donnie Cassidy (FF) and Paul McGrath (FG) were all elected for the previous Westmeath three-seat constituency, while Peter Kelly (FF) and Mae Sexton (PD) were elected for the previous four-seater Longford-Roscommon constituency.

Paul McGrath (FG) is retiring and is not contesting the 2007 election.

The Constituency: This **four-seat** constituency results from the re-creation of the traditional constituency during the redrawing of constituencies since 2002. It is composed of all of the county of Longford, together with most of the county of Westmeath, except for that more north eastern part, south and east of Castepollard, which has been incorporated into the new Meath West constituency.

2007 Candidates will include: Donie Cassidy (FF), Peter Kelly (FF), Mary O'Rourke (FF), James Bannon (FG), Peter Burke (FG), Nicky McFadden (FG), Willie Penrose (Lab), Mae Sexton (PD), Paul Hogan (SF).

In Brief: This four-seat constituency has re-emerged as a result of the redrawing of constituencies since the last election. Creative tensions within Fianna Fáil will make it the setting for one of the high-profile soap operas of the campaign, with former Fianna Fáil deputy leader Mary O'Rourke in the leading role and likely to win a seat at the expense of her party colleague, Donie Cassidy. The sitting Longford-based Fianna Fáil deputy Peter Kelly is likely to be safe. The constituency is also a crucial marginal between Fine Gael and the Progressive Democrats, with Fine Gael's Longford candidate, Senator Jim Bannon, likely to take Sexton's seat. Much will depend on whether Fine Gael can hold on to their Westmeath-based seat despite the retirement of their outgoing deputy, Paul McGrath. With Longford accounting for only one-third of the vote in this four-seat constituency, there is also the prospect of three seats in Westmeath and only one in Longford. Labour's Willie Parsons will top the poll.

Fianna Fáil: Fianna Fáil suffered a big-name casualty here in 2002, when the party's then deputy leader and outgoing Minister, Mary O'Rourke, lost her seat to her party colleague, Donie Cassidy. The Westmeath three-seat constituency was a key target for a gain for the party in 2002. All that was required was a marginal increase in the party vote and tighter management of the vote share. However, instead of increasing, the party's vote share dropped more than 4%. Furthermore, and against the national trend, the Fine Gael vote was up slightly. As a result, there was only one seat for Fianna Fáil. Crucially, Cassidy was 1,448 votes ahead of O'Rourke on the first count. This gap was reduced over subsequent counts but Cassidy was still 523 votes ahead of O'Rourke on the last count and took the only Fianna Fáil seat. In 2002 the Fianna Fáil TD in Longford, former Taoiseach Albert Reynolds, retired, but his former lieutenant, Peter Kelly, comfortably won the seat. Now that these two counties have been rejoined as a constituency, Kelly will run on the ticket here along with O'Rourke and Cassidy.

Peter Kelly was elected to Dáil Éireann for the first time in 2002. He was a long-time member of the party's national executive and had been a central figure in the Reynolds operation in Longford. He was a member of Longford County Council from 1985 to 2004 for the Longford electoral area and was formerly a publican and undertaker in Longford town.

Donie Cassidy was elected to Dáil Éireann for the first time in 2002, having been a member of Seanad Éireann from April 1982 to June 2002 and leader of that house from 1997 to 2002. He was a member of Westmeath County Council from 1985 to 2004, representing the Coole electoral area, and was chairman of the council for the year 1989–90. He is based in Castlepollard and a large portion of his local political base east of Castlepollard has been redrawn into the new Meath West constituency. He has a variety of business interests in the hotel, property and music industries.

Mary O'Rourke was a Dáil deputy from 1982 to 2002, at first for the original four-seat Longford–Westmeath constituency and then for the three-seat Westmeath constituency. Since she lost her Dáil seat in 2002 she has been a Taoiseach's nominee to Seanad Éireann and leader of the House. She was deputy leader of Fianna Fáil from 1995 to 2002. In the Dáil she was Minister for Education from 1987 to 1991, Minister for Health from 1991 to 1992, Minister of State for Trade and Marketing from 1992 to 1993, Minister of State for Labour Affairs from 1993 to 1994 and Minister for Public Enterprise from 1997 to 2002. She was a member of Westmeath County Council from 1979 to 1987 and was formerly a teacher. O'Rourke is a daughter of PJ Lenihan, deputy for Roscommon from 1965–1970, and a sister of the late Brian Lenihan, formerly a Dáil deputy and Tánaiste. She is the aunt of current Dublin West deputy Brian Lenihan and current Dublin South West deputy Conor Lenihan, both of whom are also contesting this election.

Fine Gael: Given the threat to Fine Gael seats nationwide, Paul McGrath's retention of his seat in this constituency in 2002 was impressive. In 1997 he polled 5,218 votes, which was 16% of the first preference vote. In 2002 he polled 5,570 votes, which was 16.2% of the first preference vote. However, he is not contesting this election.

James Bannon has been a member of Seanad Éireann since 2002 on the Industrial and Commercial panel. He is currently the party's spokesperson on Environment, Local Government and Heritage in the Seanad. He was a member of Longford County Council for the Ballymahon electoral area from 1985 to 2004. Based in Newtown, he is an auctioneer and farmer.

This is Nicky McFadden's second time contesting a Dáil election. In 2002 she polled 3,793 first preferences. She has been a member of Athlone Town Council since 1999. She was co-opted to Westmeath County Council in 2003, taking her father's seat. In 2004 she was elected to Westmeath County Council in the Athlone electoral area, where she topped the poll with 1,901 first preferences, which was 576 votes over the quota. She manages the family pet shop in Athlone.

Peter Burke is a 23-year-old Mullingar-based accountant. He has been a campaign worker for outgoing Longford–Westmeath Fine Gael TD Paul McGrath and in the 2004 local elections was an unsuccessful candidate for Westmeath County Council in the Mullingar West electoral area, where he polled 495 first preference votes.

Labour Party: This is a very good constituency for the Labour Party, primarily because of the phenomenal electoral appeal of their sitting deputy, Willie Penrose. He polled 20% in his first election in 1992, increased that to 25% in 1997 and increased it again in 2002 to 26%. This was Labour's second best vote share in the country, bettered only in Wicklow, where the party had three candidates. Penrose seems now to have a unique possession – a safe Labour seat.

He has been a member of Dáil Éireann since 1992 and is currently the party's spokesperson on Social and Family Affairs. He was the party's spokesperson on Agriculture from 1997 to 2002. He was a member of Westmeath County Council from 1984 to 2002 for the Mullingar electoral area and is a barrister.

Penrose is Labour's single best vote-getter in the country. For this and other reasons he was one of those who the media and commentators short-listed for the party leadership when Ruairi Quinn retired in autumn 2002. However, he decided instead to contest the deputy leadership and was runner-up for that post.

Progressive Democrats: Mae Sexton joined the Progressive Democrats in 1997, having been elected to Longford County Council as an independent in 1991. She was an unsuccessful candidate as an independent in the 1992 general election and as a PD in 1997, although she stood successfully as a PD candidate for Longford County Council in 1999, when her 12.9% vote share saw her elected on the first count. In the 2002 general election she polled 4,679 first preference votes. She had to wait for the transfers of the independent hospital candidate, Una Quinn, to see her home on the tenth count. She is the PD party spokesperson on Regional Development.

Sinn Féin: The party candidate here is 24-year-old Paul Hogan, who was elected to Athlone Town Council in the 2004 local elections.

LONGFORD–WESTMEATH 2007 FIGURES

Candidate	Party	1st Count	2nd Count	3rd Count	4th Count	5th Count	Later counts

YOUR PREDICTION 2007

	Candidate Elected	Party
1		
2		
3		
4		
5		

RESULT 2007

	Candidate Elected	Party
1		
2		
3		
4		
5		

NOTES/UPDATES

LONGFORD–ROSCOMMON 2002 FIGURES

4 seats   Quota: 9,938

Candidate	Party	1st	2nd	3rd	4th	5th	6th	7th	8th	9th	10th
Transfer of			Kilalea Lenehan	Ansbro Baxter	Flanagan	Whelan	Crosby	Connor	Quinn	Naughton's surplus	Belton
Peter Kelly	FF	7,319	+4 / 7323	+11 / 7,334	+73 / 7,407	+227 / 7,634	+238 / 7,872	+33 / 7,905	+75 / 7,980	+25 / 8,005	+1,313 / 9,318
Denis Naughton*	FG	6,660	+26 / 6,686	+36 / 6,722	+199 / 6,921	+155 / 7,076	+355 / 7,431	+2,075 / 9,506	+2,108 / 11,614		
Michael Finneran	FF	6,502	+19 / 6,521	+16 / 6,537	+75 / 6,612	+118 / 6,730	+428 / 7,158	+136 / 7,294	+887 / 8,181	+544 / 8,725	+191 / 8,916
Greg Kelly	FF	6,430	+41 / 6,471	+19 / 6,490	+180 / 6,670	+227 / 6,897	+117 / 7,014	+726 / 7,740	+719 / 8,459	+228 / 8,687	+175 / 8,862
Louise Belton*	FG	4,762	+5 / 4,767	+21 / 4,788	+133 / 4,921	+116 / 5,037	+156 / 5,193	+512 / 5,705	+127 / 5,832	+383 / 6,215	Elim'd
Mae Sexton	PD	4,679	+20 / 4,699	+52 / 4,751	+154 / 4,905	+293 / 5,198	+299 / 5,497	+61 / 5,558	+513 / 6,071	+230 / 6,301	+2,616 / 8,917
John Connor	FG	3,829	+51 / 3,880	+19 / 3,899	+143 / 4,042	+108 / 4,150	+139 / 4,289	Elim'd			
Una Quinn	IND	3,598	+52 / 3,650	+88 / 3,738	+262 / 4,000	+331 / 4,331	+528 / 4,859	+506 / 5,365	Elim'd		
Tom Crosby	IND	2,123	+10 / 2,133	+11 / 2,144	+107 / 2,251	+171 / 2,422	Elim'd				
Paul Whelan	SF	1,673	+13 / 1,686	+16 / 1,702	+170 / 1,872	Elim'd					
Luke Flanagan	IND	779	+11 / 790	+50 / 840	Elim'd						
Hughie Baxter	LAB	638	+2 / 640	+84 / 724	Elim'd						
Catherine Ansbro	GP	426	+9 / 435	Elim'd							
Vincent Killalea	IND	191	Elim'd								
Brian Lenehan	CPS	80	Elim'd								
Non-Transferable			+8	+12	+68	+126	+162	+240	936	266	1,920

*Outgoing Deputy

LOUTH

Outgoing Deputies: Dermot Ahern (FF), Fergus O'Dowd (FG), Séamus Kirk (FF), Arthur Morgan (SF).

The Constituency: This **four-seater** encompasses the administrative county of Louth. The boundaries of this constituency are unchanged since 2002.

Party	Votes 2002	Quota 2002	% Vote 2002	% Vote 1997	Swing
Fianna Fáil	20,751	2.2	43.57%	40.02%	3.56%
Fine Gael	9,635	1.0	20.235	27.90%	−7.66%
Labour	3,185	0.3	6.69%	10.50%	−3.81%
PDs				5.32%	−5.32%
Green Party	1,979	0.2	4.16%	3.12%	1.04%
Sinn Féin	7,121	0.7	14.95%	8.11%	6.84%
Others	4,952	0.5	10.40%	5.04%	5.36%

2007 Candidates will include: Dermot Ahern (FF), Séamus Kirk (FF), Frank Maher (FF), Fergus O'Dowd (FG), Mairead McGuinness (FG), Jim D'Arcy (FG), Gerard Nash (Lab), Arthur Morgan (SF), Mark Dearey (GP), Peter Short (WP), Luke Martin (Ind).

In Brief: At one time, it looked unlikely that there would be any change in this constituency in terms of the distribution of seats between the parties. However, the decision of Mairead McGuinness to declare for the constituency changes things. She may unseat her colleague Fergus O'Dowd or, on a very good day for Fine Gael, her candidature could see them win two seats here. If this happened it would probably be at the expense of Finna Fáil's Séamus Kirk. Sinn Féin's Arthur Morgan is likely to be safe. Meanwhile, the Green Party talk of this constituency as a 'long shot' for them, but it is hard to see that happening.

Fianna Fáil: The Fianna Fáil vote here in 2002 was up more than 3.5% on 1997 and the outgoing deputies, Dermot Ahern and Séamus Kirk, comfortably held their two seats. The third candidate in 2002, Frank Maher, again joins the two incumbents on the ticket for the 2007 election.

Dermot Ahern has been Minister for Foreign Affairs since September 2005. He was Minister for Communication, the Marine and Natural Resources from 2002 to 2004 and Minister for Social, Community and Family Affairs from 1997 to 2002. He was also government chief whip from 1991 to 1992 and party chief whip in opposition from 1995 to 1997. He was first elected to the Dáil in 1987 and has retained his seat on each occasion since then. He lives in the Blackrock area of Dundalk and was a member of Louth County Council 1979–1991. He was co-chairman of the British- Irish Inter-parliamentary Body from 1993 to 1995. His personal vote share dropped from 22.64% in 1997 to 20.2% in 2002, perhaps as a result of vote management efforts, although it may also be attributable to the growth of Sinn Féin in Dundalk.

Séamus Kirk is chairman of the Fianna Fáil parliamentary party. He was first elected to Dáil Éireann in November 1982 and has held his seat in each subsequent election. He was Minister of State at the Department of Agriculture and Food with special responsibility for Horticulture from 1987 to 1992. He was a member of Louth County Council from 1974 to 1985 and is a former inter-county footballer. He was one of the party's two candidates in the East (Lenister) constituency for the 2004 European elections, in which he polled 45,454.

Frank Maher received 4,653 first preferences in the 2002 general election, just under half the quota of 9,525 and doubling the vote of the party's Drogheda-based candidate in 1997. He was elected to Louth County Council for the Drogheda West election area in 2004. He polled 764 first preferences where the quota was 1,417 but took the first of the four seats on the ninth count and was the only candidate to reach the quota. He is a credit manager.

Fine Gael: Fine Gael is making a concerted effort to secure two seats here, having convinced MEP Mairead McGuinness to contest the 2007 general election.

The current sitting TD, Fergus O'Dowd, increased his vote in this constituency by 1% in 2002 from 4,486 votes in 1997 to 5,505 and took the second seat on the ninth count where he secured an impressive 48% (2,435) of Fianna Fáil Frank Maher's available transfers on elimination. He had been a senator from 1997 to 2002 and replaced the retiring Brendan McGahon as Fine Gael's only TD for Louth. He is based in Drogheda and is the party's spokesperson on Environment and Local Government. He was a member of Louth County Council from 1979 to 2003, where he represented the Drogheda West local electoral area. His brother Michael O'Dowd has been a member of Louth County Council for the Dundalk East electoral area since 1999 and interestingly is currently the 'substitute to fill Mairead McGuinness's seat in the European Parliament if she gets elected to Dáil Eireann.

The second Fine Gael candidate in 2002 was Terry Brennan, who polled an impressive 4,130 first preferences and wasn't eliminated. In 2007, O'Dowd is joined by two running mates, Mairead McGuinness and Jim D'Arcy.

Mairead McGuinnes has been a member of the European Parliament since the 2004 European elections, when she spectacularly topped the poll with 114,229 first preferances (quota 113,295). After much speculation about whether and in what constituency she might contest the Dáil election, she declared for the Louth constituency in January 2007. She is a former journalist and broadcaster specialising in agricultural matters.

Jim D'Arcy has been a member of Louth County Council since 1999. He polled 1,349 first preferences in the Dundalk South electoral area (quota 1,515) in the 2004 local elections. A former school principal, he has retired early from his job to concentrate on the election campaign.

Labour Party: Sinn Féin took Labour's seat here in 2002 with Arthur Morgan replacing outgoing Labour deputy Michael Bell. This was Labour's worst performance in a constituency where they had an outgoing deputy contesting. Michael Bell had been a Labour deputy for 20 years. However, in 2002 his vote dropped from 10.50% to 6.69% and he was eliminated on the seventh count.

Labour's candidate in 2007 is Gerard Nash. He is a member of Louth County Council for the Drogheda West electoral area, where he polled 744 first preferences in the 2004 local elections (quota 1,417). He was a mayor of Drogheda in the year 2004/2005. He is a public relations consultant.

Green Party: The Green Party candidate in 2002 was Bernadette Martin, who is based in Port Togher. The party had previously polled just 3.12% and Martin managed to push that up to just 4.16%.

On this occasion the party's candidate is Mark Dearey. Dearey was elected to Dundalk Town Council in the 2004 local elections, where he polled 802 first preferences, representing an 18.46% share of the first preference vote, and took the second seat. In 1994, he was one of three Louth people who took a court action against British Nuclear Fuels Limited (BNFL) to seek an end to reprocessing at Sellafield. This court action is ongoing. He is a former teacher and now owns and manages a bar and music venue in Dundalk.

Sinn Féin: In 1997 the party ran two candidates who together polled just over 8% of the vote. The stronger of the two was Owen Hanratty, who was the second last candidate to be eliminated and at that stage had 3,813 votes.

In 2002 Arthur Morgan was the candidate and nearly doubled the Sinn Féin vote to come in second on the first count. However, he was 2,404 votes short of the quota. Morgan proved more effective at attracting transfers than many of the party's candidates in other parts of the country. On the tenth and final count, he took the last seat without reaching the quota.

Morgan previously contested the 1987 and 1989 Dáil elections. Based in Omeath and formerly a company director in the family fish-processing business, he was a member of Louth County Council from 1999 to 2004, on which he represented the Dundalk-Carlingford electoral area. In 1999 he was the party's European election candidate in the Leinster constituency, where he polled 20,015 first preferences, which helped to raise his profile for the 2002 Dáil contest.

Others: Mary Grehan, the Dundalk GP and anti-Sellafield campaigner, who stood for the Progressive Democrats in 1997, stood as an independent in 2002 and she polled 2,384, close to the 2,395 vote she achieved as a Progressive Democrat candidate previously. She has not as of yet indicated any intention to contest this election.

Peter Short of The Workers' Party contested here in 1992 and 2002 and also ran unsuccessfully on a parental equality platform.

LOUTH 2007 FIGURES

Candidate	Party	1st Count	2nd Count	3rd Count	4th Count	5th Count	Later counts

YOUR PREDICTION 2007

	Candidate Elected	Party
1		
2		
3		
4		
5		

RESULT 2007

	Candidate Elected	Party
1		
2		
3		
4		
5		

NOTES/UPDATES

LOUTH 2002 FIGURES

4 seats   **Quota: 9,525**

Candidate	Party	1st	2nd	3rd	4th	5th	6th	7th	8th
Transfer of			McMahon O Gogain Short Maguire	Bellew Godfrey	Ahern's surplus	Martin	Grehan	Bell	Maher
Dermot Ahern*	FF	**9,603**	**9,603**						
Fergus O Dowd	FG	**5,505**	+35 **5,540**	+146 **5,686**	+2 **5,688**	+410 **6,098**	+248 **6,346**	+1,394 **7,740**	+2,435 **10,175**
Seamus Kirk*	FF	**6,495**	+66 **6,561**	+207 **6,768**	+43 **6,811**	+182 **6,993**	+651 **7644**	+316 **7,960**	2,027 **9,987**
Arthur Morgan	SF	**7,121**	+154 **7,275**	+213 **7,488**	+7 **7,495**	+310 **7805**	+669 **8474**	+518 **8,992**	+485 **9,477**
Terry Brennan	FG	**4,130**	+77 **4,207**	+235 **4,442**	+7 **4,449**	+221 **4,670**	+754 **5,394**	+652 **6,046**	+87 **6,133**
Frank Maher	FF	**4,653**	+15 **4,668**	+139 **4,807**	+4 **4,811**	+135 **4,946**	+72 **5,018**	+625 **5,643**	Elim'd
Michael Bell	LAB	**3,185**	+52 **3,237**	+151 **3,388**	+3 **3,391**	+341 **3,,732**	+385 **4,117**	Elim'd	
Mary Grehan	IND	**2,384**	+112 **2,496**	+525 **3,021**	+9 **3030**	+491 **3,521**	Elim'd		
Bernadette Martin	GP	**1,979**	+130 **2,109**	+197 **2,306**	+3 **2,309**	Elim'd			
Martin Bellew	IND	**1307**	+103 **1,410**	Elim'd					
Frank Godrey	IND	**473**	+29 **502**	Elim'd					
Aidan McMahon	IND	**294**	Elim'd						
Liam Ó Gogain	IND	**239**	Elim'd						
Peter Short	WP	**176**	Elim'd						
Michael Maguire	CSP	**79**	Elim'd						
Non-Transferable			15	99		219	772	612	609

MAYO

Outgoing Deputies: Jerry Cowley (Ind), Michael Ring (FG), Enda Kenny (FG), John Carty (FF), Beverly Flynn (Ind).

Beverly Cooper Flynn (Ind) was elected as a Fianna Fáil candidate in 2002 and was later expelled from the Fianna Fáil party. She is now running as an independent.

The Constituency: This **five-seat** constituency encompasses the administrative county of Mayo. The boundaries of this constituency are unchanged since 2002.

Party	Votes 2002	Quota 2002	% Vote 2002	% Vote 1997	Swing
Fianna Fáil	25,380	2.4	39.98%	42.95%	−2.97%
Fine Gael	23,862	2.3	37.59%	48.75%	−11.16%
PDs	919	0.1	1.45%	–	1.45%
Green Party	669	0.0	1.05%	1.52	−0.46%
Sinn Féin	2,085	0.2	3.28%	–	3.28%
Others	10,565	1.1	16.64%	6.77%	9.87%

2007 Candidates will include: Dara Calleary (FF), John Carty (FF), Frank Chambers (FF), Enda Kenny (FG), John O'Mahony (FG), Michelle Mulherin (FG), Michael Ring (FG), Beverly Flynn (Ind), Jerry Cowley (Ind), Gerry Murray (SF), Harry Barrett (Lab).

In Brief: The outcome in this constituency will be crucial to the issue of government formation and much will depend on whether Fianna Fáil wins one or two seats. Not only is it the constituency of the opposition leader and alternative Taoiseach, it is also a large five-seater with a cast of colourful characters. Among the stories will be whether Beverly Flynn, elected for Fianna Fáil in 2002 but now an independent, can hold onto her seat and, if she does, whether it will be at Fianna Fáil's expense. This is also a key target for a Fine Gael gain. Running with Kenny and the party's other sitting deputy, Michael Ring, will be the former inter-county GAA football manager, John O'Mahony, and councillor Michelle Mulherin. The prospects of the independent Jerry Cowley, prominent in local opposition to the Corrib gas pipeline, will also be of interest.

Fianna Fáil: The party ran four candidates here in 2002 – then Minister of State, Tom Moffatt, Newport-based Senator Frank Chambers, John Carty, an agricultural officer based in Knock, and the other Fianna Fáil outgoing deputy, Beverly Flynn. Flynn was the strongest of the Fianna Fáil candidates on the first count with herself, Moffatt and Carty within 200 votes of each other on the first count, and Chambers 700 votes behind. However, the distribution of both Chambers's and FG's Higgins's votes on elimination favoured Carty and Flynn over Moffatt and both were elected on the tenth count.

With Flynn running as an independent, the Fianna Fáil ticket for 2007 sees Carty and Chambers joined on this occasion by first-time Dáil candidate Dara Calleary. Dara Calleary is a son of the former Dáil deputy Seán Calleary, who represented this constituency from 1973 to 1992 and was a minister of state. Dara is a member of the Fianna Fáil Ard Chomhairle. He sought a nomination for the 2004 local elections to Mayo County Council but was unsuccessful. He lives in Ballina.

John Carty is based in Knock and was elected to Dáil Éireann on his first attempt in 2002. He was a member of Mayo County Council for the Claremorris electoral area from 1999–2004. He was formerly an agricultural officer and farmer.

Frank Chambers was a candidate in the 2002 election when he polled 5,726 (quota 10,581). He was a Taoiseach's nominee to Seanad Éireann from 1997 to 2002. He is an auctioneer and farmer based in Newport. He has been a member of Mayo County Council since 1976. In the 2004 local elections he polled 1,318 (quota 1,663) in the Westport electoral area.

Fine Gael: This constituency saw Fine Gael's best result in the country in 1997; they won 48.75% of the vote and won three out of five seats. They ran the same four candidates in 2002 with each of them well-positioned to attract different geographic support. The colourful Michael Ring, based in Westport, topped the poll and was 1,872 votes off the quota. He was elected on the transfers of the party's fourth candidate, Ernie Caffery, from the Ballina end of the constituency.

In 2002 Fine Gael's vote was down a striking 11% and it was clear from an early stage that Fine Gael was going to lose one of its three seats. However, it wasn't until the eighth count that it became clear whether it would be Enda Kenny or Jim Higgins. It was also obvious that onlookers were watching not just a contest for a Fine Gael seat, but potentially for the Fine Gael leadership. Higgins was eliminated on the ninth count and Kenny went on to win the seat and subsequently the Fine Gael leadership.

The party is again running four candidates in 2007 with the two incumbents being joined by two first-time Dáil candidates – John O'Mahony and Michelle Mulherin.

Enda Kenny has been a Dáil deputy since 1975 when he won a by-election following the death of his father, Henry Kenny, who had been a TD from 1969 to 1975. Enda Kenny has been leader of the party since June 2002 having been an unsuccessful candidate for the party's leadership in January 2001. He was Minister for Tourism and Trade from 1994 to 1997 and was Minister of State at the Departments of Education and Labour with special responsibility for Youth Affairs from February 1986 to March 1987. He was party chief whip from 1992 to 1994 and held a variety of frontbench spokesperson positions in opposition. He was a member of Mayo County Council from 1975 to 1995.

Michael Ring was first elected to Dáil Éireann in the 1994 by-election in the former Mayo West constituency which followed Padraig Flynn's appointment to the European Commission. He has comfortably held his seat since, spectacularly topping the poll in the two subsequent elections. He polled 10,066 (quota 10,310) in 1997 and in 2002 he polled 9,880 (quota 10,581). He was the party spokesperson on Agriculture from 1997 to 2000 and deputy spokesperson on Health from 2000 to 2002. He was the party's frontbench spokerperson on Social and Family Affairs from June 2002 to October 2004. Following a frontbench reshuffle he declined the offer of the post of spokesperson on Marine. Ring was a member of Mayo County Council from 1994 to 2004. He took an unsuccessful challenge to the constitutionality of the ban on the dual mandate in 2004. He is formally an auctioneer.

John O'Mahony is a former inter-county footballer who won All-Ireland football titles playing for Mayo Minors and Under 21s in 1971 and 1974, respectively. He has managed Mayo, Galway and Leitrim county teams. He was appointed manager of the Mayo GAA inter-county football team in 2006, after he had been selected as a canididate by Fine Gael. He is from Kilmovee and is a former teacher.

Michelle Mulherin has been a Mayo county councillor in the Ballina electoral area since the 2004 local elections, where she polled 1,202 first preferances. She has also been a member of Ballina Town Council since 1999. She is a solicitor.

Labour Party: The party's candidate is Harry Barrett who is a primary school teacher based in Castlebar.

Progressive Democrats: Billy Heffron, a Ballina-based auctioneer and agricultural consultant, ran for the party here in 2002 but had a minimal impact, polling just 919 votes.

Sinn Féin: The Sinn Féin candidate here in 2002 was Claremorris-based Vincent Wood, who polled just one-fifth of a quota. In 2007, the party's candidate is Gerry Murray, a councillor in the Swinford area. He was elected to Mayo County Council as a Fianna Fáil candidate on his first attempt in 1999, when he polled 1,255 (quota 1,386). He left Fianna Fáil and joined Sinn Féin and was elected for the latter in the same electoral area in 2002, when he polled 1,782 (quota 1,615).

Others: Beverly Flynn was expelled from the Fianna Fáil party in February 1999 for voting against a motion asking her father to clarify his position on allegations he had received financial contribution. She was readmitted in November 1999 but lost the party whip again in April 2001, although she was not expelled from the party following her libel action against RTÉ. She contested the 2002 election as an official Fianna Fáil candidate. She held her seat but was subsequently expelled again from the parliamentary party and later from the party organisation, so she will contest this election as an independent.

Beverley Flynn has been a member of Dáil Éireann since 1997. She was a runner-up in the 1994 by-election following the appointment of her father, Padraig Flynn, as a European Commissioner. She was a member of Mayo County Council from 1996 to 2004, where she represented the Castlebar electoral area. She was chairperson of the Western Health Board from 1999 to 2000. Pádraig Flynn was a Dáil deputy from 1977 to 1993 and held a number of ministerial portfolios.

The other outgoing independent deputy for this constituency is Jerry Cowley. He ran for election for the first time in 2002 on a western development and health services platform. He polled 8,709 first preferences and took the first seat on the third count. Prominent in the local opposition to the proposed Shell pipeline, he has also been involved in a number of other social projects and organisations. He is a doctor and is based in Mulranny.

MAYO 2007 FIGURES

Candidate	Party	1st Count	2nd Count	3rd Count	4th Count	5th Count	Later counts

YOUR PREDICTION 2007

	Candidate Elected	Party
1		
2		
3		
4		
5		

RESULT 2007

	Candidate Elected	Party
1		
2		
3		
4		
5		

NOTES/UPDATES

MAYO 2002 FIGURES

5 seats Quota: 10,581

Candidate	Party	1st	2nd	3rd	4th	5th	6th	7th	8th	9th	10th
Transfer of			Heffron Crowley King	Holmes	Wood	Caffrey	Cowley's surplus	Ring's surplus	Chambers	Higgins	Kenny's surplus
Jerry Cowley	IND	8,709	+504 9,213	+595 9,808	+765 10,573	+555 11,128	−547				
Michael Ring*	FG	9,880	+165 10.045	+339 10,384	+192 10,576	+331 10,907					
Enda Kenny*	FG	5,834	+120 5,954	+91 6,045	+97 6,142	+336 6,478	+98 6,576	+131 6707	+600 7,307	+4,615 11,922	
John Carty	FF	6,457	+55 6,512	+43 6,555	+201 6,756	+61 6,817	+5 6,822	+2 6,824	+1.460 8,284	+1,247 9,531	+626 10,157
Beverley Cooper Flynn*	FF	6,661	+80 6,741	+145 6,886	+237 7,123	+44 7,167	+11 7,178	+9 7,187	+2,330 9,517	+232 9,749	+161 9,910
Tom Moffat*	FF	6,536	+213 6,749	+143 6,892	+192 7,084	+437 7,521	+140 7,661	+36 7,697	+928 8,625	+253 8,878	+309 9,187
Jim Higgins*	FG	5,858	+113 5,971	+64 6,035	+120 6,155	+678 6,833	+165 6,998	+102 7,100	+120 7,220	Elim'd	
Frank Chambers	FF	5,729	+66 5,792	+253 6,045	+221 6,266	+41 6,307	+8 6,315	+4 6,319	Elim'd		
Ernie Caffrey	FG	2,290	+129 2,419	+67 2,486	+72 2,558	Elim'd					
Vincent Wood	SF	2,085	+96 2,181	+93 2,274	Elim'd						
Michael Holmes	IND	1,754	+119 1,873	Elim'd							
Billy Heffron	PD	919	Elim'd								
Ann Crowley	GP	669	Elim'd								
Thomas King	IND	102	Elim'd								
Non-Transferable			30	40	177	75	120	42	881	873	245

*Outgoing Deputy

191

MEATH EAST

Outgoing Deputies: Mary Wallace (FF), Shane McEntee (FG).

Mary Wallace (FF) was re-elected in 2002 for the previous five-seat Meath constituency.

Shane McEntee (FG) was elected in March 2005 in a by-election in the previous Meath five-seat constituency caused by the resignation of John Bruton (FG), who had been appointed European Union Ambassador to the United States.

The Constituency: This newly created **three-seat** constituency is made up of the eastern part of the administrative county of Meath. It includes the growing urban areas of Ashbourne, Bettystown, Laytown, Dunboyne, Dunshaughlin and Ratoath.

Party	Votes 2002	Quota 2002	% Vote 2002	% Vote 1997	Swing
Fianna Fáil	28,786	2.7	44.92%	41.88%	3.04%
Fine Gael	17,452	1.6	27.23%	36.92%	−9.69%
Labour	2,727	0.3	4.26%	7.93	−3.67%
PDs	–	–	–	2.37%	−237%
Green Party	2,337	0.3	3.65%	1.95%	1.70%
Sinn Féin	6,042	0.6	9.43%	3.53%	5.90%
Others	6,737	0.6	10.51%	5.42%	5.09%

2007 Candidates will include: Mary Wallace (FF), Thomas Byrne (FF), Regina Doherty (FG), Shane McEntee (FG), Dominic Hannigan (Lab), Sirena Campbell (PD), Sean O'Buachalla (GP), Joanne Finnegan (SF), Brian Fitzgerald (Ind).

In Brief: This new three-seat constituency has been carved out of the demographically transformed eastern part of the old Meath five-seater. Minister of State Mary Wallace is likely to hold on to her seat. Although her running mate Tom Byrne has been running an impressive and colourful campaign, there is no real prospect of a second Fianna Fáil seat. Fine Gael's sitting deputy in this area is Shane McEntee, who was elected to John Bruton's old seat in the 2005 by-election, and he too is likely to hold his seat. The Labour candidate, Dominic Hannigan, who did well in the 2005 by-election, is in the frame to win but he could be thwarted in his attempt by the former Labour TD Brian Fitzgerald, who is again running as an independent.

Fianna Fáil: Mary Wallace, who was first elected to Dáil Éireann in the Meath five-seat constituency in 1989, was unsuccessful in 1987, but has held her seat in that constituency in each election since. Wallace has been Minister of State at the Department of Agriculture and Food with special responsibility for Forestry since January 2006. She was previously a Minister of State at the Department of Justice, Equality and Law Reform, with responsibility for Equality and Disabilities from 1997 to 2002. She was a member of Seanad Éireann on the Administrative panel from 1987 to 1989. She is a former chairperson of the party's National Women's Committee. Based in Ratoath, she was a member of Meath County Council from 1982 to 1997 representing the Dunshaughlain electoral area.

Thomas Byrne is a first-time candidate based in the north eastern part of the constituency. He is a practising solicitor in Drogheda. His father, Tommy Byrne, is an independent member of Drogheda Borough Council.

Fine Gael: In the absence of John Bruton, Fine Gael's vote in this county, and especially in the part of the county covered by this constituency, can be expected to be down. However, Shane McEntee has been building his base since the 2005 by-election in which he won the Bruton seat in the five-seat Meath constituency. The party is running two candidates but it is unlikely that it can win a second seat in addition to McEntee's in this new three-seat constituency.

Shane McEntee was first elected to Dáil Éireann in the 2005 by-election. He is also a publican and restaurant owner. He is a former farmer and agricultural sales representative. Based in Nobber, he is active locally in the GAA.

Regina Doherty is based in Ratoath. She is originally from Dublin but has lived in Meath for the last nine years. She previously worked as a sales director for the Horizon Technology Group and now operates her own ICT distribution company with her husband.

Labour Party: The Labour Party organisation in Meath was decimated by the resignation of former deputy Brian Fitzgerald in 1999 in protest at the merger with Democratic Left. In 2002 the combined Labour–Democratic Left vote in the five-seat Meath constituency was down to just 4%. However, the party's prospects, at least in this part of the county, have been transformed because of the good use it made of the opportunity presented by the 2005 Meath by-election. In advance of that by-election the party persuaded independent councillor Dominic Hannigan to join and contest the by-election for the party.

In the 2004 local elections Hannigan polled 908 first preferences as an independent candidate in the Slane local electoral area and took the last of the five seats. In the 2005 by-election Hannigan polled 5,567 first preferences across the county, which was 11% of the vote and put him third on the first count. He is well placed to win a Dáil seat in this constituency, which covers the eastern portion of the county where his by-election vote was strongest. Hannigan runs a home-based business consultancy which provides advice to the health, transport, communications and entertainment sectors. An engineering and finance graduate, he worked in a private engineering consultancy in London for four years before joining Camden Council as a planner in their policy and development team.

Green Party: Fergal O'Byrne, based in Navan, was the party's candidate in the five-seat Meath constituency in 2002, and although he managed to almost double the party's vote he was never in contention. In this three-seater their candidate is Sean Ó Buachalla, a native of Dunboyne who currently works as an Irish translator. This is his first electoral contest but he has been active locally in the Save Tara Campaign.

Progressive Democrats: Sirena Campbell was the party's candidate in the Meath five-seater in the 2005 by-election, in which she polled 2,679 first preferences. She was an unsuccessful candidate in the Slane local electoral area in the 2004 local elections, polling 703 first preferences and being eliminated on the fifth count. She is a native of Julianstown and currently works in Trinity House School in Lusk, which is a secure detention centre for young males aged from 14 to 16 years. She worked previously in England with young people on the streets. She is a member of the party's delegation to the Forum of Europe.

Sinn Féin: The party's candidate in the Meath five-seat constituency, Joe O'Reilly, did very well in the 2002 election. He is running in the Meath West constituency. The party's candidate here in Meath East is Joanne Finnegan, who lives in Bettystown and is an occupational therapist working with the HSE in Coolock.

Others: Brian Fitzgerald was a Labour Party member of Dáil Éireann from 1992 to 1997. In the 1997 election, as Labour's candidate, Fitzgerald polled 3,695 first preferences and in the 2002 election he polled 3,722 first preferences as an independent. The constituency redrawing suits him in that he has a particularly strong base in this part of the county. Based in Kilcock, he has been a member of Meath County Council for the Dunshaughlin electoral area since 1985. In the 2004 local elections Fitzgerald polled 2,001 first preferences and took the second seat. He did not contest the 2005 by-election.

MEATH EAST 2007 FIGURES

Candidate	Party	1st Count	2nd Count	3rd Count	4th Count	5th Count	Later counts

YOUR PREDICTION 2007

	Candidate Elected	Party
1		
2		
3		
4		
5		

RESULT 2007

	Candidate Elected	Party
1		
2		
3		
4		
5		

NOTES/UPDATES

MEATH 2002 FIGURES

5 seats   **Quota: 10,681**

Candidate	Party	1st	2nd	3rd	4th	5th	6th	7th	8th	9th
Transfer of			Dempsey's surplus	Redmond Colwell	O'Brien	Kelly	O'Byrne	Ward	Farrelly	Fitzgerald
Noel Dempsey*	FF	11,534								
Mary Wallace*	FF	8,759	+313 9,072	+32 9,104	+180 9,284	+361 9,645	+362 10,007	+254 10,261	+113 10,374	+1,261 11,635
Johnny Brady*	FF	8,493	+258 8,751	+36 8,787	+46 8,833	+46 8,879	+108 8,987	+123 9,110	+467 9,577	+299 9,876
John Bruton*	FG	7,617	+76 7,693	+32 7,725	+155 7,880	+241 8,121	+333 8,454	+694 9,148	+1,733 10,881	
Joe Reilly	SF	6,042	+51 6,093	+51 6,144	+123 6,267	+118 6,385	+325 6,710	+412 7,122	+226 7,348	+732 8,080
Damien English	FG	5,958	+61 6,019	+52 6,071	+68 6,139	+126 6,265	+374 6,639	+737 7,376	+1,349 8,725	+1,429 10,154
John Farrelly*	FG	3,877	+15 3,892	+11 3,903	+34 3,937	+41 3,978	+74 4,052	+221 4,273	Elim'd	
Brian Fitzgerald	FG	3,722	+29 3,751	+56 3,807	+113 3,920	+185 4,105	+359 4,464	+675 5,139	+119 5,258	Elim'd
Peter Ward	LAB	2,7	+21 2,748	+21 2,769	+75 2,844	+120 2,964	+631 3,595	Elim'd		
Fergal O'Byrne	GP	2.337	+16 2,353	+53 2,406	+224 2,630	+200 2,830	Elim'd			
Tom Kelly	IND	1,373	+7 1,380	+23 1,403	+163 1,566	Elim'd				
Pat O'Brien	IND	1,199	+3 1,202	+42 1,244	1, Elim'd					
Jane Colwell	IND	263	Elim'd							
Michael Redmond	IND	180	Elim'd							
Non-Transferable				37	63	128	264	479	266	1,537

MEATH WEST

> **Outgoing Deputies**: Noel Dempsey (FF), Damien English (FG), John Brady (FF) were all elected for the Meath five-seater constituency in 2002.

> **The Constituency**: This **three-seat** constituency is created by the 2005 redrawing of constituencies. It includes that western portion of the administrative county of Meath not in the Meath East constituency, together with a north eastern section of the county of Westmeath.

Party	Votes 2002	Quota 2002	% Vote 2002	% Vote 1997	Swing
Fianna Fáil	28,786	2.7	44.92%	41.88%	3.04%
Fine Gael	17,452	1.6	27.23%	36.92%	−9.69%
Labour	2,727	0.3	4.26%	7.93%	−3.67%
PDs	–	–	–	2.37%	−237%
Green Party	2,337	0.3	3.65%	1.95%	1.70%
Sinn Féin	6,042	0.6	9.43%	3.53%	5.90%
Others	6,737	0.6	10.51%	5.42%	5.09%

> **2007 Candidates will include**: Noel Dempsey (FF), John Brady (FF), Damien English (FG), Graham Geraghty (FG), Peter Higgins (FG), Brian Collins (Lab), Brian Flanagan (GP), Joe Reilly (SF).

In Brief: This is a new three-seat constituency carved out of the western part of the old Meath five-seat constituency and a small eastern portion of Westmeath. The outcome is likely to be two seats for Fianna Fáil and one for Fine Gael. Fine Gael does have hopes of a second seat and a surprise Sinn Féin gain cannot be ruled out. The two sitting Fianna Fáil deputies, Minister Noel Dempsey and backbencher Johnny Brady, should be safe, although Brady could be vulnerable. Fine Gael is running its young outgoing deputy Damien English, new signing GAA star Graham Geraghty and Trim-based councillor Peter Higgins. However, there is likely to be only one Fine Gael seat here and English should win it.

Fianna Fáil: The party's campaign in the five-seat Meath constituency in 2002 and 1997 was characterised by stringent management of the party's vote. Distinct geographic areas were given to each of the three candidates in which they could canvass and in which party supporters were asked to vote number one for them. Vote management between Dempsey and Brady will also be important on this occasion if the party is to hold its two seats in the Meath West three-seat constituency.

Noel Dempsey was first elected to Dáil Éireann in 1987 and has held the seat in each subsequent election. He was government chief whip from 1992 to 1994 and Minister of State at the Department of An Taoiseach, Defence and Finance. In opposition from 1994 to 1997 he was party spokesperson on the Environment. When Fianna Fáil returned to power he became Minister for the Environment and Local Government from 1997 to 2002 and then Minister for Education and Science from 2002 to 2004. He has been Minister for Communications, Marine and Natural Resources since September 2004. A member of Meath County Council for the Trim electoral area from 1977 to 1992, he is a former national treasurer of Fianna Fáil.

Johnny Brady was first elected to Dáil Éireann in 1997 and was comfortably re-elected in 2002. He was member of Meath County Council from 1974 to 2004 for the Kells electoral area. In the year 1995–96 he was chairman of the county council. He was formerly chairman of the Meath GAA juvenile hurling board for six years and is also a farmer.

Fine Gael: Although the party's vote in the five-seat Meath constituency was down in 2002 from the dizzy heights it reached when John Bruton was Taoiseach, it was still one of Fine Gael's best performances in the country. Meath and Mayo were the only counties where the party won two seats in 2002.

Damien English was elected to Dáil Éireann on his first attempt. He entered local politics in the 1999 local election, when he won a seat on Meath County Council in the Navan electoral area at 21 years of age. In the 2002 general election he polled an impressive 5,958 votes, which was 9.3% of the first preferences. Importantly, he was 2,081 votes ahead of his running mate, John Farrelly. English went on to take the fourth seat without reaching the quota, becoming the youngest deputy in the 29th Dáil.

Fine Gael are also running the inter-county GAA footballer Graham Geraghty, who is based in Athboy. He joined Fine Gael in late 2006. He was captain of the Meath All-Ireland Senior Football Championship winning side in 1999 and also won an All-Ireland Senior Football medal in 1996, an All-Ireland minor medal in 1990 and an all-Ireland U-21 medal in 1993. He has also played for Ireland in the international rules series against Australia and was a GAA All-Star in 1994 and 1999.

The other Fine Gael candidate in Meath West is Peter Higgins, a Trim-based member of Meath County Council, for which he was first elected in 1999 and re-elected in 2004, taking the first and second seats, respectively. A solicitor, he is involved with a number of community development organisations.

Labour Party: The party candidate in 2007 in the five-seat Meath constituency, Peter Ward, polled 2,727 votes. This time the party candidate in this part of Meath is 31-year-old Brian Collins. He was elected to Kells Town Council in the 2004 local elections. Collins is based in Kells itself and works in the Institute of Public Administration in Dublin.

Sinn Féin: Joe Reilly had been building a base for Sinn Féin in the last number of elections in the five-seat Meath constituency and, had the county not been carved into two constituencies, he was likely to have taken a seat in this election. In 1992 he polled just 641 votes, in 1997 this increased to 2,000 votes and in 2002 his vote trebled to 6,042. Reilly proved better at attracting transfers than many Sinn Féin candidates in other parts of the country and at 8,080 votes he was 1,796 behind Fianna Fáil's Johnny Brady for the last seat.

The splitting of Meath into two three-seaters has transformed his prospects because it has split his vote. Reilly has followed the bulk of his base to Meath West, but he is competing here with three strong incumbents. Reilly has been a member of Meath County Council for the Navan local electoral area since 1999. In the 2004 local elections he polled 1,585 first preferences in the county council election and took the second of the seven seats in the Navan electoral area. He is also a member of Navan Town Council.

Green Party: Fergal O'Byrne, based in Navan, was the party's candidate in Meath in 2002 and he managed to almost double the party's vote. This time their candidate in Meath West is Brian Flanagan, whose only previous electoral outing was an unsuccessful attempt to gain a seat on Navan Town Council in 2002.

MEATH WEST 2007 FIGURES

Candidate	Party	1st Count	2nd Count	3rd Count	4th Count	5th Count	Later counts

YOUR PREDICTION 2007

	Candidate Elected	Party
1		
2		
3		
4		
5		

RESULT 2007

	Candidate Elected	Party
1		
2		
3		
4		
5		

NOTES/UPDATES

ROSCOMMON–SOUTH LEITRIM

Outgoing Deputies: Denis Naughten (FG), Michael Finneran (FF), John Ellis (FF).

In 2002 both Denis Naughten and Michael Finneran were elected for the Roscommon three seat constituency while John Ellis (FF) was elected for the four seat Sligo–Leitrim constituency.

The Constituency: This **three-seater** is a new constituency arising from the 2005 constituency redraw and combines all of the administrative county of Roscommon with the south western portion of County Leitrim.

2007 Candidates will include: John Ellis (FF), Michael Finneran (FF), Frank Feighan (FG), Denis Naughten (FG), Hugh Baxter (Lab), Martin Kenny (SF).

In Brief: The redrawing of constituencies since the last election carved South Leitrim in with Roscommon to create this new three-seater. It is now a key marginal between Fianna Fáil and Fine Gael. Since this is the constituency with the larger portion of Leitrim, it is also newsworthy because it is here that it will be decided whether Leitrim has any representative in the next Dáil. That factor is likely to assist Fianna Fáil's John Ellis who is the only outgoing deputy for Leitrim contesting. In Roscommon the two contesting incumbents, Fianna Fáil's Michael Finneran and Fine Gael's Denis Naughten, are likely to be safe although there is an outside chance that Fine Gael's new candidate, Senator Frank Feighan, could unseat Naughten.

Fianna Fáil: The retirement of Sean Doherty in Roscommon and Albert Reynolds in Longford should have put Fianna Fáil on the defensive in the Longford–Roscommon four seat constituency in 2002. However, not only did the party hold a seat in each county but it actually came close to winning two seats in Roscommon. In 2002 the party ran two candidates from the county: Michael Finneran, who was then a senator, and Greg Kelly, who is a doctor based in Castlerea. On the first count the two Fianna Fáil candidates were just 128 votes apart with Finneran in the lead. Although Finneran stayed in the lead across ten counts, the margin was never more than 250 votes. On the final count he had just 54 votes more than Kelly. Finneran is the party's only candidate from Roscommon in this new constituency and his running mate is the outgoing Leitrim deputy, John Ellis.

Michael Finneran was elected to Dáil Éireann on his third attempt in 2002 having also contested the 1992 and 1997 Dáil elections. Based near Ballinasloe, he was a member of Roscommon County Council for the Athlone electoral area from 1979 to 2004. He was a member of Seanad Éireann from 1989 to 2002. He worked previously as a health board officer.

John Ellis was first elected to Dáil Éireann in 1981. He was re-elected in February 1982, lost his seat in November 1982, regained it in 1987 and has been re-elected to Dáil

Éireann at each subsequent election. He is chairman of the Oireachtas committee on Transport. He was a member of Seanad Éireann from 1977 to 1981 and from 1983 to 1987. He is based in Fenagh and is a former member of Leitrim County Council.

Fine Gael: Fine Gael also ran three candidates in the Longford–Roscommon constituency in 2002 and again two of them were from Roscommon. In Roscommon the party's two candidates were John Connor, who had a see-saw career in and out of the Dáil between 1981 and 1997, and Denis Naughten who beat Connor for the Fine Gael Roscommon seat in 1997. In 2002 Connor's vote was down; he polled 5,104 in 1997 but that fell to 3,829 in 2002. Denis Naughten obtained almost precisely the same number of first preferences as he did in 1997, although on a lower poll this represented a percentage increase. The Fine Gael vote constituency wide was down 6 per cent points in 2002 and the party could only take one seat so Naughten was re-elected. This time Naughten is joined on the ticket by Senator Frank Feighan.

Denis Naughten was first elected to Dáil Éireann in 1997, having briefly served as a Senator. He is currently the Fine Gael frontbench spokesperson on Agriculture. He was the party spokesperson on Transport from 2002 to 2004 and party spokesperson on Enterprise, Trade and Employment from 2000 to 2001. He was spokesperson on Youth Affairs, School Transport and Adult Education from 1997 to 2000. He was a member of Roscommon County Council for the Athlone electoral area from 1997 to 2002. His father, Liam Naughten, was a member of Dáil Éireann from 1982 to 1989 and was Cathaoirleach of Seanad Éireann from 1995 to 1996.

Frank Feighan has been a member of Seanad Éireann since 2002 on the Administrative panel. He was a member of Roscommon County Council from 1999 to 2004 for the Boyle electoral area. He is the party's spokesperson on Arts, Sports and Tourism in the Upper House. He is also a newsagent and businessman and is a past president of Boyle Chamber of Commerce.

Labour Party: To date, the party has had no substantial political presence in either Longford or Roscommon. The party's candidates in the 1992 and 1997 election never got more than 700 votes and in 2002 Hugh Baxter got 653 votes when he stood in Longford–Roscommon. He is now the party's candidate in this new constituency. He was the Labour candidate in the North West constituency in the 2004 European election where he polled 13,948 first preferences. On the same day he was an unsuccessful candidate for Roscommon County Council, polling 315 first preferences in the Strokestown electoral area. He is a long time member of the Labour Party national executive with a particular interest in international affairs. He is chairman of Burma Action Ireland.

Progressive Democrats: The party's candidate in the old Longford–Roscommon was Longford-based Mae Sexton. She is contesting in the Longford–Westmeath constituency on this occasion.

Sinn Féin: Martin Kenny is the party's candidate in this newly drawn constituency. He is a member of Leitrim County Council for the Ballinamore electoral area, where he topped the poll with 860 first preferences in the 2004 local elections.

Others: Roscommon based Independent Tom Foxe had a Dáil seat here until 1997.

Una Quinn, representing Roscommon's Hospital Action Committee, polled well in 2002 and was the second last candidate to be eliminated.

ROSCOMMON–SOUTH LEITRIM 2007 FIGURES

Candidate	Party	1st Count	2nd Count	3rd Count	4th Count	5th Count	Later counts

YOUR PREDICTION 2007

	Candidate Elected	Party
1		
2		
3		
4		
5		

RESULT 2007

	Candidate Elected	Party
1		
2		
3		
4		
5		

NOTES/UPDATES

SLIGO-NORTH LEITRIM

Outgoing Deputies: Marian Harkin (Ind), Jimmy Devins (FF), John Perry (FG).

All three of these outgoing deputies were elected for the four-seat Sligo–Leitrim constituency in 2002. John Ellis (FF), who was also elected for the four-seat Sligo–Leitrim constituency in 2002, is contesting in Roscommon–South Leitrim in 2007.

Marian Harkin (Ind) was elected to the European Parliament for the North West constituency in 2004 and she is not contesting the 2007 Dáil election.

The Constituency: This constituency is now a **three-seater**, having being reduced by one seat and in size in the redrawing of constituencies since 2002. It encompasses all of counties Sligo and that part of Leitrim north east of Lough Allen.

Party	Votes 2002	Quota 2002	% Vote 2002	% Vote 1997	Swing
Fianna Fáil	19,086	1.9	38.97%	40.41%	–1.43%
Fine Gael	13,059	1.3	26.67%	36.63%	–9.96%
Labour	2,429	0.2	4.96%	10.86%	–5.90%
PDs	–	–	–	1.65%	–1.65%
Sinn Féin	5,001	0.5	10.21%	7.10%	3.11%
Others	9,396	1.0	19.19%	3.35%	15.84%

2007 Candidates will include: Jim Devins (FF), Eamon Scanlon (FF), Michael Comiskey (FG), Imelda Henry (FG), John Perry (FG), Jim McGarry (Lab), Sean McManus (SF).

In Brief: This three-seat constituency is a geographically reduced version of the former Sligo–Leitrim four-seat constituency. It is a crucial marginal between Fianna Fáil and Fine Gael, especially now that the independent Marian Harkin is not contesting. Both parties will win one seat each, with Jimmy Devins (FF) and John Perry (FG) likely to be safely returned and a battle between Senator Eamon Scanlon (FF) and probably Michael Comiskey (FG) for the final seat.

Fianna Fáil: In the 2002 election in the Sligo–Leitrim four-seat constituency, Fianna Fáil ran one candidate from Leitrim, the outgoing deputy, John Ellis, and two new candidates in Sligo, Ballymote-based auctioneer Eamon Scanlon and Sligo town-based doctor Jimmy Devins. Ellis was re-elected comfortably and Devins took the Sligo seat, which had been held for the party by Mattie Brennan, who retired at the 2002 election. With Ellis now following the bulk of his

Leitrim base into the newly created Roscommon–South Leitrim constituency, Devins and Scanlon are the party's candidates in 2007.

Jimmy Devins was elected to Dáil Éireann for the first time in 2002. He was a member of Sligo County Council from 1991 to 2004, firstly for Drumcliff and then for the Sligo Drumcliff local electoral area. He is also a former member of Sligo Corporation. He is a former chairperson of Sligo Institute of Technology.

This is Eamon Scanlon's second time contesting a Dáil election. In the 2002 election he polled 6,345 first preferences (almost 13% of the total vote). He was subsequently elected to the Seanad on the Agricultural panel. In 1991 and 1999 he was elected to Sligo County Council for the Ballymote electoral area. Eamon Scanlon was a long-time member of the party's National Executive Committee of Fifteen. He is a butcher and an auctioneer.

Fine Gael: The party won just one seat in the four-seat Sligo–Leitrim constituency in 2002, in large part due to the presence of Harkin. The outgoing frontbencher, Gerry Reynolds, who was based in Leitrim, lost his seat.

John Perry was elected for the first time in 1997. He polled an impressive 5,786 first preferences on his first attempt in 1997. In 2002, he was second on the first count with 6,897, although he was still 2,898 votes off the quota. However, intra-Sligo transfers enabled Perry to get over the quota, even though his Fine Gael running mate was never eliminated. He received one-third of the available transfers – a remarkable 2,727 votes – when Fianna Fáil's Eamon Scanlon was eliminated.

Michael Comiskey is the only candidate from the main parties running in this constituency who is from Leitrim. Although based in Newtownmanor, he is just six miles from Sligo town. Prominent in the Irish Farmers' Association, he was a former chairman of the IFA County Leitrim Executive and most recently chairman of the National Hill Farming Committee. He is also a member of County Leitrim Partnership and the county development board.

Imelda Henry has been a member of Sligo county council since 2004, having polled 688 first preferences and taken the fourth of the seven seats in the Sligo Strandhill electoral area. A self-employed businesswoman, she is also a member of the Border Regional Authority and of the committee of the National Women's Council of Ireland. She is also chairperson of Sligo Disability.

Labour Party: In 1992 Declan Bree polled 17% of the vote, but in 1997 this fell to 10.86%, costing him his seat. In 2002 his vote fell a further 5%.

The party's new candidate in 2007 is Jim McGarry. McGarry has been a member of Sligo County Council since 2004. He polled 813 first preferences in the Sligo Strandhill electoral area and took the fifth of the seven seats there. He is currently chairman of the county council. He was also elected to Sligo Corporation. He is chairperson of Shalomar housing for the homeless and secretary of Kazelain, a home for young offenders.

Sinn Féin: Sinn Féin had high hopes for a breakthrough in this constituency in 2002. Sean McManus has been their candidate here for the last number of elections and is again the candidate in 2007. In 1997 he polled 3,208 votes, which was just over 7% of the first preferences. In 2002 his support grew to over 10% and he polled 5,001 first preferences, which was just over half a quota. He attracted less than a fifth of the transfers available from fellow

Sligoman Declan Bree. When McManus himself was eliminated, almost 18% of his votes were non-transferable. Of those that were transferable, Marian Harkin was the main beneficiary, obtaining more than 38% of them. The three Fianna Fáil candidates got 42% altogether and the balance went to the two Fine Gael candidates. His transfers will be important again in this election.

McManus has been a member of Sligo County Council, where he represents the Sligo-Strandhill local electoral area, since 1999. He polled 1,140 first preferences in the 2004 local elections, which was 75 votes over the quota and seven votes off the top of the poll.

Others: In 2002 independent Marian Harkin made the news here, topping the poll and winning a seat at the cost of Fine Gael, but she is not contesting this time, choosing instead to stay in the European Parliament to which she was elected for the North and West constituency in 2004.

SLIGO-NORTH LEITRIM 2007 FIGURES

Candidate	Party	1st Count	2nd Count	3rd Count	4th Count	5th Count	Later counts

YOUR PREDICTION 2007

	Candidate Elected	Party
1		
2		
3		
4		
5		

RESULT 2007

	Candidate Elected	Party
1		
2		
3		
4		
5		

NOTES/UPDATES

SLIGO-LEITRIM 2002 FIGURES

4 seats   Quota: 9, 795

Candidate	Party	1st	2nd	3rd	4th	5th	6th	7th
Transfer of			Lacken Forde McCrea McSharry	Bree	MacManus	Harkin	Scanlon	Devins
Marian Harkin	IND	8,610	+186 8,796	+828 9,624	1773 11,397	1602 9,795	9,795	
Jimmy Devlins	FF	6,307	+120 6,427	+397 6,,824	+767 7591	303 7,894	2,727 10,621	9,795
John Perry*	FG	6,897	+86 6,465	+308 6506	+408 7,282	+224 7,509	+2516 8,499	9,271
John Ellis*	FF	6434	+31 6465	+41 6506	+776 7282	+221 7503	+996 8499	+772 9271
Gerry Reynolds*	FG	6,162	+74 6,236	+202 6,438	+501 6,939	+212 7,151	+152 7,303	+54 7,357
Eamon Scanlon	FF	6,345	+36 6,381	+82 6,463	+393 6,856	+125 6,981	−6,981 Elim'd	
Sean McManus	SF	5,001	+99 5,100	+516 5,616	−5,616 Elim'd			
Declan Bree	LAB	2,429	+101 2,530	−2,530 Elim'd				
Andy McSharry	IND	303	−303 Elim'd					
Martin Forde	IND	203	203 Elim'd					
John Lacken	CP	166	−166 Elim'd					
John McCrea	IND	114	−114 Elim'd					
Non-Transferable			53	156	998	517	590	0

TIPPERARY NORTH

Outgoing Deputies: Michael Lowry (Ind), Máire Hoctor (FF), Michael Smith (FF).

The Constituency: This **three-seat** constituency incorporates the administrative county of Tipperary North Riding and a portion of Tipperary South Riding north of Cashel and Slieveardagh on the east and a small part on the west. The boundaries of this constituency are unchanged since the 2002 election.

Party	Votes 2002	Quota 2002	% Vote 2002	% Vote 1997	Swing
Fianna Fáil	17,475	1.7	42.66%	42.29%	0.37%
Fine Gael	6,101	0.6	14.91%	11.32%	3.59%
Labour	5,537	0.5	13.52%	10.33%	3.19%
PDs	1,446	0.1	3.53%	3.48%	0.05%
Others	10,400	1.0	25.39%	32.59%	−7.20%

2007 Candidates will include: Máire Hoctor (FF), Michael Smith (FF), Michael Lowry (Ind), Noel Coonan (FG), Kathleen O'Meara (Lab), Tony Sherry (PD), Seamus Morris (SF), Jim Ryan (Ind), Michael Lowry (Ind).

In Brief: This is always a weathervane constituency and again Fianna Fáil's second seat will be in jeopardy, not only to a Fine Gael challenge but also to a strong Labour Party candidate. Máire Hoctor will probably be the stronger of the two Fianna Fáil incumbents, so the seat of former Minister Michael Smith may once more be particularly vulnerable. The most likely beneficiary of a Fianna Fáil loss would be Fine Gael's Senator Noel Coonan. Labour, however, has hopes for their candidate, Senator Kathleen O'Meara. On a good day Fianna Fáil could hold its two seats and in that scenario there is an outside possibility that Fine Gael's Coonan could still win a seat at the expense of the independent TD and former Fine Gael minister, Michael Lowry. However, this is unlikely.

Fianna Fáil: In 2002 Fianna Fáil managed their vote well and held its two seats. Former Minister Michael Kennedy retired and, with none of his family anxious to contest, the mantle fell to Nenagh-based secondary school teacher Máire Hoctor, who was selected in early 2001. The party's other candidate, Michael Smith, who was then the outgoing Defence Minister, had a minor upset when he failed to come through the candidate selection convention in 2001. He was subsequently added to the party ticket.

The Fianna Fáil vote improved marginally and, importantly, the two candidates came in close together behind Lowry on the first count, taking the second and third slots. Hoctor had just 423 votes more than Smith. When Kathleen O'Meara went out, almost half of her transfers went to Fianna Fáil and for geographic reasons Hoctor got twice as many of these as Smith. However, Smith safely took the third seat for Fianna Fáil and was more than 650 votes ahead of Fine Gael's Noel Coonan on the last count. Smith and Hoctor are again the party's two candidates in this election.

Máire Hoctor was elected to Dáil Éireann for the first time in 2002 on her first attempt. She was a member of Tipperary County Council for the Nenagh electoral area from 1999 to 2004. She was also a member of Nenagh Town Council from 1994 to 2004.

Michael Smith was first elected to Dáil Éireann in 1969. He lost his seat in 1973, regained it in 1979 and held it in November 1981. He lost the seat again in February 1982, failed to regain it in November 1982 but won it back again in 1987 and has held it in each subsequent election. He was Minister of State at the Department of Energy from 1980 to 1981, Minister for Energy from 1988 to 1989, Minister of State at Industry and Commerce from 1989 to 1991, Minister for the Environment from 1992 to 1994, Minister of State at the Department of Enterprise, Trade and Employment and at the Department of Education from July to October 1997 and Minister for Defence from June 2002 to September 2004. He was a member of Seanad Éireann from 1982 to 1987 and a member of Tipperary County Council from 1986 to 1987.

Fine Gael: The party has had no seat here since Michael Lowry resigned from the party in 1997. However, in 2002 the party improved its vote share in this constituency against the national trend. It was up 3.5% and their candidate Noel Coonan came very close to winning a seat. Coonan is again the party's only candidate in the 2007 election.

Noel Coonan is based at the Roscrea end of the constituency. He was a member of Tipperary North County Council from 1991 to 2004 for the Templemore electoral area. He was elected to Seanad Éireann on the Cultural and Educational panel in 2002 and he is the party's spokesperson on Agriculture and Food in the upper house. He is also a former member of Templemore Town Council and the Mid Western Health Board.

Labour Party: This constituency is a key target for Labour Senator Kathleen O'Meara, who is again the candidate.

Although in 2002 she improved the party's vote on what had been achieved in 1997, she was still 559 behind the Fine Gael candidate when she was eliminated on the second count. It was O'Meara's transfers which decided whether Fianna Fáil or Fine Gael would win the last seat and, interestingly, these broke down almost evenly between Fianna Fáil and Fine Gael. The internal 'rainbow' transfer rate was considerably lower than in other constituencies. This makes this one of those constituencies where a formalised pre-election transfer pact between Fine Gael and Labour will have an impact on whether the 'Rainbow' can take a seat from Fianna Fáil. O'Meara has been a member of Seanad Éireann since 1997. She is currently the party's spokesperson on Children. She was a member of Tipperary North County Council for the Nenagh local electoral area from 1999 to 2004. She formerly worked as a journalist.

Progressive Democrats: Bill Dwan was the party's new candidate in this constituency in 2002. A businessman who owns and runs a pub and a number of pharmacies in the Thurles area, and a former chairman of the local chamber of commerce, he made no real impact although he held the party's vote share. This time around their candidate is Tony Sherry.

Sinn Fein: Seamus Morris has been selected as Sinn Féin candidate for Tipperary North. He was elected to Nenagh Town Council in the 2004 local election.

Others: The independent deputy Michael Lowry again topped the poll in 2002 although his vote was down from 11,638 first preferences in 1997 to 10,400 first preferences in 2002. This represented a four percentage point drop. Michael Lowry was first elected to Dáil Éireann in 1987 as a Fine Gael deputy and has held the seat in each election since. He was appointed Minister for Transport, Energy and Communications in 1994 but resigned in controversial circumstances in November 1996. He resigned from the Fine Gael parliamentary party in 1997. He is a former chairman of the Tipperary county board of the Gaelic Athletic Association. Lowry was a member of Tipperary North County Council from 1979 to 1995. He was re-elected to the council in the 1999 local elections in the Thurles local electoral area, receiving more than 2.5 quotas. He had to resign from the council because of the dual mandate ban in 2004. However, his 27-year-old son, Michael Junior, topped the poll in the Thurles electoral area with 1,671 first preferences.

Councillor Jim Ryan is an independent member of Tipperary North Riding County Council for the Thurles local electoral area and of Thurles Town Council. He was first elected to the Town Council in the 1999 local elections as a Fianna Fáil member. He left the party in 2004 and contested the local elections as an independent having failed to secure a nomination to contest the County Council elections. He was re-elected to Thurles Town Council and won a seat on the County Council as an independent.

TIPPERARY NORTH 2007 FIGURES

Candidate	Party	1st Count	2nd Count	3rd Count	4th Count	5th Count	Later counts

YOUR PREDICTION 2007

	Candidate Elected	Party
1		
2		
3		
4		
5		

RESULT 2007

	Candidate Elected	Party
1		
2		
3		
4		
5		

NOTES/UPDATES

TIPPERARY NORTH 2002 FIGURES

3 Seats			**Quota: 10,242**		
Candidate	Party	1st	2nd	3rd	4th
Transfer of			Dwan	O'Meara	Hoctor's surplua
Michael Lowry*	IND	**10,400**			
Maire Hoctor	FF	**8,949**	*+371* **9,320**	*+1,720* **11,040**	
Michael Smith*	FF	**8,526**	*+316* **8,842**	*+800* **9,642**	*+446* **10,088**
Noel Coonan	FG	**6.108**	*+328* **6,436**	*+2,649* **9,085**	*+352* **9,437**
Kathleen O'Meara	LAB	**5,537**	**5,877**	*Elim'd*	
Bill Dwan	PD	**1,446**	*Elim'd*		
Non-Transferable			91	708	0

*Outgoing Deputy

TIPPERARY SOUTH

Outgoing Deputies: Tom Hayes (FG), Noel Davern (FF), Seamus Healy (Ind).

Noel Davern (FF) is retiring and will not contest the 2007 election.

The Constituency: This **three-seat** constituency includes most of the administrative county of Tipperary South Riding and also includes a portion of west Waterford. The sections of Tipperary South Riding which are in Tipperary North constituency are specified in that constituency profile. The boundaries of this constituency are unchanged since 2002.

Party	Votes 2002	Quota 2002	% Vote 2002	% Vote 1997	Swing
Fianna Fáil	14,121	1.5	38.51%	37.28%	1.23%
Fine Gael	8,997	1.0	24.54%	24.09%	0.45%
Labour	3,353	0.4	9.14%	16.11%	−6.97%
Sinn Féin	1,210	0.1	3.30%		3.30%
Others	8,985	1.0	24.50%	22.51%	1.99%

2007 Candidates will include: Martin Mansergh (FF), Mattie McGrath (FF), Siobhan Ambrose (FF), Tom Hayes (FG), Phil Prendergast (Lab), Richie Molloy (PD), Peadar O'Donnell (PD), Liam Browne (SF), Seamus Healy (Ind).

In Brief: No change between the parties is likely to be the outcome here. This time the Fianna Fáil ticket is without the long-time TD Noel Davern, who is retiring. The party should hold its seat however. Senator and former advisor to a number of Taoisigh, Martin Mansergh, is more likely to be elected to Dáil Éireann than his two running mates. Labour hopes, perhaps overly optimistically, to take the seat of independent socialist Seamus Healy with their new signing Phil Prendergast, formerly of Healy's organisation. Fine Gael's Tom Hayes should be comfortably re-elected.

Fianna Fáil: In 2002, the party maintained the 1.5 quotas it achieved in 1997. The party had two bad by-elections during the currency of the previous Dáil which saw the Fianna Fáil candidates eliminated on each occasion. While the sitting TD Noel Davern's personal vote was down slightly, his running mate Martin Mansergh polled over half a quota, bringing the overall party vote back up. On this occasion Davern is not contesting and Mansergh is joined by two new running mates.

Based in the Tipperary town end of the constituency, Mansergh previously worked as special advisor to a number of Fianna Fáil leaders both in government and in opposition. While he was never in contention for a seat in 2002, he still made an impact in the constituency and secured over half a quota on the first count. A farmer in whatever time he can call his own, he was subsequently elected to the Seanad on the Agricultural panel and is also the author of a number of books.

Also running for Fianna Fáil on this occasion is Mattie McGrath. He has been a member of Tipperary South Riding County Council for the Cahir electoral area since 1999. He topped the poll in 2004 with 1,902 votes, some 600 votes in excess of the quota. He had previously been a councillor from 1990 to 1991. He owns and runs a plant hire company in Clonmel.

The other Fianna Fáil candidate is Siobhan Ambrose. Ambrose is from Clonmel, where she was elected to the Town Council in 2004. She was the Munster's Ógra Fianna Fáil representative on the party's National Executive from 2000 to 2001 She is a daughter of former senator Tom Ambrose, who is a currently a member of Tipperary South Riding County Council for the Clonmel electoral area.

Fine Gael: Tipperary South was one of just eight constituencies in the country which did not see a decline in the Fine Gael vote in 2002. The party ran one candidate, Tom Hayes. He had contested the two by-elections in 2000 and 2001, respectively, securing the vacant seat in the latter.

A farmer based in Golden, he held his seat comfortably in the 2002 general election coming in some 170 votes below the quota on the first count. He is currently the party's spokesperson on the Environment with special responsibility for Heritage and Rural Affairs. He has also been chairman of the Fine Gael parliamentary party since 2002. Hayes was first elected to Tippearary South Riding County Council in 1991. He was a member of Seanad Éireann from 1997 until his election to the Dáil in 2001.

Labour Party: It could be said that Seamus Healy, the left-wing independent, now effectively holds the traditional Labour seat last held here by the late Michael Ferris. Labour's by-election performances in 2000 and 2001 were poor. Denis Landy, who contested the second by-election, was the general election candidate in 2002 and polled just 3,353, less than half a quota. Labour has hopes of regaining their traditional seat and has recruited a former member of Healy's organisation, Phil Prendergast, to run for the party on this occasion.

As a member of the Workers and Unemployed Action Group, she was elected to Clonmel Corporation in 1994 and Tipperary South Riding County Council in 1999. She topped the poll in the Clonmel electoral area in 2004 local election. She was Mayor of Clonmel in 2003–2004. In the Tipperary South by-election in 2002 Prendergast was the candidate for the Healy led organisation and she polled 7,897 first preference votes and was eliminated on the third count. She joined the Labour Party in June 2005. She works as a midwife.

Progressive Democrats: The PDs did not contest the general election here in 2002 or 1997. It ran just two candidates for election to the county council in 2004, both of whom polled poorly, each securing less than one-fifth of the quota in their respective electoral areas. On this occasion they are running two candidates, Peadar O'Donnell and Richie Molloy, neither of whom contested the council elections in 2004.

Sinn Féin: The party's candidate is 34-year-old Liam Browne. Browne is from Cashel, where his father Michael is a member of the Town Council. In 2004, he contested the local elections in the Clonmel electoral area, polled 450 votes and was eliminated on the second count. He works in the pharmacuetical industry.

Others: Seamus Healy of the Clonmel Workers and Unemployed Action Group has held a seat in this constituency since his dramatic by-election victory in 2000. He has steadily increased his vote over the course of five general elections and polled 7,350 first preferences in 2002, representing 20% of the vote. He was previously a member of both Tipperary County Council and Clonmel Borough Council.

Tom Wood, a former Fine Gael councillor who resigned from the party in January 2002, ran as an independent here in the 2002 Dáil election but his contesting did not have any real impact on the Fine Gael vote.

TIPPERARY SOUTH 2007 FIGURES

Candidate	Party	1st Count	2nd Count	3rd Count	4th Count	5th Count	Later counts

YOUR PREDICTION 2007

	Candidate Elected	Party
1		
2		
3		
4		
5		

RESULT 2007

	Candidate Elected	Party
1		
2		
3		
4		
5		

NOTES/UPDATES

TIPPERARY SOUTH 2002 FIGURES

3 seats   **Quota: 9,167**

Candidate	Party	1st	2nd	3rd
Transfer of			Ó Súilleabháin Larkin	Landy Woods
Tom Hayes*	FG	**8,997**	*−136* **9,133**	*+1,591* **10,724**
Noel Davern*	FF	**8,888**	*+197* **9,085**	*+944* **10,029**
Seamus Healy*	IND	**7,350**	*+415* **7,765**	*+1,712* **9,477**
Martin Mansergh	FF	**5,233**	*+200* **5,433**	*+455* **5,888**
Denis Landy	LAB	**3,353**	*+202* **3,555**	*Elim'd*
Tom Wood	IND	**1,515**	*+116* **1,631**	*Elim'd*
Muiris Ó Súilleabháin	SF	**1,210**	*Elim'd*	
Michael Larkin	CSP	**120**	*Elim'd*	
Non-Transferable			64	484

*Outgoing Deputy

WATERFORD

Outgoing Deputies: Martin Cullen (FF), John Deasy (FG), Ollie Wilkinson (FF), Brian O'Shea (Lab).

The Constituency: This **four-seater** encompasses the city of Waterford and the administrative county of Waterford, except for a small part of the county which is in the constituency of Tipperary South. The boundaries of this constituency are unchanged since 2002.

Party	Votes 2002	Quota 2002	% Vote 2002	% Vote 1997	Swing
Fianna Fáil	21,576	2.3	46.34%	35.79%	10.55%
Fine Gael	10,003	1.1	21.48%	24.55%	−3.07%
Labour	6,219	0.7	13.36%	11.77%	1.59%
PDs	2,137	0.2	4.59%	6.46%	−1.88%
Green Party	1,361	0.1	2.92%	1.81%	1.12%
Sinn Féin	2,955	0.3	6.35%	–	6.35%
Others	2,312	0.2	4.97%	19.29%	14.32%

2007 Candidates will include: Martin Cullen (FF), Brendan Kenneally (FF), Ollie Wilkinson (FF), Paudie Coffey (FG), Jim D'Arcy (FG), John Deasy (FG), Brian O'Shea (Lab), Brendan McCann (GP), David Cullinane (SF), John Halligan (WP), Mary Roche (Ind).

In Brief: There will probably be no change in the two Fianna Fáil, one Fine Gael and one Labour breakdown of the seats in this constituency, although there is an outside chance of a Sinn Féin gain here. Their candidate, David Cullinane, has been strengthened by his strong performance in the 2004 European elections. A Sinn Féin gain, if it happens, is likely to be at the expense of Fianna Fáil or Labour. Within Fianna Fáil, Ollie Wilkinson could be vulnerable to a challenge from his running mate, the former deputy Brendan Kenneally. Fine Gael speaks of the prospect of a gain here, but that is extremely unlikely. Although there is talk locally of intense tensions within the Fine Gael ticket, the sitting deputy, John Deasy, is again likely to be the strongest contender to win Fine Gael's one seat. Labour's Brian O'Shea should also hold his seat.

Fianna Fáil: The Fianna Fáil ticket in this constituency is the same as it was in the 1997 and 2002 elections: namely, the incumbents, Minister Martin Cullen, backbencher Ollie Wilkinson and the former deputy Brendan Kenneally. In 2002 Martin Cullen, then a Minister of State, and

Brendan Kenneally were the party's two outgoing deputies but Wilkinson was more than 1,500 votes ahead of Kenneally on the first count and was still more than 1,000 votes ahead of him on the last.

Martin Cullen was first elected to Dáil Éireann in 1987 as a Progressive Democrats deputy. He lost his seat in 1989 but regained it in 1992. During the 29th Dáil he joined Fianna Fáil and was re-elected as a Fianna Fáil TD in 1997 and 2002. He has been Minister for Transport since September 2004. He was Minister of State at the Department of Finance with special responsibility for the Office of Public Works from 1997 to 2002 and Minister for the Environment from 2002 to 2004. He was a Taoiseach's nominee to Seanad Éireann from 1989 to 1992. Cullen was a member of Waterford City Council from 1991 to 1997 and was Mayor of Waterford for the year 1993–94.

Ollie Wilkinson was elected to Dáil Éireann on his second attempt in 2002. He was a member of Waterford County Council for the Lismore electoral area from 1985 to 2004 and was chairman of the county council for the year 2000 to 2001. He polled 4,707 first preferences in 1997 and 7,312 first preferences in 2002.

Brendan Kenneally, who is based in Waterford city, was a member of Dáil Éireann from 1989 to 2002 and was Minister of State at the Department of Tourism, Transport and Communications from 1992 to 1993. He was a member of Waterford Corporation from 1985 to 1992 and Mayor of Waterford for the year 1988–89. Kenneally has been a Taoiseach's nominee to Seanad Éireann since 2002. His father, Billy Kenneally, was a member of Dáil Éireann from 1965 to 1982 and his grandfather, William Kenneally, was a TD from 1952 to 1961.

Fine Gael: Perhaps inevitably, given the national trend and the retirement of Austin Deasy, the Fine Gael vote was down in Waterford in 2002. However, the party held its one seat comfortably. They ran two candidates and the former deputy's son, John Deasy, polled almost the same first preference vote as his father did in 1997 to win a seat comfortably. The party's second candidate in both 1997 and 2002 was Waterford city councillor Maurice Cummins. Cummins is a member of Seanad Éireann on the Labour panel but is not contesting the 2007 election. This time the party is running three candidates, Paudie Coffey, Jim D'Arcy and the outgoing deputy John Deasy.

Deasy was elected to Dáil Éireann on his first attempt in 2002. He was appointed the party's spokesperson on Justice, Equality and Law Reform by the new party leader, Enda Kenny, but was removed from that frontbench position in April 2004 after a controversy about a breach of the smoking ban in the Dáil bar. He is chair of the Joint Oireachtas Committee on European Affairs. He worked previously as a legislative assistant in the United State Senate from 1990 to 1991 and in the United State House of Representatives from 1993 to 1995. He was a member of Waterford County Council for the Dungarvan electoral area from 1999 to 2004.

Paudie Coffey has been a member of Waterford County Council since 1999. In the 2004 local elections he polled 831 first preferences in the Suir electoral area, where he took the last of the three seats. He is whip of the Fine Gael group on the council, chairman of Waterford County Development Board and chairman of the Strategic Policy Committee on Housing and Emergency Services

Jim D'Arcy is a member of Waterford City Council. In the 2004 local election he ran in the No.2 ward where he polled 604 first preferences, which was just over half a quota, to take the last of the five seats.

Labour Party: The party's sole candidate in this constituency is their outgoing deputy, Brian O'Shea. O'Shea was first elected to Dáil Éireann in 1989 and has held the seat since. He has been the party's spokesperson on Community, Rural and Gaeltacht Affairs since November 2002. He was a Minister of State at the Department of Agriculture with responsibility for Food and Horticulture from 1993 to 1994, was Minister of State at the Department of Health with special responsibility for Mental Handicap and Public Health and Food Safety from 1994 to 1997 and was spokesperson on Arts, Heritage, Gaeltacht, the Islands and Sport from 1997 to 2002. From 1987 to 1989 he was a member of Seanad Éireann. O'Shea was a member of Waterford County Council representing the Tramore electoral area from 1985 to 1993, a member of Waterford City Council from 1985 to 1993 and a member of Tramore Town Council from 1979 to 1993.

Green Party: Waterford city-based Brendan McCann is again the party's candidate in this constituency. In 1997 he polled just 1.8% of the first preferences and in 2002 he increased his vote to 2.92%. This was still a relatively low vote in what might be expected to be more fertile ground for the Greens.

Sinn Féin: 35-year-old David Cullinane is again the party's candidate in this election. In the 2002 election he polled 2,955 first preferences and was eliminated on the seventh and last count. He has since been elected to Waterford City Council representing the No.3 ward where he polled 1,109, well above the quota of 861. He formerly worked in the motor trade.

Others: John Halligan is again running for the Workers Party in this constituency. He polled 1,270 first preferences in 2002, which was the first time he contested a Dáil election. He is a member of Waterford City Council. In the 2004 local elections he topped the poll in the No.3 ward, where he polled 1,123 first preferences.

Mary Roche was originally elected to Waterford City Council for the Waterford No.2 ward on the Fianna Fáil ticket but resigned from the party in 2003 over the failure to provide radiotherapy in Waterford. A former president of the student's union at Waterford Institute of Technology, she is also campaigning for the provision of a university for the South East.

WATERFORD 2007 FIGURES

Candidate	Party	1st Count	2nd Count	3rd Count	4th Count	5th Count	Later counts

YOUR PREDICTION 2007

	Candidate Elected	Party
1		
2		
3		
4		
5		

RESULT 2007

	Candidate Elected	Party
1		
2		
3		
4		
5		

NOTES/UPDATES

WATERFORD 2002 FIGURES

4 seats   **Quota: 9,313**

Candidate	Party	1st	2nd	3rd	4th	5th	6th	7th
Transfer of			Waters Kelly Halpin Walshe	Halligan	McCann	Flynn	Cummins	Cullinane
Martin Cullen*	FF	8,529	+77 8,606	+128 8,734	+120 8,854	+578 9,432		
Ollie Wilkinson	FF	7,312	+55 7,367	+16 7,383	+60 7,443	+192 7,635	+88 7,723	+481 8,204
John Deasy	FG	7,204	+99 7,303	+60 7,363	+218 7,581	+537 8,118	+1,880 9,998	
Brian O Shea*	LAB	6,219	+145 6,364	+285 6,649	+533 7,182	+467 7,649	+667 8,316	+1,208 9,524
Brendan Kenneally*	FF	5,735	+45 5,780	+140 5,920	+49 5,969	+196 6,165	+260 6,425	+692 7,117
David Cullinane	SF	2,955	+135 3,090	+320 3,410	+175 3,585	+129 3,714	+157 3,871	Elim'd
Maurice Cummins	FG	2,799	+63 2,862	+147 3,009	+112 3,121	+220 3,341	Elim'd	
Michael Flynn	PD	2,137	+50 2,187	+64 2,251	+213 2,464	Elim'd		
Brendan McMahon	GP	1,361	+172 1,533	+113 1,646	Elim'd			
John Halligan	WP	1,270	+128 1,398	Elim'd				
Declan Waters	CSP	335	Elim'd					
Jimmy Kelly	SWP	300	Elim'd					
Conor Halpin	IND	289	Elim'd					
Eddie Walsh	IND	118	Elim'd					
Non-Transferable			55	16	60	192	88	481

WEXFORD

The Constituency: This **five-seater** coincides with the administrative county of Wexford. The four key towns are, from north to south, Gorey, Enniscorthy, Wexford and New Ross. The boundaries of this constituency are unchanged since 2002.

Party	Votes 2002	Quota 2002	% Vote 2002	% Vote 1997	Swing
Fianna Fáil	24,226	2.4	40.09%	38.95%	1.15
Fine Gael	15,552	1.5	25.74%	38.58%	−12.84
Labour	7,995	0.8	13.23%	17.08%	−6.46%
Green Party	–	–	–	1.68%	−1.68%
Sinn Féin	4,964	0.5	8.22%	–	8.22%
Others	7,686	0.8	12.72	1.11%	11.61%

2007 Candidates will include: John Browne (FF), Sean Connick (FF), Lisa McDonald (FF), Michael D'Arcy (FG), Paul Kehoe (FG), Liam Twomey (FG), Brendan Howlin (Lab), Colm O'Gorman (PD), John Dwyer (SF).

In Brief: One of the sitting deputies, Fianna Fáil's Tony Dempsey, is retiring and another of the sitting deputies, Liam Twomey, who was elected as an independent in 2002, is contesting this time for Fine Gael. The published and unpublished poll data suggests that Fianna Fáil will get two seats, with Minister of State John Browne almost certain to top the poll and the party's New Ross-based candidate Sean Connick likely to be stronger than their Wexford-based candidate, Lisa McDonald. The Labour Party's current deputy, Brendan Howlin, should also be safe. Fine Gael are certain of one seat, with Paul Kehoe likely to be the strongest of its three candidates. If the party wins a second seat it could be a close contest for Liam Twomey and the party's new Gorey-based candidate, Michael D'Arcy. There will also be much interest in how the Progressive Democrats' new candidate, Colm O'Gorman, does. If there is an upset in this constituency, however, it will come from Sinn Féin's John Dwyer, who did very well in 1997 and cannot be ruled out of contention in this election.

Fianna Fáil: This was a key Fianna Fáil target for a gain in 2002 but, notwithstanding a meltdown in the Fine Gael vote, the Fianna Fáil vote only went up 1%. In 1992 the party polled 43%, which fell to almost 39% in 1997 and rose to just over 40% in 2002. In both 1997 and 2002 Fianna Fáil's John Browne topped the poll but newcomer Tony Dempsey replaced the other sitting deputy, Hugh Byrne, in 2002. Dempsey is not contesting the 2007 election so Browne has two new running mates.

John Browne was elected to Dáil Éireann in November 1982 on his first attempt and has held the seat in each subsequent election. He is currently Minister of State at the Department of Communications, Marine and Natural Resources with special responsibility for Marine matters. He was previously a Minister of State at the Department of Agriculture from 1992 to 1993, at the Department of the Environment from 1993 to 1994 and at the Department of Agriculture from 2002 to 2004. He was assistant party chief whip from 1982 to 1987.

Sean Connick has been a member of Wexford County Council since 2004. He topped the poll in the New Ross electoral area in the 2004 local elections with 1,914 first preferences. He has also been a member of New Ross Town Council since 1999. He is a businessman based in New Ross town and is a wheelchair user.

Lisa McDonald has also been a member of Wexford County Council since 2004. She polled 1,392 first preferences in the 2004 local elections and took the third of the seven seats in the Wexford electoral area. She is a solicitor and was a high-profile member of Fianna Fáil's National Executive Committee of 15.

Fine Gael: Fine Gael's vote fell by one-third here between 1997 and 2002. The retirement of their outgoing deputy, Ivan Yates, and confusion in their candidate strategy in the lead-in to the election, arising from uncertainty as to whether the MEP Avril Doyle would contest, contributed to this vote collapse. The then sitting deputy, Michael D'Arcy (Senior), suffered a particularly dramatic collapse in his vote and he lost his seat. The party's newcomer, Paul Kehoe, took the only seat the party won in that election.

Paul Kehoe is currently Fine Gael's chief whip. He was previously deputy spokesperson on Communications, Marine and Natural Resources. He is a former national chairman of Macra Na Feirme and a former youth officer with Wexford Gaelic Athletic Association. Kehoe is based in Bree near Enniscorthy and is a farmer. In the 2002 election he polled over 7,048 first preferences, which was more than 2,500 ahead of the outgoing deputy Michael D'Arcy and more than 3,000 ahead of the MEP and former deputy Avril Doyle.

Liam Twomey was elected to Dáil Éireann as an independent candidate in 2002 and his win then was at the ultimate expense of Fine Gael, whose vote collapsed. In 2002 his campaign focused in the main on health issues and in particular on the level of service in Wexford General Hospital. He joined Fine Gael in 2003 and was immediately appointed by Enda Kenny to be the party's spokesperson on Health. Based in Rosslare, he is also a family doctor.

Fine Gael's new candidate is Michael D'Arcy. Based in Gorey, D'Arcy was elected to Wexford County Council in 2004, when he topped the poll with 1,952 first preferences in the Gorey electoral area. He is a farmer and has been an apprentice solicitor and a prominent inter county footballer. His father, Michael D'Arcy (Senior), was a member of Dáil Éireann from 1977 to 1987, from 1989 to 1992 and from 1997 to 2002 and was a member of Seanad Éireann from 1992 to 1997.

Labour Party: The party's only candidate in this election is the outgoing deputy Brendan Howlin, who was first elected to Dáil Éireann in 1987 and has held his seat in each subsequent election, having been an unsuccessful candidate in November 1982. From 1997 to 2002 Howlin was deputy leader of the Labour Party and he was an unsuccessful candidate for the party leadership in 2002. He is currently the party's spokesperson on Justice, Equality and Law Reform and was previously the party's spokesperson on areas such as Health, Women's Rights and Education. He was Minister for Health from 1993 to 1994 and Minister for the Environment from 1994 to 1997. He was a Taoiseach's nominee to Seanad Éireann from 1982 to 1987. Talk of a high-profile running mate for Howlin in the months before both the 1997 and the 2002 elections came to nought.

Progressive Democrats: Colm O'Gorman is the director of One in Four, a national charity supporting women and men who have experienced sexual violence, which he founded in Ireland in 2002. Based in the Gorey end of the constituency, he is chairman of the Educate Together school in the town. He is a prominent commentator on a range of social issues and was a recipient of an ESB/Rehab People of the Year award, a TV3/*Daily Star* 'Best of Irish' award in 2002, a *Sunday Independent*/Irish Nationwide People of the Year in 2003 and he was awarded a Larkin Justice Award for his contribution to social justice in Ireland by the Labour Party in 2003.

Sinn Féin: The party ran no candidate in 1997 but in 2002 their new candidate, John Dwyer, put in an impressive performance, polling 4,964 first preferences. Dwyer, who has been a member of New Ross Town Council since 1999, has since been elected to Wexford County Council. In the 2004 local election he polled 1,368 votes and took the fourth of five seats. On the same day he was the party's candidate in the European elections in the East constituency, which covers all of Leinster. In that election Dwyer polled 39,356 first preferences.

WEXFORD 2007 FIGURES

Candidate	Party	1st Count	2nd Count	3rd Count	4th Count	5th Count	Later counts

YOUR PREDICTION 2007

	Candidate Elected	Party
1		
2		
3		
4		
5		

RESULT 2007

	Candidate Elected	Party
1		
2		
3		
4		
5		

NOTES/UPDATES

WEXFORD 2002 FIGURES

5 seats **Quota: 10,071**

Candidate	Party	1st	2nd	3rd	4th	5th	6th	7th	8th
Transfer of			Ó Bulguidhir O'Connor	S. Doyle	A. Doyle	Dwyer	D'Arcy	Kehoe's surplus	Browne's surplus
John Browne*	FF	9,150	+31 9,181	+337 9,518	+91 9,609	+569 10,178			
Brendan Howlin*	LAB	7,995	+78 8,073	+128 8,201	+723 8,924	+1,211 10,135			
Hugh Byrne*	FF	7,556	+18 7,574	+46 7,620	+135 7,755	+481 8,236	+466 8,702	+311 9,013	+59 9,072
Tony Dempsey	FF	7,520	+40 7,560	+75 7,635	+158 7,793	+403 8,196	+627 8,823	+279 9,102	+48 9,150
Paul Kehoe	FG	7,048	+51 7,099	+288 7,387	+1,404 8,791	+404 9195	3,436 12,631		
Liam Twomey	FG	5,815	+195 6,010	+203 6,213	+361 6,574	+1,488 8,062	+678 8,740	+1,342 10,082	
John Dwyer	SF	4,964	+56 5,020	+128 5,148	+69 5,217	Elim'd			
Michael D'Arcy* Snr	FG	4,564	+33 4,597	+28 4,625	+1,020 5,645	+190 5,835	Elim'd		
Avril Doyle	FG	3,940	+29 3,969	+42 4,011	Elim'd				
Sean Doyle	IND	1,274	+41 1,315	Elim'd					
Miranda Ó Bulguidhir	IND	424	Elim'd						
Michael O Connor	CSP	173	Elim'd						
Non-Transferable			25	40	50	471	628	628	0

*Outgoing Deputy

WICKLOW

> **Outgoing Deputies**: Dick Roche (FF), Joe Jacob (FF), Liz McManus (Lab), Billy Timmins (FG) Mildred Fox (Ind).
>
> Both Joe Jacob (FF) and Mildred Fox (Ind) are not contesting the 2007 election.

> **The Constituency**: This is a **five-seat** constituency. Its area incorporates the administrative county of Wicklow and a portion of county Carlow including Clonmore, Hacketstown and Rathvilly. The boundaries of this constituency are unchanged since 2002.

Party	Votes 2002	Quota 2002	% Vote 2002	% Vote 1997	Swing
Fianna Fáil	17,083	1.9	31.27%	29.87%	1.41%
Fine Gael	8,722	1.0	15.97%	19.71%	−3.74%
Labour	16,144	1.8	29.55%	23.79%	5.76%
PDs				3.30%	−3.30%
Green Party	3,213	0.4	5.88%	2.48%	3.40%
Sinn Féin	1,529	0.2	2.80%		2.80%
Others	7,935	0.9	14.53%		−6.32%

> **2007 Candidates will include**: Dick Roche (FF), Joe Behan (FF), Pat Fitzgerald (FF), Andrew Doyle (FG), Billy Timmins (FG), Liz McManus (Lab), Nicky Kelly (Lab), Deirdre de Burca (GP), John Brady (SF), Carmel McKenna (Ind), Pat Doran (Ind).

In Brief: The 'Rainbow bloc' is certain to gain at least one seat here at the expense of the 'pro-Ahern' bloc. The second Fianna Fáil seat is vulnerable following the retirement of Joe Jacob and the independent seat is up for grabs because Mildred Fox is not recontesting. Labour has a good chance of winning a second seat. Their outgoing deputy, Liz McManus, should comfortably hold her seat and the party's other candidate, Nicky Kelly, who lost out to Mildred Fox by just a handful of votes in 2002, will either win a seat or come close again. Alternatively (or even simultaneously) the Green Party's candidate, Deirdre de Burca, could win a seat. Fine Gael talk of gaining a seat but Billy Timmins is likely to win their only seat. Fianna Fáil only finalised its ticket in December 2006, with Bray councillor Joe Behan and former independent councillor Pat Fitzgerald, based in Arklow, joining Environment Minister Dick Roche on the ticket. The party will struggle to hold its two seats.

Fianna Fáil: In 2002 Fianna Fáil's strategy of only running two candidates enabled better vote management. The party's vote was up slightly and they had just under two quotas on the first count. The retirement of Joe Jacob, who has held a Dáil seat since 1987, makes the task of holding their two seats this time out much harder. It has not been made easier by a long-running row in the constituency over who the 2007 candidates should be. Because of the internal party tensions there was no constituency convention held and instead, after interviews, party headquarters announced in December 2006 that the party's Ard Comhairle had selected councillors Joe Behan and Pat Fitzgerald to run with Minister Roche.

Dick Roche was first elected to Dáil Éireann in 1987. He lost his seat in 1992, regained it in 1997 and retained it in 2002. He was Minister of State at the Department of An Taoiseach and Foreign Affairs with special responsibility for European Affairs from 2002 to 2004 and was appointed Minister for the Environment and Local Government in September 2004. He was a member of Seanad Éireann from 1992 to 1997 and is a former chairman of the Oireachtas Joint Committee on State-Sponsored Bodies. Dick Roche was a member of Wicklow County Council from 1985 to 2002, firstly for the Greystones electoral area and then for the Bray electoral area and is also a former member of Greystones Town Commission. He formerly worked as a lecturer in University College Dublin.

Joe Behan has been a member of Wicklow County Council for the Bray electoral area since 1992. In the 2004 local election he polled 1,620 first preferences and he is also a member of Bray Town Council.

Pat Fitzgerald is a member of Arklow Town Council, to which he was first elected in 1999. He is chairman of the County Wicklow branch of the Alzheimer Society. He formerly worked with IFI.

Fine Gael: In 2002 Fine Gael's two candidates, their outgoing deputy Billy Timmmins and Bray-based solicitor Raymond O'Rourke, had almost exactly a quota between them on the first count.

Billy Timmins was first elected to Dáil Éireann in 1997 and was comfortably re-elected in 2002. He was deputy spokesperson on Justice and Defence from 2001 to 2002 and was the party's spokesperson on Defence from 1997 to 2000, on Housing from 2000 to 2001 and on Agriculture and Food from 2002 to 2004. He has been spokesperson on Defence since October 2004. From 1997 to 2004 he was a member of Wicklow County Council for the Baltinglass electoral area.

Andrew Doyle has been a member of Wicklow County Council since 1991 representing the Wicklow local electoral area. In the 2004 local election he polled 2,008 first preferences, which was 168 above the quota. He was chairman of the council for the 2005–06. He is based in Wicklow town.

Labour Party: In 2002 Labour put in place an interesting candidate line-up in this constituency. They ran three candidates who were not only geographically well-positioned but also sought to attract different support bases. Liz McManus, the former Democratic Left deputy, has always had a strong base, particularly in the Bray and Greystones area. The party's west Wicklow candidate was Jimmy O'Shaughnessy, the then chairman of Wicklow County Council, who had a strong appeal to supporters of the former deputy Liam Kavanagh, and the previously independent Arklow-based councillor Nicky Kelly was the third candidate. The strategy almost delivered the two seats they were seeking. The Labour vote in 2002 was up 5.8% on the combined Labour and Democratic Left vote in 1997 and they missed winning a second seat by just 47 votes. This time the party is running only two candidates, McManus and Kelly.

Liz McManus was first elected to Dáil Éireann as a Democratic Left deputy and has held the seat in each subsequent election. She is currently deputy leader of the Labour Party and the party's spokesperson on Health. She was also spokesperson on Health from 1997 to 2002. She was Minister of State at the Department of the Environment, with special responsibility for Housing and Urban Renewal from 1994 to 1997 and was previously Democratic Left spokesperson on Agriculture and Food, Equality, Law Reform and Health from 1993 to 1994. She was chairperson of the Task Force on the Needs of the Travelling Community, whose report was published in 1993. Liz McManus was a member of Wicklow County Council for the Bray electoral area.

Nicky Kelly first won political office in 1994, when he topped the poll in the Arklow Town Council elections as an independent candidate. He contested the 1995 Dáil by-election in this constituency and then contested the 1997 general election, polling almost 5,000 first preferences in the latter. In 1999, while still an independent, he stood for Wicklow County Council in the Arklow electoral area, polling 2,403 first preferences, which gave him 700 votes to spare over the quota. He joined the Labour Party in the lead-in to the 2002 election and polled 6,529 first preferences as a candidate for the party.

Sinn Féin: Mairéad Keane was the party's election candidate in a constituency where the party has no base and she polled just 1,527 first preferences, their third lowest vote of the constituencies where they contested. The party's candidate in this election is John Brady, who is a Bray town councillor.

Green Party: Deirdre de Burca is again the party's candidate in this constituency. When she stood in the 2002 election she doubled the party's vote, polling 3,208 first preferences, which was just under half of a quota. She has been a member of Wicklow County Council since 1999. In the 2004 local elections she polled 1,638 first preferences in the Bray electoral area, which was just 151 votes under the quota. She is a psychologist based in Bray.

Others: Carmel McKenna is an independent candidate who is standing for the People before Profit organisation.

Mildred Fox, who was first elected to Dáil Éireann in the 1995 by-election caused by the death of her father, Johnny Fox, announced in 2006 that she was giving up politics and would not be contesting this election. In the 1997 general election she polled 5,590 first preferences, which amounted to 10.69% of the first preference vote. In 2002 her vote was up and she polled 6,324 votes, which amounted to 11.6% of the preferences.

Pat Doran, a former Fianna Fáil councillor in the Arklow electoral area, having failed to be selected by the party for this election, is running as an independent. He polled 1,367 first preferences in the 2004 local election.

WICKLOW 2007 FIGURES

Candidate	Party	1st Count	2nd Count	3rd Count	4th Count	5th Count	Later counts

YOUR PREDICTION 2007

	Candidate Elected	Party
1		
2		
3		
4		
5		

RESULT 2007

	Candidate Elected	Party
1		
2		
3		
4		
5		

NOTES/UPDATES

WICKLOW 2002 FIGURES

5 seats   Quota: 9,094

Candidate	Party	1st	2nd	3rd	4th	5th	6th	7th	8th	9th	10th
Transfer of			Roche's surplus	Hyland	Kenny	Kennedy Kearns Keddy	O'Rourke	Keane	De Burca O'Shaughnessy	McManus's surplus	Jacob's surplus
Dick Roche*	FF	9,222									
Joe Jacob*	FF	7,836	+63 7,899	+14 7,913	+13 7,926	+119 8,045	+28 8,073	+233 8,306	+663 8,969	+156 9,125	
Liz McManus*	LAB	7,595	+17 7,612	+24 7,636	+57 7,693	+208 7,901	+219 8,120	+190 8,310	+2,210 10,520		
Billy Timmins*	FG	7,372	+5 7,377	+11 7,388	+10 7,398	+68 7,466	+930 8,396	+80 8,476	+634 9,110		
Nicky Kelly	LAB	6,529	+3 6,532	+4 6,536	+19 6,555	+107 6,662	+29 6,691	+219 6,910	+899 7,809	+848 8,657	+12 8,669
Mildred Fox*	IND	6,324	+18 6,342	+22 6,364	+46 6,410	+232 6,642	+84 6,726	+249 6,975	+1,272 8,247	+422 8,669	+19 8,688
Deirdre de Burca	GP	3,208	+4 3,212	+28 3,240	+37 3,277	+223 3,500	+61 3,561	+465 4,026	Elim'd		
Jimmy O Shaughnessy	LAB	2,029	+2 2,031	+1 2,032	+0 2,032	+96 2,128	+20 2,148	+40 2,188	Elim'd		
Mairead Keane	SF	1,527	+3 1,530	+6 1,536	+10 1,546	+103 1,649	+10 1,659	Elim'd			
Raymond O'Rourke	FG	1,332	+1 1,333	+20 1,353	+19 1,372	+25 1,397	Elim'd				
Robert Kearns	IND	406	+0 406	+6 412	+6 418	Elim'd					
Catherine Kennedy	SWP	399	+1 400	+12 412	+13 425	Elim'd					
Charlie Keddy	IND	383	+1 384	+8 392	+12 404	Elim'd					
Brian Kenny	IND	236	+1 237	+10 247	Elim'd						
Barbara Hyland	IND	171	+0 171	Elim'd							
Non-Transferable			0	5	5	66	16	183	536	0	0

YOUR CALL

Constituency	Fianna Fáil	Fine Gael	Labour Party	Green Party	Pro Dems	Sinn Fein	Others
Carlow–Kilkenny							
Cavan–Monaghan							
Clare							
Cork East							
Cork North Central							
Cork North West							
Cork South Central							
Cork South West							
Donegal North East							
Donegal South West							
Dublin Central							
Dublin Mid-West							
Dublin North							
Dublin North Central							
Dublin North East							
Dublin North West							
Dublin South							
Dublin South Central							
Dublin South East							
Dublin South West							
Dublin West							
Dun Laoghaire							
Galway East							
Galway West							
Kerry North							
Kerry South							
Kildare North							
Kildare South							
Laois–Offaly							
Limerick East							
Limerick West							
Longford–Westmeath							
Louth							
Mayo							
Meath East							
Meath West							
Roscommon–South Leitrim							
Sligo–North Leitrim							
Tipperary North							
Tipperary South							
Waterford							
Wexford							
Wicklow							
TOTAL SEATS							